Security and Privacy for E-Business

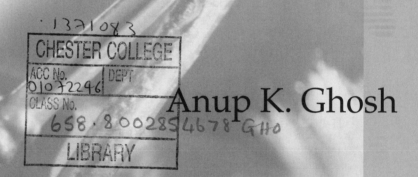

Anup K. Ghosh

Wiley Computer Publishing

John Wiley & Sons, Inc.

NEW YORK · CHICHESTER · WEINHEIM · BRISBANE · SINGAPORE · TORONTO

This book is dedicated to Nita, who first captured my eye, then my heart, and now my future with the birth of our son, Jay.

AKG

Publisher: Robert Ipsen
Editor: Margaret Eldridge
Managing Editor: Angela Smith
Text Design & Composition: Publishers' Design and Production Services

Designations used by companies to distinguish their products are often claimed as trademarks. In all instances where John Wiley & Sons, Inc., is aware of a claim, the product names appear in initial capital or ALL CAPITAL LETTERS. Readers, however, should contact the appropriate companies for more complete information regarding trademarks and registration.

This book is printed on acid-free paper. ⊗

Published by John Wiley & Sons, Inc.

Published simultaneously in Canada.

This publication is designed to provide accurate and authoritative information in regard to the subject matter covered. It is sold with the understanding that the publisher is not engaged in professional services. If professional advice or other expert assistance is required, the services of a competent professional person should be sought.

Library of Congress Cataloging-in-Publication Data:

ISBN 0-471-38421-6

Printed in the United States of America.

10 9 8 7 6 5 4 3 2 1

Advance Praise for Security and Privacy for E-Business

"This book is essential reading for everyone interested in jumping on the e-business bandwagon without getting run over in the process."

> —Peter G. Neumann
> Principal Scientist, Computer Science Lab, SRI International
> Moderator of the ACM Risks Forum
> Author of Computer-Related Risks

"Ma... es a difficult topic very approachable ... ...d dec... ... ... who want to secure th... ... ... want to get ... ..."

"A ... ... and the exp... ... ...d. This boo... ... ...ng secu... ... ...al exe... ... ...today's eve..."

"An ... ...d priv... ... ... e on the Inte... ... ...t now attr... ... ...ks to both ... ...mselves on t... ... ...rough sev... ... ...tech... ... ...riously."

"The global e-business wave continues to spark passionate debate about important personal and consumer-rights issues, such as Internet security and individual privacy. As organizations and individuals become increasingly connected through various networks in the coming decades, clearly the need for more intelligent safeguards—at both the organizational as well as consumer levels—has never been more apparent. *Security and Privacy for E-Business* offers its audience a front-row seat allowing a view into the realities and dangers that exist in today's universal electronic marketplace."

> —*Richard Dean*
> *Internet Security Professional*

CONTENTS

Although the Internet has been around in one form or another for over 20 years, it was not in a form accessible to the mass market until the birth of the World Wide Web (WWW), or simply, the Web, in 1993. Even then, the Web was largely the domain of computer enthusiasts, researchers, and students—people we now call early adopters. By 1995, e-mail had already become the preferred communication medium of business and the Web was on its way to radically changing the way we do business.

By simply providing a means for widely distributing documents in a simple markup language called HTML, which also supports live linking to other Web documents, the Web provides a powerful and cheap communications medium that not only powers business, but more importantly, empowers the individual to publish multi-media documents on a medium whose global reach is growing at exponential rates. The advent of Java in 1995 provided a crucial boost to the Web by providing the ability to move beyond simple typesetting and linking to full-featured programming functionality. Java became the most popular programming language in a new paradigm of programming, known as mobile code, where programs are seamlessly distributed and executed on end users' machines, as easily as linking to a Web page.

Electronic commerce, or simply e-commerce, entered the popular lexicon in 1996 with much hype, but little content and few successes. By 1997, e-commerce was struggling in its infancy as businesses were trying to adapt physical-world notions to the electronic medium resulting in notable failures such as virtual malls. The WWW was rapidly becoming known as the Wild Wild West, where few survived and lawlessness was the rule. In 1998, Internet stocks, or "dot com" companies, became the darling of Wall Street investors. Showing profits were was strictly optional. Banking on the future of e-commerce, investors, large and small, poured money into the dot com companies, whose defining characteristic is that their business depends wholly on the Internet. The

Christmas of 1998 became known as the Internet Christmas because of the billions of dollars that were spent in online shopping. By 1999, e-commerce was no longer simply a neat phenomenon, but a real economic force to be reckoned with by the traditional brick and mortar establishment. In 2000, the distributed denial of service attacks against the top e-commerce sites, was followed coincidentally by the dot com crash, which re-adjusted everyone's expectations of what makes for a viable e-business.

Throughout this period of amazing growth in e-commerce, the security and privacy risks have grown in scope and magnitude. Three driving factors have increased the risks of e-commerce: first, the sole reliance on the electronic medium for a company's core business; second, the growing complexity of the software systems needed to support e-commerce; and third, the value of the digital assets brought online to an inherently insecure medium—the Internet.

While the market capitalizations (market caps) and price to earnings (P/E) ratios of profitless Internet companies baffled many stock analysts before the dot com crash, the valuations were merely a reflection of investors' beliefs in the future potential revenue and profits from Internet-based commerce. The most successful dot com companies have not simply transferred physical world products and services to the Internet; rather they have found ways of delivering new products and services that exploit the best features of the Internet: easy and cheap access (from work or home), global distribution, and freedom from geographic boundaries. While the new paradigm of building a business solely on the Internet caused many investors to swoon, it also entails the risk of putting all of a company's eggs in the Internet basket. Companies like AOL, eTrade, eBay, and scores of others have learned how precarious an e-commerce existence can be when the business is wholly dependent on the fragility of software and Internet service. Service to dot com companies can go down simply because of the inability to meet peak customer demand, problems in software, problems in the Internet infrastructure, or even malicious denial-of-service attacks.

The Internet, a communications medium originally built for open collaboration among academics, is an inherently insecure medium. As a result, systems built on top of the Internet must be designed and developed with intrinsic security. Providing a full-service e-commerce business is not as simple as putting up a Web page anymore. The complexity of Internet-based systems has grown from e-mail to Web publishing to intranets and extranets, to full-blown electronic commerce, including front-end Web service, complex middleware, and back-end data warehousing, to logistics and supply chain management. As the complexity of Internet-based software systems has grown, so has the risk that even simple errors in software design, development, and configuration can lead to complete compromise of system security. Even common off-the-shelf software such as Web servers from major software vendors have been rife with flaws that have permitted full compromise of system privileges to hackers armed only with off-the-shelf Internet browsers. Beyond the risks of commercial off-the-shelf software, custom development of some software is generally necessary, particularly in coding the business application logic for the online site. The increasing sophistication of business application logic has led to more complex custom middleware that more often than not leaves gaping holes in the site's security and the site owner's digital assets.

The value of the digital assets brought to the Internet gives new incentive to malicious computer hackers (or even competitors) to sabotage online systems or simply steal intellectual property. Hacking into online systems has proven all too easy for teenagers equipped only with a $500 personal computer, a 56Kbit modem, and Internet service. While computer security became an issue the first time two computers became networked together, the stakes of computer security have risen enormously with online commerce. The cost per security incident is rising steadily as hackers are moving on from hacking into university systems to the Pentagon to dot com sites. A company whose Web pages have been vandalized by joyriding teenagers can find itself with 30 seconds on CNN for all the wrong reasons. The fallout can shake investor and consumer confidence as well as incur legal liability for the company.

The risks of Internet-based e-commerce, however, do not mean businesses should shy away from e-commerce. Rather, the upside for bringing new revenue streams, decreased operational costs, and increased profitability make e-commerce the preferred, and sometimes, the only way of doing business for both novice entrepreneurs and Fortune 500 CEOs. It is important to understand that while there are risks in e-commerce, they can be effectively managed as long as they are well understood.

This book presents the various issues in engaging in e-commerce from both a business and a consumer point of view. The goal of this book is not to discourage either businesses or consumers from e-commerce, but rather to educate the reader as to what the pertinent security and privacy concerns are in engaging in e-commerce. Consumers need not worry about sending their credit card numbers over the Internet. The standard data transaction protocols such as the Secure Sockets Layer (SSL) provide more than adequate confidentiality of data. The real risks are for business losses due to breaches in security in online sites and for loss of privacy for consumers engaging in e-commerce. These topics are covered in this book.

In *E-Commerce Security: Weak Links, Best Defenses* (Wiley, 1998), the notion that e-commerce was rendered secure by "secure" transaction protocols such as SSL was dispelled. Since then, it has become widely acknowledged that there are several weak links in both the server and client software that enable e-commerce. *E-Commerce Security* explained in detail where the weak links are and what defenses can be employed to secure e-commerce systems. For a practical, hands-on guide to identifying weak links and securing e-commerce systems, *E-Commerce Security* is still the best reference to reach for.

In this book, we cover new ground in e-business security and privacy. Most importantly, we talk about the security and privacy issues that we face as businesses and consumers in e-commerce. This book is targeted to the business professional in the technology industry. This new breed of professional must understand the risks new technology brings to their business, while not necessarily having been trained formally in computer science and engineering. For the business professional, software, and Internet-enabled software, in particular, introduces new risks to the business, previously unseen, and even now rarely well-understood. This book sheds light on the security and privacy risks of Internet-enabled software in the enterprise at a level that does not require detailed technical knowledge as a prerequisite, but deep enough to illuminate the core and substantial issues in "e-enabling" the business.

We begin in Chapter 1 with a study of what we mean by e-business, understanding the roles that e-business players have, and where e-business is heading. We present case studies of the successes and perils of e-business in order to better understand what has worked and what has not. We conclude the chapter by looking at new paradigms of e-business that move away from the general purpose desktop machine to using embedded Internet devices as enablers of e-business. Examples include palm computing devices, cell phones, smart cards, and the Internet kiosks that are replacing the tried-and-true vending machine.

In Chapter 2, we examine the technology that enables all of e-commerce—software—and the risks it poses to e-businesses. In this chapter, we discuss why e-commerce security is so hard, and how easy it is to break software systems. Software is by far the most complex creation of our human minds. We do not have the capacity to understand all the different states any non-trivial software program, like those that enable e-commerce, can find itself in. We are just now beginning to create the science, engineering, and tools necessary to design and analyze secure software systems. We present two detailed case studies of significant software problems that have plagued e-businesses.

Chapter 3 turns the discussion from software problems to solutions. We present a software risk management strategy for e-businesses that necessarily depend on software. The meat of Chapter 3 is served up with a discussion on engineering secure e-business systems from the ground up. We conclude with a discussion of what it takes to provide assurance that our e-commerce systems will be secure, reliable, and available to our business partners and consumers.

Chapter 4 applies the knowledge from Chapter 2 and Chapter 3 to e-business systems. Here, we present the nuts and bolts of building a secure e-business. We begin by presenting the basic three-tier architecture of e-businesses: server, middleware, and back-end databases, then talk about a layered approach to securing the software that comprises this architecture. This chapter includes an in-depth discussion on how to assess the security of the middleware that represents the business application logic and forms the bulk of custom development of e-businesses.

Where Chapter 4 was primarily concerned about server-side e-business systems, Chapter 5 concerns itself with the client-side risks and specifically the risks of mobile and malicious code. In particular, we examine how mobile code can compromise individual and corporate security and privacy. We begin with a discussion of what mobile code is and its common forms such as Java applets, ActiveX controls, Web scripts, e-mail attachments, software agents, and even push software. We pose the question of do you know when you are running someone else's mobile code and answer it for you: often not. The final topic of Chapter 5 addresses one of the most significant emerging risks of mobile code:

code-driven attacks. We describe how code-driven attacks can seamlessly and transparently compromise your security and privacy, and what you can do to thwart malicious mobile code.

In Chapter 6, we address the risks to the newest form of e-commerce: mobile e-commerce or m-commerce for short. We show how m-commerce has many of the same risks of desktop-based e-commerce, plus new ones. Risks in wireless devices, networks, and servers are systematically analyzed. Finally, the risks of scripting-based attacks against cell phones are described.

Finally, in Chapter 7, we describe privacy risks in an online world. We begin with a discussion of the security-privacy relationship—one that has confused people time and again. We present four privacy-friendly businesses practices. We assert that the biggest problem in online privacy is simply the lack of knowledge about what information is being collected about users and how it is shared. We present a sample of the information that can be learned about you when you surf the Web and engage in e-commerce. As in Chapter 4, we systematically decompose e-commerce systems and describe both the client-side and server-side privacy risks. The chapter describes why and how online businesses profile their site visitors, how ad banners are generated based on your profile, what Web bugs are and how they can compromise your privacy, and what spyware and E.T. applications are. Finally, we look at privacy-enhancing tools and future paradigms of online commerce that involve bartering privacy for some return.

Since the writing of *E-Commerce Security*, the e-commerce market and industry have radically changed and grown up. However, the core issues in securing e-commerce have not changed. By contrast, as online systems have grown more complex, the security and privacy issues have become even more important. In this book, we cover new material in this rapidly changing business paradigm that addresses the core issues of performing commerce over an untrusted medium. Soon, the label "e-commerce" or "e-business" will be an anachronism. It will simply be the only way we do business. This book will arm the reader with the knowledge and tools to securely participate in the new way we do business.

ACKNOWLEDGMENTS

Though the cover indicates one author, this book is written in first person plural deliberately. This book represents the cumulative effort and support of many individuals. When "we" is used in this book, it refers to the people acknowledged here. Though this book draws on the collective knowledge of many researchers at Cigital, Inc., any errors of omission or inaccuracy are solely my own. Apologies to those who are victims of my first error of omission: those I fail to acknowledge here.

My first debt of gratitude goes to my family and friends. Without the unconditional support and love of those closest to me, a project such as this is simply not possible. I thank you not only for your support, but also for your patience as I continue to pursue my labor of love.

I'd like to thank Marjorie Spencer, formerly of Wiley Computer Publishing, for making the call to arms to write this second book. Without her insistence, I would not have even considered taking on this project. I'd also like to thank my editor Margaret Hendrey Eldridge, also of Wiley Computer Publishing, who showed tremendous patience through deadline after missed deadline. Thanks to the staff at Wiley Computer Publishing, who behind the scenes, pull together books that serve a greater good—educating the public through accessible technical literature.

There are many individuals at Cigital, Inc. (www.cigital.com), who made this book possible. First, thanks to John McManus, Jeffery Payne, and Jeffrey Voas, not only for your patience and support of this project, but also for providing a nurturing environment that encourages the art of writing. Thanks to Mike Firetti for being a good friend, supporter, and promoter. Thanks to Gary McGraw for pushing the envelope at Cigital and encouraging creative works such as our books. Last, but certainly not least, thanks to all of those at Cigital who directly and indirectly contributed to the collective knowledge shared in this book:

B. Arkin, D. Berrier, J.T. Bloch, R. Craven, S. Goodwin, F. Hill, T. Hollebeek, R. Leslie, R. MacMichael, C. Michael, S. Millet, J. Norman, M. Pelican, M. Schatz, M. Schmid, V. Shah, T. Swamintha, J. Viega, and P. Wallace.

With gratitude and respect,

AKG

CHAPTER 1

E-Commerce in the Twenty-First Century

"Uncertainty—in the economy, society, politics—has become so great as to render futile, if not counterproductive, the kind of planning most companies still practice..."

PETER DRUCKER
WALL STREET JOURNAL
JULY 22, 1992

Electronic commerce, or simply e-commerce, has overwhelmed so much of today's business news that we often forget the humble beginnings of what is now a multibillion dollar industry. E-commerce hit the popular lexicon when businesses began using the Internet for commercial purposes. Prior to e-commerce, universities and research laboratories used the Internet largely for communicating and exchanging documents. Previous initiatives in e-commerce were largely over proprietary networks using Electronic Data Interchange (EDI) formats for automating order processing. These networks, though, were expensive and often dedicated to one particular service. As a result, e-commerce over proprietary networks was limited to closed communities of large businesses that could afford the up-front costs of being a player.

The Internet changed this model drastically. Business could perform the same types of EDI transactions over the Internet—and much, much more. With pervasive Internet service, the entry costs are significantly cheaper than EDI, while at the same time, Internet service provides a much larger field of business partners. To sweeten the pot considerably, consider that the general public has largely become Internet savvy at home and work. The benefits that accrue with widespread adoption are non-linear, like a snowball effect. That is, each additional Internet node provides a disproportionately high return of value. Like the fax machine, having a single Internet node is more or less useless. The more widespread the adoption, the greater the utility will be to everyone. In economic terms, each new Internet node creates positive network externalities. Or, in other words, the act of creating one additional Internet node creates positive side effects—everyone else on the Internet can now reach that new node. This type of positive externality, long known to economists when studying telephone networks, has an even more magnified effect than traditional phone networks because of the sheer bandwidth and range of services that can be offered through that one additional Internet node, when compared to the same bandwidth and services offered over traditional telephone service.

Another significant change has been in the thinking of what e-commerce is. Since the Internet started replacing EDI and proprietary value-added network (VAN) systems, "e-commerce" became the term for describing transaction-based commerce over the Internet. The industry grew quickly to encompass the broad range of activities that support business over the Internet. The term "e-tailing" is now being used to describe the purchasing and selling of goods and services over the Internet, while "e-business" is sometimes used to describe the myriad activities involved with doing business on the Internet. E-commerce encompasses both these terms and describes the whole range of Internet-based activities that support businesses, transaction-based commerce, research, information brokering, and business communications.

Although it is true that the Internet changed e-commerce from what it was to what it now is, it is also true that e-commerce changed the Internet. One truly remarkable effect that the commercial sector has had on the Internet is the phenomenal rate of adoption it has spurred. As an indication of the kind of phenomenon Internet rate adoption is, consider that it took radio 38 years, the television 13 years, and the Internet merely 5 years to achieve 50 million subscribers. The high rate of adoption has created the business-to-consumer (B2C) market. It is the B2C marketing phenomena that has received the most hype, if not generated the most sales. In fact, business-to-business (B2B) e-commerce outpaces B2C e-commerce by a rate of 5:1 in terms of sheer dollar values, if not in numbers of transactions, and this trend is expected to continue in the near term. Over the long term, it is certainly possible that the B2C economy may eventually outpace B2B sales, but that model remains to be borne out.

Three Waves of E-Commerce

As Peter Drucker noted in 1992, the amount of uncertainty in today's economy can make planning for the future an effort in futility. While predicting the future is usually an exercise in futility, if not vanity, given the amazing history of e-commerce and the amount of uncertainty over its future, it is also worthwhile thinking about where we are heading. In this section, we lay out a vision for where we believe e-commerce is headed in the twenty-first century, over the next 10 years. Uncertainty has traditionally been fiend to corporate planners. Uncertainty is also a favorite among savvy entrepreneurs because it provides opportunities for business. This has never been truer than in today's Internet-driven economy, where opportunities abound and creative ideas can hit the market quickly. Even though the predictions of where e-commerce will take us in the future may be wrong, the uncertainty over the predictions of e-commerce also provides opportunities for agile and entrepreneurial businesses.

We can discuss e-commerce in three waves: screen scraping, machine-to-machine e-commerce, and Web-based distributed computing. The first wave has already swept us up off our feet, and now that we have been there and done that, we're ready for the next wave, which is now just swelling. The second wave will replace the ad hoc fashion in which e-commerce is currently performed between humans and machines to a machine-to-machine–based computation model that will automate much of what is now only a Web façade on a traditional brick-and-mortar business. The third wave will radically change the way we currently do business to more closely reflect the way we want to do business: E-commerce will be performed anytime, anywhere, by many different types of devices besides the personal computer. IP everywhere will be more than a vision—every type of device that is currently used and envisioned will have its own computational resources and its own Internet connectivity. The individual will be empowered over the business. Agents will act on behalf of the individual's interest to find the optimal service provider for a particular request. Service providers will fragment into specialized services that come together to either cooperate via just-in-time loose federations or compete for any given transaction request. Software and computation will be distributed among collaborative resources that use the Web as the basic fabric of communication. Before we get too far into the Utopian vision of the future, let's take a look at what we have today.

Screen Scraping

The first wave to sweep e-commerce is colloquially known as screen scraping because during this phase, the Web was largely used to display data, which subsequently is "scraped" by browsers. The Web caught on quickly because of its ability to share documents rapidly and easily. The first wave of e-commerce was mostly about taking catalogs of product and service offerings and putting them up on the Web. Partially, there was a novelty factor to having a Web presence, but there are also obvious advantages to screen scraping over the traditional way of printing and distributing the information on paper. For instance, distribution of Web content is much cheaper than distribution of hard copy. The obvious disadvantage is that screen scraping is largely based on a "pull" model of commerce. That is, you have to get the customers to visit you in the first place in order to show your wares, unlike direct marketing. Of course, e-mail spammers have tried to change that situation, much to everyone's chagrin.

Web content can be fairly dynamic. That is, you can change content easily, frequently, and cheaply. For instance, you can easily fix an error in content, and it may even go unnoticed. Once hard copy has been printed and distributed, it cannot be changed—only retracted. Finally, the usual properties of the Internet hold: no geographic boundaries and 24×7 round-the-clock access. For these reasons and more, the first wave of e-commerce was mostly about putting printed catalogs up on the Net and hoping for the dough to start rolling in.

Though much ado was made about e-commerce in 1996 and 1997, little money was actually made by the companies that rode the first wave of e-commerce. As we find out later in this chapter, this trend still holds true. Since the early days of e-commerce, almost every business has found the InterNIC and registered one or more domain names. Interestingly enough, the rush to usurp domain names created incredible demand and instant riches for those quick and creative enough to register domain names early. Although the first wave of e-commerce promised much, it delivered little more than enhanced text, images, and audio. Nonetheless, screen scraping is still the predominant form of e-commerce today. The reason is simplicity. Consumers like being able to navigate Web pages to find information at their own convenience. Getting news, sports, weather, and stock quotes in near real-time from work is a real bonus. Not to mention that the Web is an incredibly convenient tool for research. Businesses find it cheaper to put up frequently asked questions (FAQs), product catalogs, business offerings, and documentation rather than fielding questions on these over the phone. For all of these reasons, e-commerce has emerged from its infancy and into mainstream acceptance.

So far, we have been riding the first wave of e-commerce relatively happily. In other words, we are still in the honeymoon phase because we continue to be enamored with the neatness factor of putting everything up on the Web and playing with cool new technologies such as active content and multimedia formats. The grumblings are beginning to be heard more frequently that while this has been fun, we also need to make some money. During this stage there have been few winners and many losers, as the dot com crash of 2000 painfully reminds us. The impact on business of the first wave has largely been localized to a few dot.com companies whose stock valuations shot through the roof and whose bottom lines have largely been red. To sustain e-commerce, businesses need to make profits and consumers need a value proposition. The hard truth is we are not there yet.

Today, the Web-based model of e-commerce presents a Web interface to which people read and respond—that is, the screen-scraping model. On the other end of the transaction, a machine reads data sent in by a person and processes it. In some cases, the model is even worse. Stories abound in industry of where data sent in via Web forms is then re-typed by hand into traditional order forms. In other words, the human enters back in the loop on the merchant side in order to interface with legacy back-end transaction processing systems. The human-to-machine model is bound to change in order to facilitate e-commerce. One of the reasons is that HTML, the markup language used to write Web pages, cannot represent application semantics. HTML is a structural markup language whose main purpose is to support publishing and linking of text in electronic form. HTML distinguishes elements of a Web page by using markup tags, such as <H1>HEADER</H1> to distinguish a first-level header from a second-level header, <H2>HEADER</H2>, or to distinguish <I>italicized</I> text from normal text. Tags are also provided to organize the document physically, such as markers to distinguish paragraphs, list items, create forms, provide buttons, insert graphic images, and link documents. Although HTML is useful for organizing and displaying information to be human-readable, it does not provide the necessary constructs to make the same information machine-readable. As a result, every e-business that collects information via HTML must custom-write software that attaches semantic meaning to the collected data, or else it opts to the old-fashioned way of hand-typing in the data sent in via a Web form.

Consider a T-shirt shop that is taking its business to the Internet. The business needs fields in a Web form to represent the article of clothing (shirt, pants, shoes, etc.), size, catalog number, customer information, shipping type, and possibly other data. In HTML, the business would need to create its own placeholders for these fields. Even worse, the business has to write a middleware layer of software to process the data received (unless, of course, a human is transcribing the data). This requires a completely new set of variables to be custom-created according to the collected data. The problem with this approach is that each business creates its own software (Web front-end and middleware) and then must process this data using legacy transaction processing software according to standard business practices. Custom-creating all this software is a bad business practice in general.

To understand why, consider a bike industry that did not standardize on bike models, but rather sold only bike parts to bike stores. Every bike shop would have to sell bikes by taking orders for seats, handlebars, wheels, frame, brakes, and other bike components. The bike-savvy consumer may get a custom-built bike, but the bike owner would face significantly higher costs selling bikes piecemeal versus selling standard models of bikes. Furthermore, most consumers would be daunted and put off by the complex and non-standard process of ordering bikes. The lack of standard bike models would further complicate the process. Every shop would end up assembling different bikes from different manufacturers' components. Obviously, having standard models of bikes makes shopping an easier experience for consumers and bike sellers.

This is the situation we face today in e-commerce. We are still in the pre-industrial era of e-commerce. Every merchant is essentially assembling custom bikes in the form of custom e-commerce sites. The components of most e-commerce sites are fairly standard (front-end Web servers, back-end databases, and a middle application layer), but the way in which the components are used (or assembled in the bike analogy) is completely ad hoc. As a result, the shopping experience from one site to the next varies wildly. Besides Web services, merchants need to develop several other types of software services to build an effective e-commerce site. These may include online transaction processing, supply chain management, customer relationship management, enterprise resource planning (ERP) software, ordering, inventory management, shipping and logistics, and data mining. Without a standard way of doing e-business, merchants face a complex and uncertain process in developing e-commerce sites.

Machine-to-Machine Commerce

The second wave of e-commerce will begin to address its current shortcomings by driving forward the means for facilitating business within given market segments while providing a value proposition for consumers. The fundamental change in the second wave will be a shift from the screen-scraping human-to-machine model of Web commerce to an application-specific machine-to-machine model of e-commerce. That is, rather than merely presenting the consumer with a Web interface to product offerings, e-commerce applications will be developed around the business semantics of the transaction. The enabling technology will be software that runs on both ends of the transaction—the client and the server—that vendors will develop for specific business applications.

Currently, e-commerce site developers are using generic technologies for application-specific functions. The end result is the ad hoc e-business practices described previously. Rather than asking more of HTML and CGI than can be reasonably delivered, the next wave of e-commerce will be enabled by advances in the software that is specific to particular industries and applications. The key technologies that will enable this transition are XML, application servers, distributed software components, and mobile code. In the short term, this shift will occur in B2B commerce, the major growth area in e-commerce; then once the technology matures and migrates to end users' machines, it will influence the B2C market.

One of the key technologies facilitating the shift to machine-to-machine e-commerce is XML, the Extensible Markup Language. XML, like HTML is a markup language, and it is a proper subset of the Standard Generalized Markup Language (SGML). Where HTML is concerned with organizing and displaying information to be human-readable, XML is concerned with representing information to be machine-readable. The key attribute of XML that distinguishes it from HTML is that XML provides *semantic meaning* to the information that is represented. That is, XML provides constructs to describe information and give it meaning. This meta-information allows programs to understand and distinguish different types of information used in e-commerce. For instance, while humans are trained to recognize a mail address and its components (name, street address, city, state, zip code), this same information presented to a computer is just a stream of ASCII characters with no meaning in particular.

XML provides semantic markup constructs to enable structuring and labeling of content in a way that machines can process. Furthermore, in order to meet the diverse needs of different applications, the representation is extensible. That is, content developers can develop new structured tag and attribute names. Two other nice features XML derives

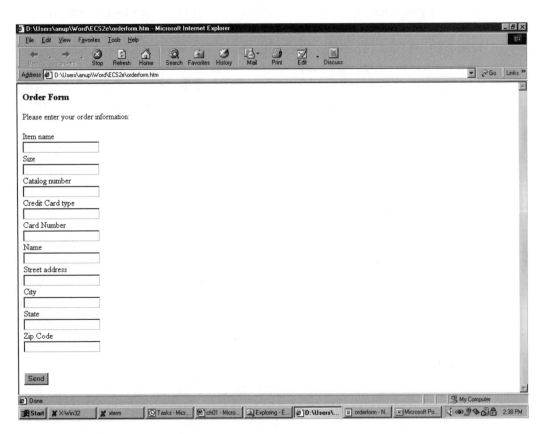

Figure 1.1 HTML order form.

from SGML are the ability to structure documents such that they can be containers for other documents and the ability to validate that the document conforms to its specified structure. The first of these features allows arbitrary nesting of documents within documents such that complex documents can be constructed easily from simpler ones. The second feature allows an application to validate a well-formed XML document (according to its published grammar description) before using it.

To give a concrete example, consider the example of the Internet-based T-shirt business. Using the screen-scraping model of e-commerce, the business would develop a Web page using an HTML form that asks for specific fields. Consider the order form that a merchant might put up (see Figure 1.1).

The fields in this order form reflect the types of data that a clothing merchant might need to process an online order for clothing. The HTML code for this Web page is shown in Figure 1.2.

```
<HTML>
<HEAD><H3> Order Form </H3></HEAD>
<BODY>
<p>
Please enter your order information:
<FORM METHOD="POST" ACTION='/cgi-bin/processOrder.pl'>
Item name<BR>        <INPUT TYPE='text' NAME='Item' VALUE=''><BR>
Size<BR>             <INPUT TYPE='text' NAME='size' VALUE=''><BR>
Catalog number<BR>   <INPUT TYPE='text' NAME='ID' VALUE=''><BR>
Credit Card type<BR> <INPUT TYPE='text' NAME='card' VALUE=''><BR>
Card Number<BR>      <INPUT TYPE='text' NAME='card_num' VALUE=''><BR>
Name<BR>             <INPUT TYPE='text' NAME='name' VALUE=''><BR>
Street address<BR>   <INPUT TYPE='text' NAME='street' VALUE=''><BR>
City<BR>             <INPUT TYPE='text' NAME='city' VALUE=''><BR>
State<BR>            <INPUT TYPE='text' NAME='state' VALUE=''><BR>
Zip Code<BR>         <INPUT TYPE='text' NAME='zipcode' VALUE=''><BR>
<BR><BR>
                 <INPUT TYPE='submit' NAME='submit' VALUE='Send'>
</FORM>
</BODY>
</HTML>
```

Figure 1.2 HTML code for Web order form.

Again, this order form is conjured for this example. In practice you would want to present a menu selection for some of the fields, you would want to ensure that the data is well formed (such as 16-digit numeric characters for the credit card numbers), and you would also limit the length of the data accepted by the program that processes this data. This form, though, represents the type of code that is used today for accepting orders over the Internet. One of the problems with this approach is that the requested fields are ad hoc, though the type of information requested for a particular market segment (such as apparel ordering) is fairly standard. This point goes back to the discussion of the necessity for standard practices in obtaining and processing information within a given market segment. Second, notice that the markup tags in the HTML form, delimited with the "<" and ">" characters, do not provide any semantic information about this application. Instead, they are generic tags such as INPUT TYPE, NAME, and VALUE. As a result, the Web page designer must come up with his or her own ad hoc naming scheme to aid the CGI script that ends up receiving this data. In this case, the CGI script, processOrder.pl, uses these NAME tags to determine to what kind of data the posted input corresponds. From the CGI script's perspective, the NAME tag "zipcode" is no different from the NAME tag "card_num." That is, these names have no semantic meaning associated with them. Therefore, custom logic must be written by the e-commerce site to process these fields according to the business logic for the application.

In XML, we would represent the same type of information using a clothing industry standard template for ordering clothes. The XML template shown in Figure 1.3 may be included within an HTML document for populating when placing an online order.

While the document may not be any more readable to a human than HTML, it is now easily processed by a program. Note that the tags we use describe the information we captured about the order. For instance, with this labeled data, a program can now find out how many orders came from a particular zip code. Also note that the tags are hierarchical in nature—a natural structure for databases and programs to store and process data. The key to making XML successful will be adoption of industry standard templates for e-commerce transactions. These templates are known as Document Type Definitions (DTDs), and they can

```
<?xml version="1.0"?>
<Order>
  <Item> </Item>
  <Size> </Size>
  <Color> </Color>
  <CatalogNum></CatalogNum>
</Order>
<Customer>
  <Name>
      <Last> </Last>
      <First> </First>
      <MI> </MI>
  </Name>
  <Address>
      <Street> </Street>
      <City> </City>
      <State> </State>
      <ZipCode></ZipCode>
      <Country> </Country>
      <Phone></Phone>
  </Address>
  <Card>
      <Type> </Type>
      <Number></Number>
      <Expiry></Expiry>
  </Card>
</Customer>
```

Figure 1.3   XML code for order form.

be either explicitly included with the XML document or simply referenced. The DTD specifies the names of the markup tags in an XML document, relationships between document entities, and the required and optional elements of an XML document. Aside from enabling standardization for data exchange in a particular industry, DTDs also enable validation of documents to ensure that they are well formed (that is, they are syntactically correct) and consistent with the specified format of the DTD (that is, a check to ensure that required fields are present and that new fields are not).

Currently, every different business within a given industry has developed its own schema for storing transactional data. One key role that XML will play is in standardizing an exchange format for data. Once an industry standard template for exchanging data is agreed on, each vendor needs only write a program to write data to the standard XML format from the current database schema and conversely to read from the XML standard format to write to the proprietary database schema. Businesses that are already working together need not wait for an industry standard to emerge, however. Business partners that are already engaged in B2B relationships can agree to a mutually satisfying DTD and begin using XML. The result will be that vendors will be able to exchange information in a compatible way without having to overhaul existing databases.

Finally, you may have noticed that while XML provides semantic markers for the captured information, it does not provide display or organizational markers for displaying the information as HTML does. For this purpose, XML provides the facility to use style sheets for any given XML document. A style sheet specifies how data within an XML document is to be displayed on a given client (such as a Web browser). Different style sheets can be used for a given XML document to give different views of the same data. This approach has the advantage that if you wanted multiple views of the same data (such as a table and a graph of the same data) you need not recreate the data multiple times. You only need to create different style sheets for different views of the data that can be reused across different XML documents. Internet browsers are now being released that contain parsers for XML code. Using the built-in parsers, client-side Java and Javascript programs, for example, can be written to obtain elements from an XML document and perform client-side processing.

Hyper Distributed Computing

The third wave of e-commerce will change the way we do business and the way we think about Web computing. First, instead of a business- or server–centric model of e-commerce, we will likely have an individual-centric model of e-commerce, where businesses cater to the needs of the individual rather than vice versa. That is, in today's model of Web commerce, consumers (which can be businesses, too, in a B2B type of transaction) attempt to find service providers, often unsuccessfully, to meet some need. This need, of course, is what we call market demand. This model is roughly based on the physical world model of how we do commerce. If we want to buy a car, we go to car dealerships, instead of having them come to us. To make life easier, centers of commerce evolved in the form of malls so that we can do "one-stop shopping." The point is, though, that market demand is met by businesses displaying their products and services and consumers finding them. In the physical world, we have little alternative. In the virtual world, however, we have as many alternatives as we have ideas.

Thus far, though, the virtual world of Internet-based commerce has modeled itself on the physical world, even going as far as to develop virtual malls. In the future, this model will be flipped on its head. Instead of consumers finding service providers, consumers will advertise (in a virtual sense) their needs, and businesses will compete to meet them. Instead of one-stop shopping where consumers go to one location for all their needs, businesses will develop specialized services and likely work in coalition to meet customized consumer needs. Ultimately, the individual will be empowered over the business, and commerce will be more efficient for both businesses and consumers.

As Internet usage becomes all pervasive and new Internet technologies emerge, it is certainly possible that business might be cut out of the loop in transactions. Consumer-to-consumer (C2C) transactions describe this model of commerce. eBay facilitates one of the best-known examples of C2C commerce. The basic model is that end users offer up goods for auction on which other users can bid. eBay serves as the intermediary, making it possible for individuals to put goods up for sale on the eBay site and taking either a small percentage of the transaction or a fixed fee.

In the future, we may not need the eBays of the world to facilitate these types of transactions. The hub-and-spoke model of C2C commerce will likely be replaced with a fully connected peer-to-peer model that will effectively cut intermediaries—and possibly even major Internet content providers—out of the loop. A distributed client/server model where individuals' computing devices serve as client *and* server will eventually replace the current server-centric model of e-commerce. The first generation of this distributed content model that facilitates C2C commerce—enabled by Napster and its variants, Wrapster, Gnutella, Freenet InfraSearch, and other variants—will revolutionize the e-commerce world.

Napster is a client/server software program that gained a cult-like following among digital music aficionados. Napster allows users to share and exchange digital music files of the MP3 format. End users download the Napster client, which shares MP3 files on the user's hard drive with other Napster clients. Napster users can search every participating user's hard drive for a particular MP3 music file. Once found, the file can be uploaded from one user's machine via the Napster server and downloaded to the requesting user's machine. While a Napster server is still necessary to facilitate the transfer, the intermediation is almost transparent. Furthermore, the servers can be highly distributed, which means a very large number of Napster servers can be deployed.

The uproar from the recording industry is that Napster facilitates illegal copying and distribution of music. While copyright law retains a consumer's rights to copy a CD or other music media for one's own purpose, it does not allow users to distribute these copies. Napster technically does not actively distribute the copies; rather, it facilitates the possibly illegal distribution of copies.

Napster really was just the beginning of this new model of reversing the current paradigm of Internet-based commerce. Today's Web commerce is server-centric; that is, users go to a server to download content. With Napster, users no longer have to hit MP3 sites to download (and pay for) music in digital format. They go through Napster servers to get to music files on other people's machines, rather than from major content providers. Napster still requires users to go to a Napster server. Gnutella takes it to the next level in terms of both the distributed model and content type. Gnutella allows anyone to share and download any type of file—music, software, documents, even pornography. With Gnutella, everyone is a client and a server. Once you sign up into the Gnutella network you agree to share files on your disk as well as have files downloaded to your disk—even files you do not care for. Anyone can search and download files from your disk and vice versa. Gnutella offers anonymity and protection against violation of copyright laws. Because there is no single server that shares content, prosecutors have a hard time identifying whom to target. Furthermore, if files are encrypted, each user will not even know what files he or she is sharing and can therefore potentially claim no knowledge of copyright violation.

Gnutella and its brethren are threatening traditional businesses and industries in several ways. First, they threaten to replace the server-centric model of Internet commerce with a highly distributed model for C2C-based commerce. Now, one need not go to a major content provider to find and download content. Second, those who make money by controlling release of content stand to lose this controlling interest. Third, the individual will become empowered at the expense of the business, at least as it currently stands. Not surprisingly, several industry associations from movie studios to recording labels and artists to software publishers are fighting the release and use of this technology vehemently in court and in Congress. As the expression goes, though, the horse is already out of the barn. There is no stopping technology's progress. Nevertheless, as in the days when the movie studios fought video technology as its biggest threat, but then found a way to make it their leading source of revenue, innovative businesses will find a way to harness this technology for commercial profit. Just don't tell the anarchists who, for now, have found a way to free the information.

Changes that are more significant are likely to occur in the way we do Web-based computing. Today's client/server model of Web computing will be replaced by a hyper-distributed model of computing where computing is performed on any number of different resources to meet some need. The key distinction between today's distributed computing models and the hyper-distributed model is that the distribution of computing will be performed using the Web (HTTP) protocol. Though current versions of HTTP are not well equipped to distribute computation, this will doubtless change. The notion of "IP everywhere" will be instrumental in ushering in this fundamental change in computing. As all devices—not just those we conventionally think of as computers, which are, in fact, mostly general-purpose computing machines—are assigned IP addresses (and by extension, Web addresses), we will have the ability to distribute computation (that is, distribute programs and data) among any number of different resources according to both our computational needs and available resources.

The traditional client/server model, where many clients make requests to a given server, will be replaced by a hyper-distributed model where any given computing resource can be a client or a server in the old client/server model. Rather than a server-centric model of computation, computation will be distributed among many different computing resources ("servers" in the traditional sense) in order to service any given requesting "client." In many cases, these same "clients" will be a "server" or, more appropriately, some component of a "distributed server" to service other "client" requests. This hyper-distributed paradigm of addressable devices will include our watches, articles of clothing, household appliances, office furniture, and perhaps even celestial bodies, as Internet inventor Vinton Cerf is fond of citing. As common devices become "intelligent" or, more accurately, programmable, the security and privacy issues will be staggering in proportion and traditional means of securing computing assets, such as firewalls, will not be of much use in a hyper-distributed architecture.

To properly frame the hyper-distributed computing paradigm, it is important to understand the current limitations of Web-based computing and distributed computing. Web-based computing is performed using the Hyper Text Transfer Protocol (HTTP). The main hyper media technology in use is HTML documents. In other words, Web-based computing today primarily consists of using HTTP to access HTML documents. As we discussed earlier, HTML is a markup language designed to enable distributed authoring and publishing of documents. As such, it does not support traditional constructs of programming languages such as file input/output and maintaining and manipulating variables. HTTP was designed as the transport layer for HTML documents. As such, it is also very limited in its functions. For instance, HTTP is a stateless protocol, which means that each HTTP connection (or HTML document request) has no memory of prior connections. To overcome some of these hurdles, cookies were created to retain memory between HTTP connections by saving prior connection data to users' disk drives. HTTP also lacks the extensibility and modularity of a more general-purpose protocol because it was designed specifically for document transport. The number of methods supported by HTTP is also very limited (for example, GET, PUT, POST), though some ad hoc extensions to the methods have been proposed (such as DELETE), though not widely implemented and supported. The main point here is that HTML and HTTP were designed for the specific purpose of document authoring and large-scale distribution. Attempts to use HTTP for more general-purpose computing have had to work within this fairly limited paradigm of Web-based computing. Regardless, HTTP is what we use almost universally and inevitably what we must work with if we are to develop Web-based technologies.

Distributed computing is widely used today. Distributed computing is a paradigm of computing where program computations are performed and coordinated by a number of different software components, which need not reside on the same machine. One of the keys to distributed computing and component-based software in general is the "glue" that binds the interactions between different software components. Like general-purpose computing, software components are written in a particular programming language, such as C, C++, or Java. In order to support communication between software components as well as other component services, such as naming and persistence, a distributed component infrastructure is necessary. This is the role that the distributed object technologies we know as CORBA, COM/DCOM, and Java/RMI serve. They provide the infrastructural services to enable software components to interact whether the components are on the same machine or distributed over a network.

Distributed object technologies were built to extend existing component technologies that link local software components together. For instance, much of today's Microsoft Windows software is component-based software. The common desktop applications we use actually consist of a bunch of distinct COM components that are hooked together under a familiar graphical interface. Provided that the underlying components are fairly robust, this is a great way to rapidly build industrial-strength applications from reusable components. It also makes it easy to import a spreadsheet into a word processor application or a table into a presentation. With Microsoft's COM-based technologies, it just so happens that the components of an application reside on a single machine. Distributed computing extends this notion to make machine boundaries transparent. The idea is to make accesses to remote components indistinguishable from accesses to local components. Therefore, the user need not be concerned about where the software actually resides, be it on his or her own computer or networked on a distant machine. For instance, using DCOM, desktop applications can be built from components that physically reside on different machines.

To take it a step further, some component models also provide location transparency to application developers. That is, the application developer also need not be concerned where the components used by the application physically reside, so long as the name of the component is known. The actual location of the component—that is, the machine— is handled transparently by the component infrastructure.

The way current distributed object technologies work is based on remote procedure calls (RPCs) or remote method invocations (RMIs). That is, an application or component makes a request to another component using the particular communication mechanism of the distributed object technology infrastructure. The requesting mechanism will vary depending on whether you are using COM/DCOM, CORBA, or Java RMI. One limitation of using existing distributed object technologies for Web-based computing is in the manner in which these remote method invocations are made. When making a request to a component, the network and machine addressing used to reference the component is generally technology-specific and sometimes platform-dependent. The referencing scheme will vary depending on which distributed object technology and potentially which platform type is used.

In Web-based computing, we require naming services to use the domain name service (DNS) conventions and the technology to be universal and platform-independent. For instance, to invoke the services of a distributed component in the Web-based model, we would want to include the full domain name of the Web site we are requesting, together with the name of the component, in order to be compatible with existing DNS conventions and to retain the valuable branding of domain names that currently exists.

Thus, today, we have two technologies, a universal protocol in HTTP that is unable to support distributed computation and several distributed object technologies unable to support universal computing, which on their own are not able to fulfill the needs of Web-based hyper-distributed computing. This is likely to change in order to meet the changing paradigm of e-commerce. Over the long term, as e-commerce shifts to an individual-based market where a multiplicity of services collaborate in real time to meet the dynamic needs of the individual, hyper-distributed computing will replace the aging client/server model. Distributed computing will be performed on all manner of devices using the Web as the fabric for interprocess communication. XML will likely have a role in transitioning from today's screen-scraping model to tomorrow's hyper-distributed model. In a sense, all components will be remote clients *and* servers, and all components will interoperate over the Web. XML will be used to translate Web-based requests into appropriate RMIs and vice versa.

Principal Drivers of E-Commerce

In the preceding section, we laid out a vision of where e-commerce is heading in the future. In order to better understand the engine driving e-commerce today, however, it is meaningful to understand the principle drivers of e-commerce. Three principle drivers of business in e-commerce are as follows:

1. The opportunity for new revenue streams through new services, products, or business methods.
2. The potential to reduce operating costs.
3. Increased profitability as an outcome of the first two drivers.

Perhaps the most significant business driver is the opportunity to derive new revenue streams. Businesses that innovate and provide new services, new ways of doing business, or even value-added services are more likely to succeed in the online world. One of the main reasons why e-commerce did not emerge more significantly in its early days of 1996 and 1997 was because the business model was to simply map prevailing brick-and-mortar business practices to a Web interface. For the most part, consumers did not buy into this model. Businesses that have done well in e-commerce are the ones that have innovated in using the Web to deliver new types of products and services. For instance, the reverse auction concept reverses the role of consumer and provider, by having providers of services and products bid on a consumer's business requests. For established businesses, simply bringing their catalogs to the Web is often not sufficient to bring in consumers. Value-added content appears to be the minimum effort required to make surfing the Web to a particular site worthwhile. For instance, major retailers Wal-Mart and Kmart provide *free* Internet access service. Obviously, this move is an attempt to bring consumers to their own sites and probably to signal a shift to an electronic marketplace for these two traditional brick-and-mortar retailers.

Numerous examples exist and many more are to come in value-added services made possible by the Internet. Another instance of value-added retailing in the business-to-consumer space is the concept of aggregating and leveraging high consumer demand for certain products to reduce the cost of the product for each consumer by buying the product in bulk from the manufacturer. Companies like mercata.com and accompany.com provide this type of value-added service, previously unavailable to consumers, by using the Internet and a Web interface to order high-demand products in bulk from manufacturers. The savings in cost is passed on to the consumers in real time. As more consumers sign up to purchase a product, the price of the product drops (shown in real time) and all consumers that have signed up to purchase the product benefit. Likewise, the retailer benefits by purchasing only the quantity demanded by its consumers, which brings real meaning to just-in-time purchasing and acquisition.

Many companies are building electronic communities from their Internet sites. One of the true virtues of the Web mentioned earlier is that it makes a researcher out of everyone. For instance, many sites offer "buyers guides" to products and services they resell to enable consumers to make informed decisions, like the *Consumer Reports* magazines that have been around for years and years. This is a great value-added service to provide, but some sites take it a step further. For instance, electronic communities leverage the Internet to share their own experiences with products. In a town hall style reminiscent of yesteryears, visitors share their experience with and wisdom about particular vacation destinations, cars they purchased, or differences between brands of a particular product. For many consumers, there is nothing like a testimonial from real users of a product. Obviously, the Internet and the Web make this kind of sharing possible and the e-commerce experience worthy for doing product research and due diligence.

While the most successful method of making money on the Internet involves generating new revenue streams, some companies are attempting to make money by reducing the costs of their operations by going to the Internet. The banking industry is a good example. For instance, as banking transactions have become increasingly electronic over the years, from ATM banking to telephone banking to Internet-based banking, the cost per transaction has decreased significantly. One source states that the cost per transaction drops from roughly U.S. $1.00 for a cash-based transaction to about $.25 per transaction using electronic bill presentment (see *E-Commerce Security*, Chapter 3). If e-cash were widely used, the cost could drop to just a few cents per transaction.

One of the original business drivers for doing business on the Internet was to cut costs by eliminating brick-and-mortar operations and associated personnel. This is the second principle driver mentioned earlier for doing business on the Internet. At one extreme you have companies like Egghead Software closing all of its retail outlets in order to become a pure Internet play and more effectively compete for people's dollars in the commercial software business. In practice, though, many retailers have kept their retail outlets open but have supplemented their offerings with Internet access to their services and products. This "click-and-mortar" model proved to be successful during the Christmas of 1999, when some of the most popular e-tailing sites were not necessarily new Internet businesses, but traditional brand-name retailers who opened Internet sites for their clientele to do their shopping online in addition to shopping in physical stores.

In banking, many banks have kept their branches open but have provided Internet access to accounts for their customers as a value-added service, if only to be competitive in a tight market. In the short term this has increased the banks' costs, but in the long term it may save banking costs by automatically handling common transactions over the Internet. There are now a number of pure Internet firms providing banking and financial services. That is, these firms have no brick-and-mortar buildings (that we need know about). Time will be the best judge of whether this pure Internet play works for the banking industry or if customers are going to demand the human interface in banking.

With recent legislation eliminating legal barriers previously erected to prevent a company from offering banking, investing, and insurance services, an opportunity awaits large companies that can offer "one-stop shopping" for all these services on the Internet. As predicted by the first principal driver of e-commerce, e-businesses are more likely to be successful by innovating and creating new services and revenue streams previously not possible in typical retailing. There are a number of Internet businesses whose role is not to sell you their insurance or loan you their money, but rather to find you the *best* insurer or the best loan based on *your* needs. This is the role of intermediation for e-businesses. The intermediary essentially pitches your needs to the lowest bidder or best suitor. The argument is that with many suppliers willing to bid for your business, the customer is likely to end up with the best deal (that is, a low loan rate or insurance premium) from a company that can best cater to your individual needs. This is the model in which the way consumers and businesses interact is reversed so that businesses cater to the needs of the individual and compete on a per-transaction basis.

While the case for intermediation in e-commerce is substantiated by novel business practices otherwise not possible, there is also a case to be made for disintermediation—eliminating the middleman that exists in traditional commercial transactions. Disintermediation will not be universally applicable, for as demonstrated previously, there is often a role for which a broker can add considerable value to a transaction. In some market segments, pundits have claimed that entire industries might be radically changed by disintermediation that occurs as a result of e-commerce. The travel industry is ripe for disintermediation. Travel agents set up and broker deals between consumers and the multiplicity of airlines, hotels, and rental car companies. For their efforts, travel agents get a small percentage in every transaction. More recently, the airline industry is trying to gain direct access to the consumer by offering online booking services directly to the consumer, thus cutting out the middlemen. Of course, a number of new middlemen have also set up shop on the Internet (such as Travelocity and Microsoft Expedia) to facilitate online booking. In either case, the travel industry will likely be radically changed by the ability to efficiently book travel online.

Dell Computer Corporation has also exploited (if not invented) the concept of "buying direct" to bypass intermediaries, which, in this case, are computer retailers. Rather than going to a computer retailer to purchase a computer off the shelf, the idea of buying direct is to customize the computer yourself over the Web by specifying your desired configuration (CPU type, memory, hard drive, monitor, modem, and peripherals). Dell will build the computer according to your specified configuration (or you can choose a preconfigured computer) and then ship you the machine. The buy direct model is appealing because you configure the computer according to your own needs, as opposed to having to buy a computer already configured (perhaps to someone else's needs) off the shelf at a retail store. Also appealing about the Web interface is that different computer configurations can be "built" online to balance desired features against cost limits. Of course, if you feel intimidated by having to configure your own computer, preconfigured computers are offered, much like the ones you might buy off the shelf. The key benefit of cutting the middleman out of the transaction is reducing costs. To the extent that buying direct will catch on, the computer retail industry could radically change from selling computers to selling computer peripherals, software, and support. Even this may change with time as consumers already often buy software directly from the software publisher.

Buying direct is also beginning to catch on in the multibillion dollar automobile market. One of the most frustrating experiences for consumers buying cars today is the uncertainty over how much you should actually pay for the car. We've all been trained that "sticker price" is way too much and that you should be able to cut a deal for less. But how much less? Often, the fear that someone else is buying the same car for less—that is, the fear of getting ripped off—is far worse than the actual amount you end up paying. For this reason, among many others, a Web-based alternative to the typical car purchasing experience may have the potential to change this industry. Buying direct from the manufacturer or buying cars online through an intermediary are possible alternatives. Currently, almost every car manufacturer has Web pages with pictures and features of their cars. One still needs to go to an affiliated dealership in order to purchase the car. This might well change within the next year. Car manufacturers have already openly talked about selling directly to the market at fixed pre-established prices.

Web-based car sales intermediaries may actually blaze the trail for car manufacturers to sell their cars directly online. Currently, there are a growing number of online car sales sites that have no apparent affiliation with any given car manufacturers. These sites serve as intermediaries between the consumer and the manufacturer, while still keeping the car dealer in the loop. What is innovative about some of these sites is that, similar to Dell, they let the customer "build" the car online. That is, the car buyer specifies the desired features in the car he or she wants while checking the associated price point. Once the customer builds the car to his or her own specifications, the order is made via the intermediary and the car is shipped to the customer, via the local dealer. The invoice price, the Manufacturers Suggested Retail Price (MSRP), along with the intermediary's price, is shown. The benefit of the Web-based buying experience is that there is no high-pressure sales pitch to buy anything; you can buy the car you want—not just the cars the dealer has in stock—and you know the exact price of the car ahead of time. The downside, of course, is that you can't test drive the car on the Web (at least not today!). Typically the cost of the car you buy falls between the dealer's invoice and the MSRP, which is the point to which most informed car buyers try to bargain.

Other online car sites act as an intermediary in different ways. Auto-By-Tel made its name by letting the customer specify his or her desired car and leveraging a group discount for Auto-By-Tel buyers to get a better price (in theory) from the local dealer. A more recent approach is to let car dealers vie for a customer's business by bidding the lowest price for the buyer's desired car. Again, value-added service is what makes online sites successful. Dealers that simply put their car pictures online are not adding much value. Intermediaries that work in the consumers' interests are going to be most successful. Those that change the current paradigm of buying cars at dealerships are using the Web in different and innovative ways that will likely lead to a successful online business. Buying direct and reversing the traditional relationship between car dealers and consumers are just two ways of innovating on the Web. Building electronic discussion groups on cars is another way to add value: Car buyers can share experiences with buying cars (online and offline), owning cars, and driving cars to the benefit of prospective car buyers. Finally, while car auctions have been around for quite some time, before now, selling your car at an auction was rarely possible. eBay.com now gives consumers the ability to sell their cars in an online auction format.

As stated at the beginning of this section, one of the principal business drivers of e-commerce is profitability. As the examples above illustrate, the Web is enabling business innovation by creating new models of business previously not possible. While many of these new businesses have garnered tremendous brand names, Web traffic, and stock valuations, few have managed to turn a profit. Following the "Internet Christmas" of 1998, many expected the fourth quarter of 1999 would be the biggest ever. They were not disappointed. Forrester Research estimated U.S. $10 billion in sales in the fourth quarter alone in 1999. While revenues were high, profits were scarce. Amazon.com provides a good case study. By standard metrics, Amazon.com had an amazing fourth quarter in 1999. Its fourth quarter sales of $650 million was 2.5 times its fourth quarter sales of 1998 and, in fact, exceeded the $610 million in sales it did in all of 1998. In the process, Amazon.com shipped 20 million items and gained 2.5 million new customers. In spite of the increases in revenue, Amazon.com still has not been able to turn a profit. It lost $140 million in the same quarter. Furthermore, Amazon.com has not been able to project a profitable quarter in the foreseeable future. Yet, Amazon.com's market capitalization at the beginning of 2000 was over U.S. $20 billion.

If some of the biggest e-tailers have yet to turn a profit, how is it that e-commerce businesses can drive such high market valuations? Is the answer "irrational exuberance" over dot.com companies? These questions have no clear-cut answers. The one thing we do know is that the valuation given to a company at any given time is based on its expected future profitability. Dot.com companies have such high valuations because their investors believe that in the future, these companies will be profitable over the long haul. Only time will tell just how well these companies will perform. Their current share prices and valuations will be a continuously adjusting expectation of future profitability.

The Changing Paradigm of Computing

We have all been weaned on the desktop computing model of e-commerce. That is, today, most of us still sit at our desktop machine and surf the Net using a Web browser. Looking to the future, this model will be changing significantly to a world of more wireless and embedded devices. In the section on hyper-distributed computing, we hinted at the fact that the server-centric model of computing is rapidly changing to a hyper-distributed model, where objects, and computing, are all distributed. The network, as we know it today, will really be the platform of computing tomorrow. What is striking about this change is the way we view technology and the way we use it. Previously, we thought about computing in terms of computational power (CPU cycles or millions of instructions per second). Probably the most important shift in our technology and thinking is that it will no longer be about *computing*, as much as it will be about *communicating*. That is, in the next evolution of computing, we will be more concerned about harnessing technology for communicating between corporations, individuals, and objects, than for crunching numbers.

To this end, we will see significant advances in the market with wireless and embedded devices that are Internet-enabled. Although the desktop machine will not disappear all together, its importance will be relegated to office hours. In the new digital economy, the twenty-first century worker will no longer be tethered to the desk. Wireless technologies will provide seamless Internet access to network computing when you are in a car, on a plane, commuting by train, or in someone else's office. Early adopters have already been consuming personal digital assistants (PDAs) such as the Palm Pilot and Internet-enabled mobile phones in droves. Today, one can check e-mail, surf the Web, get the local weather and traffic conditions, and determine optimal routes to the new restaurant you found on your hand-held PDA. As liberating as PDAs are from the klunky deskbound PCs, PDAs still have some technical hurdles to overcome to make surfing the Web the same experience as on a 17-inch monitor, or composing e-mails a manageable experience without the benefit of a keypad. As the display technology, software, and Internet connection to hand-held devices improve over the next few years, these devices, or some variants of them, will outnumber their desktop counterparts. Or more appropriately, they will become as standard as the telephone. After all, these devices are really about communicating, rather than about computing.

To effectively cut the tether to the desktop, several enabling technologies will be needed. Beyond wireless connectivity to the Internet, devices will need to be able to seamlessly connect to e-mail servers of choice, to file servers on the home or corporate LANs, and they will need some processing capability themselves to perform various client-side processing for e-commerce-related functions, such as dispatching intelligent agents to book the best ticket across the country. As most travelers will attest to, connecting to the office LAN is still a non-trivial process, one that generally involves installing and configuring complicated software on a laptop, dialing up to an office modem bank if Internet access to the office LAN is not supported, authenticating to firewalls and file servers, and then ensuring that the files you actually need were made available on a remote access share. Usually, a few phone calls to technical support are necessary as well. As more and more of the twenty-first century workforce become mobile, the notion of the LAN and a fixed office becomes more antiquated. Ideally, connecting to file servers and Internet services should be as easy from a hand-held or portable computing device as it should be from within the office.

The other important technology enabler will be the ability to host and execute software within small devices that are Internet-enabled. Embedded Internet devices will become more pervasive not just for the traveling worker, but also within the home in the form of intelligent appliances, in cars for families who are doing "just-in-time" research while shopping, in kiosks in convenience stores, in music stores, in town centers, and in vending machines. Taking embedded Internet to the next level, we may very well have Internet-enabled clothing in what is called "wearable computing" to provide hands-free Internet access. For instance, if you can't lug around a 17-inch monitor, you may be able to pull down a visor over your eyes that provides a display for your Internet surfing. These devices will require the ability to host and execute software that can not only support communication to Internet servers, but can also perform some of the computing necessary to make local decisions (such as to book a particular ticket after considering all offers). Furthermore, in a hyper-distributed object model, other devices may invoke objects within an embedded device in order to perform collaborative computing. For instance, in a completely wired home, a grocery manager program may poll the refrigerator to determine which groceries need to be ordered from the online grocery delivery service. Likewise, a house manager program may automatically adjust lighting, heating, ventilation, and air conditioning, depending on whether and where occupants are in the house.

Considering the many forms of wireless and embedded Internet access that consumers are demanding and vendors will be providing, seamless access to home and corporate servers will be essential. The LAN will need to be opened up and firewalls will need to be tumbled, simply because they will have no place in a wireless and fully connected society. The advances made in smartcards over the last few years will significantly jump-start these efforts. Smartcards have the ability not only to authenticate users to PCs and firewalls, but also to perform client-side computing for e-commerce transactions. Programs can be downloaded and executed on a credit-card-sized PC.

The notion of firewalls, or logical guards in general, is becoming antiquated very quickly for several reasons. One of the most important reasons is that users want ubiquitous access to their corporate networks and file systems from wherever they are and whatever type of device they are using (desktop PCs, cell phones, or handheld PDAs). Firewalls are artificial barriers that no longer meet the needs of ubiquitous networks. That is, the distinction between inside and outside is quickly fading. Second, resources are becoming widely distributed. That is, one may use resources or services from many different vendors or Internet sites, where again firewalls cannot really serve their purpose in distinguishing who is inside or outside. Finally, as HTTP becomes the pervasive protocol of Web-based commerce (including distributed computing), firewalls are ill-equipped to provide any type of security against these types of transactions because, they let *all* HTTP traffic through.

In a hyper-distributed model of computing, firewalls will be more an impediment than a solution. As a result, they will become obsolete. In their place, access control will be performed at the object level, rather than at the network entry level as it currently is performed. Smartcards provide the ability to perform strong authentication using public/private keys. As a result, one will be able to perform personal computing from public kiosks or shared devices by authenticating one's credentials via the smartcard. Biometrics may be used in place of passwords to provide even stronger authentication based on immutable and unforgeable properties of the human anatomy.

Marrying encryption, authentication, and access control services with maturing distributed object technologies, today's networks will change from physical enclaves and clusters of machines to clusters of virtual networks. Your personal data and software may be physically stored on any number of systems that you may or may not own. Firewalling networks and subnetworks against attacks from within and without will not make sense in this model. Interestingly enough, with data and resource objects widely distributed, the system as a whole will be more secure. Compromising a single server will give only partial access to confidential data and privileged services.

To realize this vision of the future of network computing, we need to shift our thinking about security from guards, fortresses, and firewalls to application-based security—at a more microscopic level, object-based security. The basic idea is that security is enforced based on access to system resources regardless of the protocol used to access the object.

In summary, the digital economy of the twenty-first century will radically change the way we think about and perform computing. Wireless devices, embedded Internet, and hyper-distributed objects will all enable an Internet-based economy that is driven by advances in communicating between corporations, people, and objects. While these advances will no doubt enable greater efficiencies in all walks of life and greater profitability for business able to capture the changing paradigm of computing, this new paradigm also introduces significant new challenges to securing both business proprietary information and individual privacy. The rest of this book is devoted to these two topics.

Risks in E-Commerce

Without question, electronic commerce is changing the way we think about and do business. The impact of e-commerce on the economy and society is only now being felt. In spite of the profound potential of businesses engaging in e-commerce to revolutionize business paradigms as we know them, the security and privacy risks still present major stumbling blocks to realizing the twenty-first century vision of a robust digital economy.

While not quite the "electronic Pearl Harbor" predicted by so many, the denial-of-service attacks against many of the best known names in e-commerce in February 2000 presented a startling wake-up call that the Internet infrastructure on which e-commerce is based is fundamentally vulnerable to simple attacks. E-commerce luminaries including Yahoo!, eBay, Amazon.com, E-Trade, Datek, Buy.com, ZDNet, and CNN.com all fell victim to distributed denial-of-service attacks, rendering these sites unavailable for one or more hours, resulting in losses estimated in the millions of dollars for these companies. These attacks exposed the vulnerability of any company doing business on the Internet. Denial-of-service attacks have long been called the "Achilles heel" of the Internet because of the inability to defend against them. While some specific defenses can be employed against specific types of denial-of-service attacks, it is not very hard to bring down an online server by harnessing the power of PCs and other servers to make many, many requests to the target server. Interestingly enough, one of the best solutions to this problem is self-policing of the Internet. Because most perpetrators of these types of attacks attempt to disguise the origin of the attack by changing the origination header field in the network packets, Internet Service Providers can perform a simple check to eliminate those packets that attempt to "spoof" the identity of another origin. This approach requires the cooperation of the entire Internet community, which is perhaps a better alternative to policing by federal governments.

A burgeoning type of e-commerce crime is Internet fraud. Internet fraud has risen dramatically since 1997. In particular, Internet-based auctions are a major source of fraud. The number of complaints of fraud to the Federal Trade Commission's Bureau of Consumer Affairs over Internet auctions rose to more than 10,000 in 1999, compared to just over 100 in 1997. Most of these complaints are about promises "e-con artists" never delivered on for goods that were purchased at auction or for delivery of goods significantly different from what was advertised. The problem has gained the attention of federal and state authorities that have promised to crack down on Internet fraud.

Another type of Internet crime that strikes fear in many consumers' hearts is online credit card theft. A recent example of theft and extortion from a popular online CD site illustrates this risk well. A cracker allegedly broke into a popular online CD site and managed to steal more than 300,000 credit card profiles of members, including their credit card numbers and other personal information. Having been refused the money the cracker was seeking from the site's owner, the cracker allegedly posted the credit card numbers to other Web sites and attempted to sell them for profit. The reality is that this problem is not new. Most Internet hacks are made possible by flawed software. It appears to be the case here, again, that flawed software allowed the cracker to get access to the system he otherwise should not have had. These problems will not go away in the short term, either. Many sites are vulnerable to either poorly configured systems or flawed software that can be exploited for malicious gain.

Aside from intruders and malicious software, one of the most pervasive, least acknowledged, and least defensible attacks is from trusted insiders. Insiders often have unrestricted access to sensitive and proprietary information. An insider can be anyone with access to network and file resources, ranging from corporate executives to administrative support staff. Disgruntled employees are a source of major concern in corporations today. A disgruntled employee who may be on his or her way out can easily plant a logic bomb that destroys local and networked file systems. Given today's competitive environment, it is not too unusual for an employee to take company proprietary material with him or her on his or her way to a competitor. We don't have good mechanisms to detect or prevent this kind of theft of digital assets. Even well-intentioned employees can become unwitting accomplices to pernicious outsiders. For example, running an e-mail attachment (even desktop documents that have the ability to run macros) sent from the outside can result in confidential documents being shipped out to potential competitors or adversaries. The Melissa virus demonstrated this capability on a large scale.

Another tried-and-true practice that predates computer cracking is social engineering in order to obtain access that would otherwise not be granted. Social engineering is using non-technical techniques in order to obtain unauthorized access. Social engineering may be used to convince a system administrator that you are an ISP contractor who needs access to a router. Simply gaining physical access to a site by posing as cleaning services is often enough to grab post-it notes that have user names and passwords scrawled on them from terminals.

The problem is, however, much more severe than that painted by these specific incidents. How severe is the subject of much study and debate. The Computer Security Institute, based in San Francisco, surveys more than 500 corporations, financial institutions, and government agencies annually; see www.gocsi.com/prelea990301.htm. In the 1999 CSI survey, over half of the respondents reported they had suffered financial losses due to computer attack. However, only 31 percent could actually quantify these financial losses, which were estimated to be over $100 million in 1999. Corporations' reluctance to report such crime has made gathering accurate statistics about computer crime difficult, at best, and, at worst, almost impossible to prosecute by law enforcement. After the 1994 Citibank hacking incident, in which a Russian cracker was able to successfully move $10 million out of Citibank's accounts, many financial institutions have been loathe to report computer crime, even though all but $400,000 of the stolen money was recovered. A U.S. House Banking Committee estimated that the financial sector lost $2.4 billion due to computer attacks in 1998.

Awareness of law enforcement in computer crimes is only now beginning to drive up reporting to law enforcement. The 1999 CSI survey found that reporting of incidents has increased to 32 percent from 17 percent three years ago. Even with increased reporting, the chances of catching and prosecuting computer criminals still remain slim. Federal authorities with limited resources and technical prowess will prosecute only the largest cases of computer crime. Further complicating the prosecution is the lack of good auditing at host sites on which to establish the damage perpetrated by the criminal. Probably, most significantly, the lack of good auditing and intrusion detection tools means that most computer crime is perpetrated unbeknownst to the victims. Thus, the figures reported from companies on losses is probably far too conservative an estimate, discounting for those who do not report and those who do not even know they have lost assets.

Financial losses are only part of the picture, however. Theft of proprietary information is perhaps one of the greatest threats to most companies' portfolios of intellectual assets. The U.S. Chamber of Commerce estimates that nearly 80 percent of corporate intellectual assets are stored digitally. With Internet connections to every employee's desktop, the risks of losing proprietary information increase significantly. What makes this problem worse is that the information can be stolen without any trace of the crime committed. Digital information can be perfectly copied without changing the original. As a result, most victims are unaware that they have even lost the information. The 1999 CSI survey found that 26 percent of the respondents reported theft of proprietary information. Malicious software plays a large part in these losses. Software downloaded surreptitiously from Web pages, run as innocuous-looking e-mail attachments, or spread by floppy disk or other media can corrupt files or even ship them out over an Internet connection. Recent examples include the Melissa virus, Explorer.zip worm, Back Orifice 2000, NetBus, and the BubbleBoy virus. A study by Computer Economics of Carlsbad, California, found that in just the first two quarters of 1999, businesses worldwide lost an estimated $7.6 billion due to malicious code.

Regardless of which of these figures paints the most accurate picture of the amount of losses, it is clear now that security and privacy in e-commerce are as important to the industry as the business that is conducted on the Internet. Building e-commerce sites without understanding the security and privacy risks to both corporate digital assets and personal information is simply irresponsible. To this end, the rest of the book addresses and tackles the security and privacy risks in e-commerce.

CHAPTER 2

Security Is a Software Problem

"We can create powerful and pleasurable software-based products by the simple expedient of designing our computer-based products before we build them. Contrary to popular belief, we are not already doing so."

ALAN COOPER
"FATHER" OF VISUAL BASIC[1]

L et's set the record straight from the beginning. Security and privacy in e-commerce are inextricably intertwined with the software that runs e-businesses and the Internet infrastructure. The problems with and solutions to e-commerce security begin with software. At the heart of our digital economy is software. Software is pervasive in every component that enables the information economy, from the ubiquitous Web browser to telecommunications switches, network servers, middleware, databases, and supply-chain logistics. The greatest risk to electronic commerce and to the growing new economy is failing software, be it from inadvertent flaws in design and implementation or from malicious attacks. Denial-of-service attacks against leading e-commerce players underscore the fragility of the Internet. To put it succinctly, security is a software problem.

Over the past few years, several events have conspired to create one of the biggest problems humankind has faced—poor software. CNET recently published its top ten list of great bugs in history that details some of the most expensive and interesting failures due to software bugs.[2] The top ten list in reverse order is as follows:

Mariner 1 Venus probe failure (1962). A faulty line of Fortran code written in 1962 veered the rocket off course, which forced NASA to self-destruct the rocket before it endangered human lives.

Therac-25 radiation treatment machine (1985–87). A combination of poor software engineering, software interlocks, and flawed user interface code caused four patient deaths by massive radiation overdoses.

AT&T long distance outage (1990). A single line of faulty code in AT&T's call handlers resulted in a meltdown of the company's long distance network, affecting significant portions of the country.

Patriot missile defense misses (1991). A software bug that resulted in clock drift accumulated to 0.34 seconds—enough to throw the tracking system far enough off that the missile battery could not track an Iraqi Scud missile that killed 28 U.S. soldiers in barracks.

Intel Pentium chip floating-point bug (1994). A bug in the Pentium chip's floating-point operations, discovered by Lynchburg College Professor Thomas Nicely, sometimes would give erroneous answers to complex operations. The bug brought national attention to the reality that software bugs had now become a problem in the design of complex chips.

Intuit's MacInTax bug (1995). A bug in Intuit's MacInTax software leaked users' financial information available on personal tax returns. Debug code left in a file allowed Unix users to log into the Intuit master computer where all MacInTax returns were stored. Users could then view, delete, or modify other people's tax forms prior to being submitted to the IRS.

Denver airport baggage handling (1995). Bugs in the new Denver airport's computerized baggage handling system not only chewed up baggage, but also caused the airport to open 16 months late and $3.2 billion over budget.

Java security holes (1996–97). A series of obscure holes in the Java Virtual Machines in both Netscape's and Microsoft's Web browsers put into doubt the security of running mobile code on users' desktops. The publicity these holes received in the media helped create an environment of distrust for Internet-based software.

Power grid bug in California (1998). Problems in debugging the software that runs a new power grid in California delayed the deregulation of the California power industry by three months. The deregulation would allow consumers and businesses to choose from as many as 200 different power providers. Bugs found during a seven-day simulation of the new power grid halted the scheduled January 1, 1998 deregulation, costing an estimated $90 million, much of which will be borne by consumers.

Millennium bug (2000). The best known software bug in history was the Y2K bug, caused by programmers who represented the year used by many applications with two numeric fields, instead of four. Thus, when the century date turned over, these software applications believed the date was 1900 instead of 2000. The Y2K bug fix has also been called the most successful emergency management operation in the history of humankind.

Other examples abound. *Business Week* published its Software Hell edition in its December 6, 1999 issue that listed 21 major failures due to software bugs since January 1998.[3] Scanning the dates on the preceding list, it is clear that software bugs have been a problem for a long time. It has only been in the last several years, though, that software has become pervasive and so incredibly complex that it is too difficult to grasp and test in its entirety. This means that the bugs listed here only hint at the types of spectacular failures we will likely see in the future.

While many of the bugs listed here are related to reliability and safety, software bugs also affect security. To put it simply, when it comes to security, it's all about the software. All too often, we focus on encryption protocols, firewalls, and other point solutions when it comes to security, when in fact we are overlooking the root cause of most security problems: bad software.

Software in the Stone Age

To give some perspective on how radically things have changed in software, we need to think back to the days before the PC revolution. In the pre-PC era of the 1970s, software was primarily run on "big iron" mainframe systems from IBM and the seven dwarfs—the lesser-known mainframe competitors that have largely gone by the wayside, but whose story was chronicled by Tracy Kidder's Pulitzer Prize winning book, *Soul of a New Machine*. Mainframe software was generally regarded as robust and as reliable as the hardware itself. Bugs were rare, and when they did occur in the field, the developers took the reports personally. It was a different environment then, though. Hardware was fairly homogeneous. That is, the platform on which the software ran did not change drastically from installation to installation. Because there were a limited number of software vendors, market pressures did not mandate quick release cycles. Dependability was valued over features.

Before the PC revolution, the computing paradigm was the client/server paradigm. Like fashion trends, we see the same computing paradigm again 20 years later with Internet-based computing. In the early days of client/server computing, the client was known as a dumb terminal, typically a VT100 monochrome monitor with a keyboard. Today, we would call these "thin clients." The dumb terminal got its computing cycles from a mainframe server. What is important to note is that users did not have much control over the software that was installed with the server, including the operating system and application software. Users were simply users, while system administrators had control over the software that ran on the servers. This dumb client/smart server paradigm—while seemingly ancient—had the benefit that users could not very easily corrupt the server through inadvertent deletions or modifications of files. Also, without the ability to install software on the servers, users could not very easily install malicious software or viruses—intentionally or not. By and large, the client/server paradigm of the mainframe days worked reliably, with security as an unintentional side effect of good software and stringent control of the server machines.

The PC Revolution

The PC revolution changed this paradigm for better and worse. Consumers of PC software were considered early adopters and thus were willing to accept buggy software. Over time, this grew to be the culture of PC software: quick releases with new features that are likely to be buggy. The number of software vendors grew in proportion to the penetration of the PC onto desktops in the office and at home. Patches to fix bugs are now *de rigueur*. New versions of software are as much about fixing known bugs as they are about introducing new features. Microsoft introduced its customers to the innocuous sounding term "service pack," as a way of fixing bugs in the operating system. Heretofore, most consumers were not even aware of operating system bugs. Service packs tended to introduce as many new problems as they fixed, though, presenting an interesting quandary for customers: Should I upgrade to the next service pack level (which might fix a security hole to which I am vulnerable) at the risk of introducing new bugs and holes, or should I stick with the current level whose vulnerabilities I know?

Software has grown into the most complex machine ever assembled by humans. Unlike the physical science disciplines, such as physics and chemistry, there are no laws that govern software except one: the more complex the code, the more flawed it is likely to be. Today, programs contain millions of lines of instructions that lead to an effectively infinite number of different ways the program can be executed. Exhaustively testing a program is infeasible. Thus, there is no way to know all the ways in which a software program can behave. We often characterize software in terms of its correctness—Does the program respond correctly to a given input or set of inputs? A program's behavior, however, can be described with respect to reliability, safety, and security properties. Bugs are usually described as flaws in programming or design that result in incorrect outputs. Program bugs also result in unreliability of a program (such as when it crashes), in safety hazards such as when a control system becomes unstable, or in insecurity (such as when an unauthorized user can gain privileged access to system resources). In practice, most Internet security and reliability problems result from buggy software. Addressing this problem at its source—that is, reducing the number of flaws in software—is the best solution to addressing insecurity and unreliability in the Internet.

The PC itself presented new challenges over the traditional mainframe computing model. Any given PC can be configured in myriad different combinations of hardware and software. As a result, the environment in which any given software application will run will change from installation to installation, making it extremely difficult to test under all different configurations. Further complicating the problem are the interdependencies that exist between software components that run on the same machine. Bugs in one software component often adversely affect other software programs that use the component. The result is that it is very difficult for software vendors to adequately test the software if the environment in which it runs is unknown and dynamic.

To make matters worse, users are often given administrator or super-user privileges on their PCs. In the hands of someone technically skilled, this level of privilege is desirable. In the hands of the average user, though, it is the equivalent of giving users a power saw when the user really needs a precision screwdriver. For instance, users are able to delete system files that can crash the operating system. This is a bad idea. Many PC users are familiar with the routine of reinstalling the operating system—a practice rarely performed in the past on other computing platforms.

Users diligent enough to use "uninstall" utilities for programs, as opposed to simply deleting executables, are often confronted with daunting questions and decisions. For instance, a common dialog box that pops up during software de-installation asks the user if he or she wants to remove a shared library (known as a DLL) that came with the application that is being uninstalled. Usually the dialog box comes with the ambivalent warning that it is possible, though not likely, that some other application could use that library, and thus removing it can cause instability for another application. What is the user to do, when half the application the user is attempting to remove consists of shared libraries? This dilemma goes back to the problem of hidden software dependencies. Deleting, modifying, or corrupting a DLL or shared library has the potential to break any number of other applications that may be using that library. This dependency also means that a buggy or corrupted core DLL (such as one of the key DLLs that make up the Win32 system) can cause program instability across many different applications that use the shared library for basic operating system management.

The Internet Revolution

The Internet revolution superseded the PC revolution and made an already tenuous software quality problem untenable. The Internet has brought a whole new segment of the population to computers. Early Internet adopters were seasoned users who typically programmed computers as part of their jobs. The growth of the Internet illustrates how it has changed the demographics of computer users. The thousand percent per annum growth rate of the Internet over the past few years is indicative of the number of new computer users created every day.

Stepping back to before the Internet revolution, users who wanted to install new software either had to buy packaged software off-the-shelf in stores or through mail order, or they could download software through dial-up bulletin board systems (BBSs). BBSs were an electronic trading post where savvy programmers would post their programs for free use. The Web ultimately replaced the BBS, and the Internet replaced dial-up access.The key difference is that downloading and installing a program was an action a user was not only cognizant of, but it also required user effort. In most corporate environments, downloading free software onto corporate machines was not allowed. As a result, users who were interested in downloading software from BBSs would do so on their own computers at home. Thus, the spread of malicious content was controlled fairly well because it generally was not possible to download and install software unbeknownst to the user, and a cultural environment existed that frowned on downloading non-commercial software that was not approved through the usual corporate procurement channels.

The Internet has created a new and efficient distribution channel for software. In the pre-Internet era, running new software often meant a trip to Egghead or some other software retail outlet to pick up a piece of shrink-wrapped physical media. The Internet changed not only the distribution channel and media for software, but also the way in which software is installed and run. Today software is downloaded, installed, and executed on users' PCs all the time, often unbeknownst to the user, let alone the corporation or entity that owns the machine. That is, the Internet will often bypass any corporate software procurement process. Mobile computing paradigms, to be discussed later in this book, allow programs to download, install, and run, via Web pages and e-mail attachments, often without the user's knowledge and approval. The corporate owner of the equipment and the individual responsible for it (such as the CIO or system administrator) rarely even know what software is running on their machines, let alone are given a chance to control software installations. Fundamentally, the Internet has changed the entire nature of how software is distributed, installed, and executed on our machines to the point where we have little control over and knowledge of the programs we are running.

Another immediate impact of the Internet revolution is that most commercial and mass-marketed software is "Internet ready." Or, in other words, most software that runs on the desktop today can communicate over TCP/IP network ports to download, export, and generally share data. This is great for collaboration; however, it also introduces new risks. Internet-enabled software is, by association, security-relevant. That is, Internet-enabled software introduces new risks over its predecessor generation of PC software. The security and privacy implications of sharing data or access to a program with the outside world are significantly different from those of a program that has access to only the local machine on which it runs. Again, the CIO has little control over what data and programs are shared from corporate machines to outside and untrusted entities.

One of the main drivers of Internet software proliferation is the time-to-market pressure placed on vendors of Internet software. The demands of Internet time production—currently estimated to be seven Internet years in one calendar year—have reduced software release cycles to three months in many software houses, virtually eliminating any time for software testing and quality assurance. End users have become the *de facto* software quality assurance group. To underscore the point, Netscape Communications offers a "Bugs' Bounty" reward to end users who find bugs in Netscape software.

Software consumers should share part of the blame for the shoddy state of commercial software quality. In the rush to consume new and innovative software, consumers have developed a very high tolerance for buggy software. As long as the market will accept buggy software, software publishers have little incentive to develop higher-quality software. In fact, software publishers make money on software upgrades (that fix bugs in previous release versions), so there is little incentive for software publishers to get it right the first time. In order to force software publishers to produce higher-quality software, the software industry will need a radical collective shift in mentality toward software quality similar to the shift that consumer advocate extraordinaire Ralph Nader forced on the U.S. auto industry 20 some odd years ago.

A People Problem

While time-to-market pressures of Internet software are a major factor, several people-related problems have contributed to the current state of insecure software. First and most significantly, we have a general lack of understanding about how to write secure software. Second, we have an inadequate number of trained personnel to maintain our current systems. Third, we deal with security problems reactively, rather than proactively.

Cracking into computer systems is made possible by flawed software. When we realize that bad software is the underlying reason why our systems are vulnerable, we can begin to address the problem at its core through good software engineering practices that emphasize defensive programming, testing, and assurance activities over flash-in-the-pan and fly-by-night programming.

The Internet has created a whole new generation of programmers. New languages oriented toward Internet programming, such as Java, JavaScript, and Visual Basic, have also placed commercial software development within the reach of college freshmen. Even though Internet software is security-relevant for its user base, rarely is thought given to developing Internet software securely. Developers of Internet software are rarely trained in writing secure code. Again, the overriding driver for software vendors is time-to-market, rather than security of the application and privacy of the data that they use.

Weak and strong programs look identical on the shelf. That is, we have no way of distinguishing whether one program is going to be stronger, weaker, or malicious by looking at its packaging or Web page, or even by knowing who developed the program. As a result, consumers of software often have little basis on which to know whether one program is likely to be more secure or dependable than another. Without any standard to certify software as secure, consumers have only the reputation of the vendor to rely on, or sometimes just the packaging. The Internet also makes it easy to impose the façade of a big software corporation on a lone programmer writing programs in his spare time with little or no quality control.

Universities have traditionally been the primary educational institution for software developers. Recently, that trend is changing, partially because of the strong market for software developers and the shortage of qualified personnel. Now many software developers are self-trained, while many others have achieved software credentials through non-accredited certificate programs. Many corporations are taking matters into their own hands by creating corporate training programs in the art of software development.

While many computer science departments focus on teaching programming languages, operating systems, compilers, and algorithms, few take engineering seriously. The result is computer science graduates who enter industry with a toolbox of programming languages and tools, but who lack the engineering knowledge to build reliable, safe, and secure systems. From a consumer product perspective, we see a proliferation of software bloat where new and rarely used features are emphasized over software quality.

Probably the most significant long-term solution to the problem of producing higher-quality software is the development of an interdisciplinary curriculum that emphasizes engineering of software systems to be robust, dependable, and secure. The U.S. government is now proposing the development of a curriculum and allocation of scholarship money to train a cadre of "security engineers" to help defend against cyber attacks. Rather than spend significant amounts of money on defending a brittle infrastructure, a wise use of this investment would be to train tomorrow's software engineers to develop secure and survivable information systems.

Compounding the lack of software engineering curricula is the shortage of trained information technology professionals. The problem is so severe in certain parts of the United States that the number of unfilled IT jobs nears 100,000, resulting in millions of dollars of lost revenue for the firms that need these people. This demand for people has caused a wave of non-technical personnel to attempt to quickly gain technical credentials through the non-traditional training programs just described in order to benefit from the high-tech economy. Even so, companies today are badly short-staffed for qualified and experienced personnel. One of the areas hardest hit is system administration. While many companies in the high-tech sector do not develop commercial software products, almost all need to maintain computer systems. The need to administer these machines has resulted in a tremendous demand for system administrators.

One of the key problems in securing our systems is that there simply are not enough qualified system administrators to go around. The shortage of trained IT personnel has resulted in too few system administrators for too many machines. Because system administrators need to respond to many user requests, ranging from software installation and configuration to application problems, few have the time to keep on top of the security of their systems, let alone patch their systems every time a bug fix is released (about one per week) to fix a security hole. The result is that most installations are vulnerable to any number of attacks at any given time.

The solution to the problem, however, is not necessarily to train and hire more system administrators (though that would help in the short term); rather, the solution is to take a proactive approach to securing our systems. Our current approach to securing our systems is reactive. We attempt to bandage our broken systems, rather than building them to be secure from the ground up. The reactive approach to security today is known as "penetrate and patch." Buggy software is released on tight schedules driven by time to market. Clever hackers then find holes in the software that enable them to obtain greater privileges. An exploit script is written, then widely disseminated in underground networks. Large numbers of junior crackers, called script kiddies, run the exploit scripts to penetrate into installations. Once enough installations are penetrated, the software vendor becomes aware of the problem, finds the bug, and releases a piece of code called a patch to fix the problem. It is then up to system administrators everywhere to monitor newsgroups where the patch is released, download the patch, and fix all affected systems in the enterprise. As you can guess, this rarely happens in practice due to all the other demands on the system staff. Furthermore, even though the patch may fix one problem, 30 percent of the time it will introduce others. As a result, system administrators are reluctant to fix what appears not to be broken—especially if they have not noticed any penetrations through the known bug.

A proactive approach to securing our systems is to break the penetrate-and-patch cycle. That is, rather than putting bandages on a broken machine, we need to engineer the machine from the ground up to be secure. To do this, we need to understand how to write secure software, we need to incorporate this knowledge within a software engineering program, and we need to train the next generation of software engineers to learn how to develop secure and survivable systems. Until we decide to break the penetrate-and-patch cycle, we will continue to treat the symptoms of the disease, rather than working on a longer-term cure.

Case Studies in Software Security Vulnerabilities

To illustrate how e-commerce is vulnerable to software problems, two case studies are presented: the denial-of-service attack and the buffer overrun attack. Both of these pervasive threats against e-commerce sites illustrate vulnerabilities in software that undercut the security and reliability in e-commerce.

The Standard Denial-of-Service Attack

Internet-based *denial-of-service* (DoS) attacks work in either one of two ways: (1) sending malformed packets that crash servers or (2) overloading a machine with more requests than the machine can handle. The first strategy exploits vulnerabilities in network packet processing software, known as the network stack, which runs on server operating systems. The second DoS strategy exploits weaknesses in server software, protocols, and protocol implementations to overload network machines with more traffic than they can handle. It is the brick-and-mortar equivalent of a street protest that seeks to stop the legitimate business of an organization by tying up street traffic with so many people or vehicles that potential customers and partners cannot gain access to the organization's facility.

The network stack has been a notorious source of denial-of-service problems for both Unix- and Windows-based systems. The network stack is an essential part of all Internet-enabled devices. It is the portion of the operating system that processes network packets sent to and from network services. Various implementations of the TCP/IP network stack in different operating systems have been flawed such that a single malformed packet can crash the server, resulting in a denial of service for other legitimate requests. Well-known DoS attacks, such as Tear Drop, Bonk, and Ping O'Death, exploit flaws in the network stack to crash systems and deny service. In some cases, attacks exploit the way IP service allows data packets to be fragmented and reassembled to overrun buffers at the server. While this kind of buffer overrun attack does not necessarily give the attacker root privilege (as described in the next section), it can cause a segmentation fault and result in the service or machine crashing.

What makes these attacks particularly pernicious is that it does not take a powerful machine, the cooperation of many machines, or the ability to overwhelm powerful servers to bring them down. Rather, in some cases, a single malformed packet can cause the software receiving the packet to choke and crash. The root cause of this vulnerability is bad software. To date, most operating system vendors have fixed the known bugs in the network stack that have permitted these attacks. In the future, we may see more of these types of attacks that exploit operating system bugs.

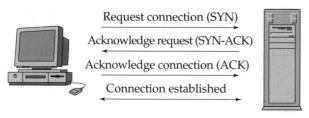

(a) Normal TCP/IP connection

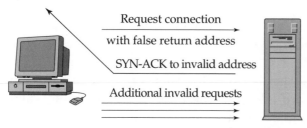

(b) Standard Denial of Service attack

Figure 2.1 Standard denial-of-service attack.

The most prevalent kind of DoS attack uses the Internet to overwhelm Internet services with a deluge of requests. Most DoS attacks leverage the time-out on incomplete connections to fill up the victim server's buffer of connections. The basic denial-of-service attack works as illustrated in Figure 2.1. During a normal TCP/IP connection, illustrated in Figure 2.1(a), a client will request a connection to a network service known as a synchronize (SYN) packet. The network service will respond with an acknowledgment to the SYN request (SYN-ACK). The client, in turn, will send an ACK command that ends the three-way handshake necessary to set up the connection. At this point, the connection is established and data is transferred back and forth between the client and server.

In the standard SYN flood DoS attack shown in Figure 2.1(b), the client sends a request to the server with an invalid origin. When the server responds to the client, it uses the invalid origin field as its destination. Because the origin address the client sent was invalid, the server will not receive the expected SYN response. The server holds the connection open while waiting for the final handshake for a time-out period, typically up to 90 seconds (to account for varying network latency conditions). During this period, the attacking client sends a deluge of other similar invalid requests, effectively filling up the capacity of the server to service incoming requests. This game continues for the duration of the attack. As the server times out on connections, the attacker is sending more and more invalid requests that the server has to process. The attacker is effectively able to defeat the server at this game because, by exploiting the time-out period, the attacker is able to send more requests than the server can process. As a result, legitimate requests to the server by others are effectively blocked by the attack.

The standard DoS attacks exploit weaknesses in Internet protocols to leverage these attacks. The SYN flood attack illustrates how the time-out on incomplete connections is leveraged to fill up incoming connection buffers. Also, because Internet connections are not authenticated before they are allowed, these attacks can use spoofed IP addresses as origin fields. Similarly, the Domain Naming Service (DNS), which is essentially a Yellow Pages for Internet addresses, is not secure or authenticated. As a result, it may be possible to compromise a DNS server such that legitimate sites can be taken offline or spoofed to significant segments of the Internet. This type of attack is sometimes called domain hijacking, and it is becoming increasingly popular amongst hackers. Similarly, the Internet counts on "good citizens" to provide security for everyone. In other words, every node on the Internet should do its own policing to ensure that malformed or spoofed packets are not sent from their sites. To date, Internet Service Providers (ISPs) have been reluctant to do this because of the performance penalty involved in scanning each packet for legitimacy. With recent advances in routing hardware, however, it may be possible to perform simple checks in the future at line speed.

The Distributed Denial-of-Service Attack

The distributed denial-of-service (dDoS) attacks represent a logical evolution in the standard DoS attack. A distributed DoS attack simply leverages the scaling power of the Internet in order to magnify the intensity of a DoS attack against a particular victim. To give an idea of the power of dDoS attacks, consider its most prominent victims. In early February, 2000, Yahoo!, eBay, CNN.com, Amazon.com, ZDNet, E*Trade, and Excite were all victims of dDoS attacks. These sites represent only some of the victims; however, they are also some of the most heavily visited sites on the Web, and many are portals to other sites. As a result, very high-bandwidth servers host these sites, which in the past meant they could overpower most standard DoS attacks. In the case of the dDoS attacks, some of the victim servers were inundated with data at rates up to 1 gigabit per second—more than even the highest-volume servers can handle. The collective downtime of these sites resulting from these attacks is believed to have caused a loss in revenue in the millions of dollars. The Canadian youth apprehended in the case in mid-April of 2000 is facing up to two years in juvenile detention and a fine of roughly $680.

What is often overlooked in considering dDoS attacks is that they are made possible by breaking into systems via flawed software. A distributed denial-of-service attack takes a standard DoS attack and multiplies its power by first cloning the attack machines, then magnifying their power on a particular victim. Figure 2.2 shows how a dDoS attack works. The attack works at the behest of the über hacker. The über

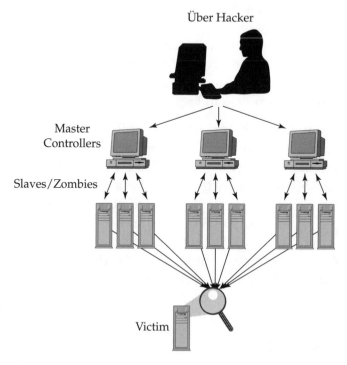

Figure 2.2 Distributed denial-of-service attack.

hacker sets up a few master controller machines, which serve two functions. First, these machines put distance between the victim machines and the hacker, making it harder for a network trace to lead back to the hacker. Second, these machines, which are typically other people's machines compromised by the hacker, serve as the master controllers that direct hundreds, thousands, or potentially tens of thousands of other zombie machines to act in concert to cripple a victim computer.

The key to implementing the dDoS attack is to compromise a large number of machines that serve as the army ants or soldiers in the dDoS attack. This is where the underground hacker community and the Internet can be leveraged. As junior hackers try out other hackers' tools on different sites, they will frequently post the sites they have compromised in underground mailing lists. These compromised sites then become caches for malicious software, pirated software, and other warez (the term colloquially given to illicit software and files) that the hacker community will put on other people's machines. With cooperation, the scripts that both launch DoS attacks and implement the controlling infrastructure shown in Figure 2.2 can be placed on a large number of compromised machines. These machines are called zombies because the scripts sit idly until resurrected by command from one of the master controllers. They are also called slaves because they follow the instructions of the master computers, including instructions to attack specific sites, to download new software, and even to remove traces of their activity from system logs.

Typically, the zombie machines are powerful network servers that often reside in open environments, such as universities, where liberal access is granted and security is generally lax. Even corporations running vulnerable software on network servers are at risk. Running buggy network services can permit hackers to obtain the privilege necessary to set up a zombie machines on corporate networks. Thus, companies may be complicit in a dDoS attack without their knowledge or involvement. What is most disturbing about the dDoS attack is that at the whim of a single attacker, the resources of thousands of machines can be focused on a single server to bring it down.

Denial-of-Service Defenses

The DoS attacks are among the least defensible of all Internet-based attacks. One of the main reasons is that many of the standard DoS attacks leverage vulnerabilities in Internet protocols to block service. Some security experts have called these vulnerabilities the "Achilles heel" of the Internet because there is little defense against protocol weaknesses. As a point of fact, though, a number of defenses can be employed against DoS attacks, most of which require widespread cooperation and good Internet citizenship.

The first defense against DoS attacks is ensuring that your own individual systems are secure. As mentioned earlier, sites whose servers have been compromised make dDoS attacks possible. If every site secured its systems, it would be difficult to launch dDoS attacks on the large scale necessary to bring down high-volume servers. While many books discuss how to secure server systems, including *E-Commerce Security: Weak Links, Best Defenses* (Wiley, 1998), simply upgrading software to the latest release/patch version can go a long way toward eliminating the types of holes that allow server systems to be compromised. Again, most security violations are made possible by bad software. The reality is that most security breaches are copycat crimes, rather than novel exploits. This fact can be leveraged in defending systems by simply closing well-known holes in software. Today, this is considered best practice, meaning that if companies are not doing this, their practice can be considered negligent and a danger to the Internet community at large. In other words, if all Internet sites practiced security as a responsibility, then overall we would have a more secure infrastructure for the community at large. Asking every site to secure its servers is like asking for world peace—it's not likely to happen.

Perhaps a more realistic defense against DoS attacks is to implement ingress and egress filtering at routers by ISPs and major Internet nodes. Ingress and egress filtering allows sites to process packets entering and exiting a node (or router or gateway) against a set of rules. Because most DoS attacks spoof origin addresses, simply checking IP origin addresses for validity will detect a large number of these attacks if this practice is widely deployed. For instance, if packets entering a network from the outside have an address coming from the inside (a common attack mode), then ingress filtering can either drop these packets or log the anomaly to be processed by an intrusion detection tool. This tactic would be a defensive measure to protect internal networks against outsider attacks. Conversely, egress filtering would drop packets (or log them again) exiting a network whose origin address is not a valid address from inside the network. This tactic would be a proactive approach to stopping attacks from being launched within a domain under your control.

If every node were to practice egress filtering, most DoS attacks would be stopped in their tracks at some point between themselves and the target victim. So, why don't we do this now? The main reason is that it is expensive performance-wise to perform filtering at the packet level. ISPs struggle to provide enough bandwidth to meet the ever-growing demand of their customer base. Implementing packet filtering rules to scan every packet for potentially malicious behavior would simply be too expensive and result in significant slow-downs for their customers. There is hope, however. Recent advances in routing chips have enabled very high-speed filtering of packets. In previous-generation routers, rules were implemented in software and thus resulted in significant performance degradation. By implementing rules in silicon, such as denying packets that violate basic ingress and egress "good citizen" rules, the performance degradation can be minimized significantly. Expect to see router vendors releasing new generations of routers designed to stop DoS attacks by incorporating these rules within the hardware. Bear in mind, though, that not everyone needs to implement these rules in order for the strategy to be effective. Simply getting a critical mass of major ISPs and major Internet nodes (universities included) to perform these types of checks can result in a significant reduction in the threat of DoS attacks.

Another approach to the problem is to fix the weaknesses in the protocols that permit these kinds of attacks. The basic problem with IP spoofing is one of authentication. That is, packets that spoof their identity could be effectively stopped if every connection authenticated the node making the connection. So, if before making connections, the protocol required authentication of the requesting node (that is, the IP address of the packet sent from the node must match the IP address of the requesting node), then most illicit connection attempts would be stopped dead in their tracks. The next version of the Internet Protocol, called IPv6, will support authentication of connections. In addition, IPv6 supports end-to-end encryption of connections, also called IPSec. As IPSec becomes more widely adopted, some of the attacks that use IP spoofing will be effectively countered. IPSec will not be a silver bullet solution to Internet-based attacks, but it will certainly help in many areas, particularly as it becomes more widely adopted.

In addition to IPSec, work is underway with the Internet Engineering Task Force (IETF) to develop a secure DNS protocol called DNSSec. As mentioned previously, the DNS serves as the Yellow Pages for the Internet domain system. This allows us to look up Web sites and companies by their domain name, rather than by their IP address. A DNS server simply looks up the IP address for the requested domain name in order to route packets to the proper domain. In its current implementation, the DNS is susceptible to spoofing. For instance, it is possible for attackers to replace an authentic DNS server with a corrupted DNS server. This would allows hackers to spoof a site such that when someone requests a Web page from a site, the request is sent to a different site with different content (or even the same content, but under the control of a different organization that may steal confidential information such as passwords and account information). Alternatively, all packets to a given site can simply be dropped to implement a DoS attack.

Spoofing the DNS system is the equivalent of dialing your friend using her correct number, but the phone system routes the call to someone else. We don't expect this kind of behavior from the phone system, and we shouldn't expect it from the Internet domain system. A major security vendor fell victim to this kind of DNS attack early in 2000. The attack seemed aimed at embarrassing the vendor. What leaves the victim powerless is that the victim site need not be hacked—only the DNS servers that serve requests to the site need to be changed. Because DNS servers periodically update their records from upstream servers, a change in one DNS server is propagated to others over a period of time. In the past, denial of service has occurred inadvertently on a very large scale when a corrupted master DNS server propagated its corrupted DNS list to a large number of subordinate DNS servers. Today, the DNS system works on the basis of trust. That is, a DNS server must trust that it is getting correct information from other DNS servers. To add some rigor to the trust, a secure DNS system will require authentication before accepting new DNS records. Because most authentication systems also support data integrity checks, inadvertently corrupted DNS records can be caught before corrupted records are propagated.

The Buffer Overrun Attack

The buffer overrun attack is one of the most pervasive modes of attack against computer systems today. According to statistics released by the

Computer Emergency Response Team (CERT) Coordination Center (CC) out of Carnegie Mellon University's Software Engineering Institute, about 50 percent of computer incidents reported today in the field involve some form of buffer overrun. In 1998, 9 of 13 CERT CC advisories were related to buffer overrun attacks. Moreover, buffer overrun attacks dominate remote network penetrations, where an anonymous Internet user is able to leverage superuser privileges by exploiting a software flaw.[4]

One of the most notorious cases of exploiting a buffer overrun flaw occurred in 1988 via a program known as the Internet Worm. The Internet Worm was a program written by Robert T. Morris, Jr., to exploit a flaw in the finger server, which runs on many networked machines and provides information to remote clients about the local users. Normally, the finger server is queried through a command of the following format:

```
finger userID@machinehost.domain.com.
```

The information returned by the finger server may include the identity of users who are logged on to the queried machine, the length of time a user has been idle at the terminal, the last time a user read mail, the status of mail received, and sometimes additional information that users will provide about themselves such as phone numbers, office hours, public encryption keys, and philosophical statements about life. The finger server can also provide information about which users are currently logged on to a host machine. Although this information may reveal more than is necessary, the Internet Worm did not exploit any of this information in its attack. Rather, the Internet Worm exploited a flaw in the finger server that allowed it to overflow an internal buffer.

The finger server allocated an array in memory (the buffer) of 512 bytes to store the argument of the finger client command. The argument to the finger client command is normally just a user ID and machine name or simply the machine name itself. The function the finger server used to read the argument did not check the length of the buffer it was reading it into, nor did it limit the length of the argument to the limit of the buffer. As a result, if the argument the finger client sent was greater than 512 bytes, the buffer allocated in memory would be overwritten. This flaw is exactly what the Internet Worm exploited to overflow the buffer and overwrite the stack on many machines it attacked. By overwriting the stack, the worm was able to execute its own code that it sent in the argument to the finger command. The code written by the worm created a shell from which arbitrary commands could be executed. Because many finger servers run with root privilege, the worm was able to execute its commands as the superuser. The worm made its point, not by damaging the systems it violated, but by launching the same attack on other machines from each successive machine it conquered through this program flaw. This case has been studied and well documented in the literature.[5] Despite its prominence in the annals of computer security, a very large number of attacks today exploit buffer overrun flaws in programs. The lesson learned from this attack is that input should always be checked for proper length and format before being further processed in a program.

The buffer overrun attack is simply an attempt to exploit a logical flaw in software in order to gain higher privileges. Buffer overrun attacks are generally aimed at software that runs with superuser privileges. The objective of the attack is to be able to inject attack code into an executing program in order to run it with the privileges of the victim program. For instance, network services will often run with superuser privileges because they listen to privileged ports and need access to privileged files. If an attacker is able to inject his or her own code into a network service, then the attacker can get the network service to run a shell or command window with superuser privileges. This allows the attacker to interactively run commands with all the privileges of the superuser.

What is a buffer overrun attack? A buffer is simply a contiguous portion of memory that stores data used by a program. A buffer is overrun when more data is read into it than space is allocated for the buffer in memory. When input is read into a buffer and the length of the input is not limited to the length of the buffer allocated in memory, it is possible to overflow the buffer. Overrunning the buffer results in overwriting memory that is not assigned to the buffer. The consequences of overrunning a buffer can range from no discernible effect to an abortion of the program execution, to execution of instructions contained in the input. If no adverse effects result from an overflowed input buffer, the program is tolerant of or robust to this type of attack.

In the second case of overflowing buffers, it may be possible to crash a program during execution. As an example, consider the Ping O'Death denial-of-service attack, mentioned in the preceding section. The ping program is often used on platforms to determine if a remote host is "alive." The ping server responds to a network packet, which is usually

64 bytes in length but can be up to 65,536 bytes—the maximum packet length allowed by an Internet Protocol (IP) datagram. The Ping O'Death attack involves sending several IP datagrams and reassembling them at the target server as a single input with length greater than 65,536 bytes.

Unfortunately for many servers, the ping service does not respond very well to input this large. Rather than limiting the length of the buffer it will read, the ping server attempts to read the entire input and ends up choking on it. On some machines, the ping server shuts down; on others, the entire system shuts down or reboots. Thus, even though this buffer overrun attack does not result in the execution of the attacker's code, it does result in a serious denial of service.

The third case of overrunning buffers can result in serious security problems for a site. Depending on where in memory the buffer is allocated, it is possible that overrunning a buffer will result in writing over a special section of memory called the program *stack frame*. The stack frame is the section of memory that is used to restore the state of the executing program after returning from a function. During the execution of a program, when a call is made to a function, the current state of the program, which includes program variables and internal registers, is saved on the stack. In addition to the program state, the address of the next instruction to be executed after returning from the called function is "pushed" on the stack. This address is known as the instruction pointer. When the program finishes executing the called function, the next instruction to be executed is "popped off" the stack and loaded in the program counter to execute the next program instruction.

The attack works by overwriting the stack frame with code contained in the input. The goal is to first overwrite the instruction pointer such that it points to the code contained in the input. Now, when the program returns from the called function, the next instruction to be executed is one embedded in the user's input. This technique is known in the underground hacker community as "smashing the stack."

Smashing the stack is illustrated in Figure 2.3. In the program's "main" function, an array variable "large" is defined to have length 2000. This array is filled with 2000 "X" characters. Next, the function "overflow" is called with a pointer to "large" passed as an argument. In "overflow," a new array, "small," is defined with length 100. The stack in the right side of Figure 2.3 shows how the memory is allocated for the overflow

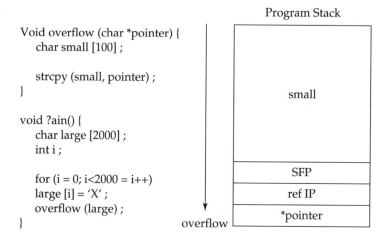

```
Void overflow (char *pointer) {
    char small [100] ;

    strcpy (small, pointer) ;
}

void ?ain() {
    char large [2000] ;
    int i ;

    for (i = 0; i<2000 = i++)
    large [i] = 'X' ;
    overflow (large) ;
}
```

Figure 2.3   Smashing the stack.

function. The variable "small" is allocated 100 characters. After "small," memory is reserved for the stack frame pointer (SFP), the return instruction pointer (IP), and the pointer that was pushed on the stack when overflow is called. The "overflow" function simply copies the contents of the large variable array to the small variable array. Unfortunately, the function, strcpy, does not check the length of the variable it is copying before copying it to small. As a result, the 2000 characters are written over the 100-character-long array, buffer. This means that after copying the first 100 X's, the rest of the 2000-character-length array will overwrite the SFP, the return IP, and even the pointer.

After the overflow function finishes executing, it will pop off the return IP address and execute the instruction located at that address. In this example, the address pointed to by "X" is probably not an instruction, and as a result, this program will probably crash. However, the "large" array could have been intelligently loaded with input that places a meaningful instruction address at the return IP memory location. After overwriting the return IP address, the next instruction that will execute could be an instruction of the attacker's choice, most likely one included in the rest of the buffer that was overwritten.

This technique is as effective as being able to access and modify the program source code, recompile it, and execute it on the server without ever having access to the source code. Smashing the stack is one of the primary attacks launched against privileged set user id (SUID) root programs. In the case of e-commerce applications, the problem can be especially dangerous if a network server program such as a Web server, mail or news server, login, or ftp server is susceptible to this type of attack. The implication is that a remote attack launched over the Internet by an unprivileged user can potentially execute arbitrary commands on the server with superuser privileges.

Again, the root of the most pervasive computer security problem is bad software. In the case of the buffer overrun vulnerability, the problem is a programming error that allows a larger buffer to overwrite a smaller buffer. Unfortunately, because C is an unsafe language, it is easy and common for programmers to mistakenly code buffer overrun vulnerabilities. C provides a number of unsafe string manipulation functions in its standard library. Among them are these commonly used functions: strcpy(), strcat(), sprintf(), and gets(). These functions are pervasive in programs that read user input, which, of course, is how hackers attack programs. The fundamental problem with these functions is that they do not check the length of the input before copying it into a buffer. Therefore, they must be used with extreme care or preferably not used at all.

The C standard library now provides an alternative set of equivalent functions, strn*(), that do check the length of the input before copying. Problems still persist, though, for many reasons. First, a generation of programmers learned to program with the unsafe functions, and bad habits are hard to unlearn. Also, as we learned from the Y2K bug, a lot of bad legacy code still runs on servers. Second, the form of the strn*() function calls is different from their equivalent unsafe functions. For instance, strncpy(dst, src, sizeof dst) includes a third parameter to limit the size of the buffer being written to, whereas strcpy(dst, src) does not. As a result, one cannot simply replace strcpy() with strncpy(). Instead, the context of the write is important and must be considered. Further complicating matters for programmers is that the family of strn*() functions behaves dissimilarly in both form and function.[6] For instance, while strncpy(dst, src, sizeof dst) is correct, strncat(dst, src, sizeof dst) is not. Rather, the correct usage of strncat() is strncat(dst, src, sizeof dst - strlen(dst) −1). Even though these details are programming trivia, the end result is that the language makes it hard for programmers to get it right.

What defenses do we have against this pervasive problem? The best defense is to use safe languages, such as Java, which ensure that during runtime buffers cannot get overwritten. Alternatively, using a safe subset of C (such as Safer C) or a safe compiler (such as the StackGuard gcc variant; see endnote [4]) provides higher assurance against buffer overrun attacks. Finally, good software engineering can go a long way to developing more secure software. A software engineering view of writing secure software is described in the next chapter. One of the traditional activities in software engineering—code reviews—is important for finding these types of bugs. Doing source code inspections by hand, looking for buffer overrun vulnerabilities, is not only tedious, but it can also be rife with error, particularly when trying to address the subtleties of the strn*() functions. Here, using source code analysis tools to flag potential buffer overrun vulnerabilities can help eliminate these bugs during development before the software is released for consumption. See endnotes [6,7,8] for information on automated analysis of source code for security vulnerabilities.

Last Word

This chapter tried to drive home the fact that bad software is responsible for a vast majority of the security problems we have today. The case studies in denial-of-service and buffer overrun attacks illustrate how software flaws underlie the Internet's most pervasive problems. The other most pervasive problem, configuration errors, is also a software problem, but one that is left to the user to correct.

Once we realize and accept the fact that security is largely a software problem, we can begin to put to apply decades of software engineering and testing practices for Internet software. The next chapter presents good engineering practices and a software risk management approach for developing secure and robust Internet software.

Notes

1. *The Inmates Are Running the Asylum* (SAMS Books, MacMillan Publishing)
2. "10 Great Bugs in History," CNET. Online: http://coverage.cnet.com/Content/Features/Dlife/Bugs/ss05.html.
3. "Bad Bug Bites," *Business Week*. Online: www.businessweek.com/1999/99_49/b3658017.htm.

4. C. Cowen, et al., "Buffer Overflows: Attacks and Defenses for the Vulnerability of the Decade," in *Proceedings of the DARPA Information Survivability Conference and Exposition*, January 25–27, 2000, Hilton Head, SC.

5. E. Spafford, "The Internet Worm Program: An Analysis," *Computer Communications Review*, Vol. 19, No. 1 (January 1989): 17–57.

6. D. Wagner, et al., "A First Step Towards Automated Detection of Automated Buffer Overrun Vulnerabilities," in *Proceedings of the Network and Distributed Systems Security (NDSS) 2000 Symposium*, February 3–4, 2000, San Diego, CA.

7. See the ITS4 tool for this purpose (www.rstcorp.com/its4/).

8. V. Shah, T.J. Walls, and A.K. Ghosh, "Towards Certifying Software for Security," in *Proceedings of the 2nd International Software Assurance Certification Conference (ISACC2000)*, September 24–26, 2000, Reston, VA.

Securing Software

> *"The mass-market marketplace is overly concerned with features;*
> *it tends to be long on fancy features and to ignore critical*
> *requirements such as rudimentary robustness. However, robust*
> *features can be achieved with good design and good*
> *programming practice, rather than the business-as-usual*
> *practice of sloppy development and a rush-to-market mentality.*
> *If automobiles were recalled as often as computer system flaws*
> *are detected, we would still have horses and buggies."*

PETER G. NEUMANN[1]

It should be clear by now that software is a critical weak link in e-commerce systems. The more complex the software gets, the more likely it is to be prone to error—errors that an adversary can use to advantage. Two familiar adages play an important role in understanding how to secure e-commerce systems: (1) A chain is only as strong as its weakest link, and (2) in the presence of obstacles, the path of least resistance is always the path of choice.

Encryption protocols generally provide the strongest perceived security in all the components involved in e-commerce transactions. In e-commerce, as in other real-world systems, the security of the system is only as strong as its weakest component. On the whole, the security of server-side systems is much weaker than the security provided by secure data transaction protocols such as SSL. Considering these two adages together in the context of e-commerce security, it becomes clear that malicious perpetrators rarely will attempt to break encryption codes, when breaking into an e-commerce site is much easier and has a much higher return on effort.

The recent trend in e-commerce sites has been to outsource the development, maintenance, and hosting of the site to Web hosting providers. The reason is economics. Large Web hosting providers can spend the money required to buy very high-bandwidth fiber and servers. A Web hosting provider can recover the cost of this investment by leasing space on their servers to host commercial e-commerce sites. In order to be economically viable, most Web hosting providers will host multiple sites on a single server—introducing interesting risks we get into here.

It is always interesting to take a tour of one of these Web hosting providers, if given the opportunity. Web hosting servers typically reside in "data bunkers" that tend to remain fairly anonymous in location. Specifications for these facilities call for 12-inch thick cinder block construction, usually without windows. They should be able to withstand not only natural disasters from tornados, floods, and hurricanes, but also physical attack against the facilities. They are typically guarded by armed security personnel, and visitor identification is checked rigorously. What makes this whole set-up fairly comical is that these measures (like firewalls, in many respects) place a façade of security on a house of cards.

While strong physical security is better than no physical security, one should not be lulled by the appearance of strength into a false sense of security. Just as all shrink-wrapped encryption packages look identical on the outside, it's what's on the inside that really counts. In reality, e-commerce sites are not attacked from a physical infrastructure vantage (though they could be). Instead, they are attacked through data. All the physical security in the world is not going to buy you any protection against a data-driven attack, against which, incidentally, firewalls also provide little protection.

The most favored strategy of Web hosting providers to protect their e-commerce sites against computer intrusions is to use firewalls. Firewalls are great in closing down services that should not be offered to everyone. For instance, RPC services, NetBIOS, DNS, intranets, and other services that might be necessary for internal trusted users, but not necessary for outside untrusted users, can be protected by firewalls. Firewalls, though, provide little protection against data- and code-driven attacks through services that *need* to be offered. For instance, firewalls need to let Web service, e-mail service, and sometimes news and IRC service through, or else we wouldn't have any use for the Internet. Hackers that leverage these offered services to launch these attacks go right through the firewall, unimpeded. Data-driven attacks through offered services are sometimes called tunneling attacks because they "tunnel" their way through a legitimate protocol to breach security. A buffer overrun attack against a Web server is an example of a tunneling attack over HTTP. Similarly, e-mail worms, such as Melissa and Bubble Boy, are code-driven tunneling attacks over SMTP (the simple mail transfer protocol).

The point is that while combinations of physical security and firewalls provide security against some classes of attack, they do not address the most common form of attack against e-commerce sites: data- and code–driven attacks against software. The dDoS attacks from February 2000 emphatically make this point. Consider again the fact that many Web hosting providers host multiple sites on a single server. A data-driven attack against one e-commerce site that exploits a software vulnerability can give the attacker system privileges on that machine. Now the attacker can modify, capture, or delete information on another e-commerce site hosted on the same server. The economic argument of co-hosting one e-commerce site with others has to be weighed against the risk of being penetrated via a flaw in the *other* site's software.

The key question is how do we design our systems so that they are resistant to all manner of data- and code–driven attacks? That is the subject of the rest of this chapter. The answer lies in software risk management and good security engineering through software design, implementation, configuration, and maintenance.

Design for Security

We have learned the hard way in safety-critical systems that safety must be designed into the product from the earliest stages. Like safety, security is not an add-on feature that can be appended once the product has been designed and implemented. Researchers and practitioners who have been designing fault-tolerant systems for decades know that fault tolerance begins very early in the lifecycle of a product. Developers of safety-critical and high-reliability systems know that fault tolerance is incorporated into system requirements, specifications, and design, not to mention implementation, configuration, and maintenance.

For a long time now, practitioners of computer security have believed that security can be layered into products. In fact, the Internet was designed based on this principle, and perhaps that is why this belief still prevails. The Internet relies on higher-level protocols in the ISO-OSI model of network services to provide additional services (such as TCP) that lower-level services do not (such as IP). The basic idea is that each service layer adds some additional property to the quality of service above it and uses the services of the layer below it. While this strategy works well in certain situations, such as requesting retransmissions for dropped packets, it does not substitute for flawed designs. As the DoS attacks, the ILOVEYOU e-mail worm, and its ilk have demonstrated, the Internet is extremely vulnerable to attacks. The fact is that the Internet was not designed to be a secure protocol. Rather, it was designed to accommodate the lowest-common-denominator platform so as to be all-inclusive of many different types of platforms at the expense of other properties, such as security, dependability, predictability, and real-time behavior.

Today, when many vendors talk about application security, they are usually talking about adding security features to otherwise insecure applications. For instance, many online applications do not provide strong authentication services, but they need them. In the financial sector, it is very important to provide positive identification of parties involved in transactions, not to mention to provide non-repudiation of transactions. In addition, confidentiality and data integrity are often desirable properties in financial transactions. These types of properties can be layered onto existing applications, and many applications will benefit from these types of security services. But it is important to realize that if the application itself is vulnerable to attack, then adding these security properties will not make up for these deficiencies. For instance, if the application is vulnerable to a buffer overrun attack, these properties will not make the application any more secure. Even worse, if the software that provides these security services is vulnerable itself, then the application can be potentially weakened in the effort to strengthen it. Whenever new functionality is added to a system, the potential exists that the code that implements the new functionality may be buggy and might provide an avenue for compromise.

The hard reality is that Internet-based systems must be designed from the ground-up with security as an integral part of the design. Of particular concern are legacy systems that have been Internet-enabled. In the rush to Internet-enable everything, many companies are bringing legacy back-end systems to the Internet by providing front-end Web pages. Essentially, they are bolting the Internet onto the side of an existing legacy system built to be run in a closed, proprietary environment. Bolting Internet functionality onto any system without considering the security ramifications is extremely dangerous. Furthermore, attempting to add security after the fact is usually a failing strategy.

Another key risk area is software developed on Internet time. Many software vendors are under severe time constraints to develop and release software in extremely compressed time schedules in order to achieve first-mover status and significant market share. For these vendors, security is often a secondary consideration, well behind time-to-market and functionality considerations. Furthermore, most software developers, while trained in the art of programming, know little about the security risks of the software they are developing. Because most commercial software developed today is Internet-enabled, many software vendors are releasing security-critical software without even realizing it until after incidents are reported in the wild.

Although market pressures on software vendors are tight, they don't begin to compare to the pressures on e-businesses. As new e-businesses are hatched every day, the critical requirement is to get a Web presence, then to develop interactive content. While much of the software that runs e-businesses is Commercial Off-The-Shelf (COTS) software, one of the key pieces that requires custom development is the implementation of the business application logic. This represents the core offering of the online site and will necessarily vary from site to site depending on what services and products are offered. The more unique the offering, the more customization is required. The more complex the offering, the more code is required. Business application logic is typically implemented in a middleware layer via CGI scripts, application servers, Enterprise Java Beans, and other component-based solutions that sit between front-end Web servers and back-end software systems, such as databases. Chapter 4, "Weak Links in E-Commerce," goes into detail about the weaknesses involved here. From a risk area perspective, e-businesses will have to develop this software (even if it is outsourced) in a hurry, often with little to no security analysis of this software. The business application logic is a key weak link in the security of many online sites. Typically, application subversion attacks as well as data-driven attacks exploit weaknesses in this software. In the following, we describe good engineering practices for developing secure software systems.

Engineering Secure Business Systems

As with all software development, good design and engineering practices are important for software quality. This point is particularly important for development of security-critical software such as e-commerce applications. Rather than thinking of security as an add-on feature to software systems, security should be designed into the system from the earliest stages of requirements gathering through development, testing, integration, and deployment. The goal of designing for security is to break the penetrate-and-patch mindset that pervades commercial software security today and replace it with a process for finding and removing security-related bugs prior to release. The cost of finding and fixing bugs in software after release is orders of magnitude more expensive than correcting them early, during the software development lifecycle.

One unfortunate consequence of the huge pressure to reduce time-to-market for e-commerce services is that good software engineering practices are dropped (or, more often, never started). As described in the preceding section, the demand for e-commerce applications is driving the complexity of business application logic. Developing software for one user at a time—for example, a typical desktop software application—is a lot different from developing an e-commerce application that needs to handle tens of thousands of concurrent requests. Today's e-commerce applications need not only to handle vast numbers of simultaneous users, but also to deal with malicious threats.

Taking Speculative Risks

One often overlooked but essential activity in engineering an essential software system is risk analysis. First, let's start with what is risk. According to Merriam Webster's 10th edition dictionary, risk is simply the possibility of loss or injury. There are, in fact, two types of risk to consider: pure risks and speculative risks. Pure risks are risks that can result only in losses—for example, airplane crashes. Pure risks are often used by mathematicians and engineers in designing systems with acceptable levels of loss. Speculative risks are risks taken on the premise of a possible upside as well as the possibility of a downside. These are risks that can result in loss or profit. Businesses and individuals make speculative risk decisions every day. For instance, playing the lottery, or gambling in general, is a speculative risk. You are willing to risk some amount of money on the gamble that you might win the jackpot. Similarly, investing in companies and real estate can be considered speculative risks.

Speculative risks are of interest to e-commerce because we understand that there is no guarantee of perfect security. As a result, we are willing to take on some risk of security breaches in order to bring our business to the Internet for the upside of potentially high valuations and earnings. It is useful to discuss security in terms of speculative risks because ultimately the decision to develop and deploy e-commerce systems is a business decision. In making business decisions, rather than focus on absolutes (perfect security, no security), it makes sense to analyze the trade-offs in functionality, ease-of-use, and security, in order to make informed business and engineering decisions.

Software companies and consumers make speculative risks. From a consumer perspective, we make speculative risks in software whether we realize it or not. Software is embedded in practically every electronic device today. Software is the intelligence that controls appliances, runs our cars, flies our planes, controls our building's temperature, automates factory manufacturing, and runs nuclear power plants. The risk we take is that the potential upside in using software is greater than the likelihood of the potential downside of the software failing. For instance, most of us have experienced software application and even operating system crashes (for example, the infamous blue screen of death on PCs). While this happens occasionally, and maybe too frequently for many of us, we are willing to accept the potential loss of data and revenue in downtime for the automation benefits of desktop software. As software replaces traditionally hardware-controlled systems, such as appliances and cars, we will be less likely to forgive software failures. There are some software risks that most consumers are unwilling to accept, such as a nuclear meltdown because a software interlock mechanism on a nuclear trip control failed.

Businesses assume speculative software risks on every software project. Higher-quality software products can be released at lower risk to the business (in terms of reputation and liability for losses due to bad software) and consumers by increasing the amount of product testing before release. More testing is more expensive, which may result in product delays and loss of market share and profits. Thus, businesses must make speculative software risk decisions about what level of assurance is necessary before releasing software products. The greater the product liability, it stands to reason, the less risk the business is willing to assume, and the more product assurance the business may require. Conversely, for markets where high product quality is not expected (such as the current state of affairs in desktop software), businesses will make decisions to release poorer quality software in order to maximize profits because of the lower business risk involved.

In the scope of e-commerce systems, software vendors must make speculative software risk decisions as well. The consequences of flawed e-commerce software products may be greater than for typical consumer-oriented software products. Flaws in e-commerce software can result in significant business losses either through brand damage due to security breaches or through lost revenues in downtime due to failing software systems. In almost every Internet-based software product, a trade-off is made between security and functionality. There is no such thing as 100 percent secure systems, except perhaps a system that is powered down and buried in a concrete bunker 30 feet underground, as an old security joke goes. Any time new functionality is added to a system, particularly an Internet-based system, new security risks are added.

Case Study: Visual Basic Worms

A didactic case study in security versus functionality is the phenomena of Visual Basic Internet worms. The most famous examples include the ILOVEYOU worm (estimated damage on the order of U.S. $8 billion), the Melissa worm, and the Bubble Boy worm. These viruses are the payload of Internet e-mails. They are smart enough to mail themselves out from users' accounts using the addresses contained in the Microsoft Outlook and Outlook Express address books. Their least benign behavior is that they can simply mail a text message to recipients. The most dangerous is that they can replace, corrupt, or erase documents on the recipients' hard drives. Some even go to the extent of downloading other malicious software off Web sites to capture passwords and even faxing messages to recipients' fax machines.

To understand the trade-off between security and functionality for this class of virus, one must look back to the days before all desktop software became Internet-enabled. In order to automate rather mundane and common tasks in its desktop software, Microsoft gave its software applications the ability to run macros. Macros allow users to define a series of actions for an application to perform. Essentially, macros are a higher-level language in which users write the instructions for an application to execute. To provide uniformity, Microsoft used the Visual Basic language as the common language for developing macros across its desktop applications. A Visual Basic interpreter actually resides in many of these common desktop applications. Its scripting language is known as VBScript. As with many programming languages, this level of automation made life easier for serious users who wanted to automate common tasks. For instance, in Microsoft Word, the easiest way to list available fonts is to write or use a macro.

The picture became muddled, however, when scripting was enabled for Internet applications. What was a useful feature suddenly became a major security risk. For instance, VBScripts and JavaScripts are commonplace on Web sites. Unless you specifically configure your browser not to, it will download and run these scripts without warning. More subtly, desktop applications have new risks in the form of being scripted from other Internet-enabled applications. For instance, Microsoft Outlook is hooked extensively into the Windows Scripting Host. This Windows component allows applications or users to script the behavior of the applications that use it. For instance, one can write a VBScript to instruct Outlook to send out a massive mailing over a period of time. This function is certainly a useful and time-saving device if you are an e-mail spammer. The same functionality, however, can be used by virus writers to send out a message to everyone in your Outlook address book.

One need only write a VBScript and attach it to an e-mail and write a short message to persuade the user to run the VBScript. The VBScript, in this case, runs like any other program you attach to an e-mail. When it is double-clicked, the operating system invokes the Visual Basic interpreter that lives in the operating system and executes the VBScript commands. The VBScript has all the rights and privileges you do, and thus it can overwrite files as well as script other applications, such as scripting Outlook to send out e-mails on your behalf. Running executable attachments of unknown content is always dangerous. Now, with scriptable Internet applications, these attachments can propagate their maliciousness on an Internet scale in Internet time.

Another case of using VBScripts in Internet applications is also dangerous and subtler, and it illustrates the risks of allowing scripting of Internet-based applications. In addition to supporting attachments, MS Outlook and Outlook Express support scripting from e-mails, similar to how Internet Explorer supports scripting from Web sites. This means that the application itself can be scripted by e-mails. In this case, the VBScript is part and parcel to the mail message (usually an HTML message). The VBScript is run when the mail is opened. This execution mode is different from the previous case of the VBScript attachment where the user must decide to open the attachment, which results in the VBScript interpreter in the operating system running the attachment and ultimately scripting Outlook. What makes this type of scripting more dangerous is that it does not require user participation in order to execute the VBScript. In MS Outlook's preview pane, the script runs when the user selects the e-mail message. The Kak worm is an example of this type of threat.

The crux of the problem is that an application is taking code in the form of data downloaded from untrusted sites and executing it. Before e-mail clients became HTML-enabled, this was not much of a problem. Most data was received as plain text, and none of it was executable. When attachments became a popular way to send working documents and multimedia files, e-mail clients became more "intelligent" and provided the ability to launch applications based on the data type—typically specified as a MIME type. In the case of scriptable applications, a separate application need not be launched. In this case, an application can directly execute an embedded script.

Recognizing the potential dangers of executing untrusted code, many browser/mailer software vendors have coded limits on the types of actions that scripts can command. Software flaws in these protection models have enabled malicious code exploits to gain access to system command shells in order to execute arbitrary commands. For instance, Microsoft's Internet Explorer 5.0 browser was vulnerable to scripting attacks because of two ActiveX controls installed on the Windows desktop. The controls, called scriptlet.typelib and Eyedog, are configured by default to be scriptable, or marked as "safe for scripting." In addition, one of Eyedog's methods has a buffer overrun vulnerability. As a result, a Web page or e-mail can harbor malicious scripts that can instruct these controls to overwrite files on the desktop, query information about the user's machine, and even modify the system registry.

These bugs are not an isolated incident, however. Another serious vulnerability in scripting attacks exists because of a control, the UA ActiveX control, which is shipped with the Microsoft Office 2000 suite.[2] The control is used as part of the Office Assistant "Show Me" functionality. The problem, again, is that the control is marked "safe for scripting." The control allows scripting of almost any functionality in the Office 2000 suite that a legitimate user can perform from the keyboard. Because the control is marked safe for scripting, any script downloaded from a Web page or one running in an e-mail can script any Office 2000 application. Of course, the Office 2000 suite of applications is very powerful. For instance, confidential documents can be mailed directly from Office 2000 applications.

What is also interesting is how one vulnerability can blaze the trail for other malicious scripts to do their damage. For instance, many of the Office 2000 applications have built-in functionality to prevent macros from running without the user's knowledge. Usually when opening a document with an embedded macro, an Office 2000 application will notify the user that the document has a macro present and ask the user whether he or she wishes to execute the macro. While this strategy does not really give the user enough information to make a good security risk decision, the safest course of action is to prevent the macro from running, unless the user knows for sure the macro is safe. It is possible to write a script to lower the security settings for an Office 2000 application so that the user is never offered the opportunity to deny a macro before it runs. This is exactly what some researchers with AtStake L0pht Research Labs did to demonstrate how the UA control vulnerability can be exploited. They wrote a script (downloadable from a Web page) that will open a Word document, script the UA control to attach to the Word application instance, script Word to change the macro security level to Low (including clicking through the OK dialog box for you), then pointing Word to download a document from a Web page with an embedded macro. The macro will run without any intervention from the user. This new vulnerability has now opened the floodgates to a whole class of macro vulnerabilities Microsoft previously tried to mitigate by informing the user when a macro was running.

The speculative risks the software vendor took here are many. First, the vendor provided strong functionality—by giving users the ability to script applications—for the small fraction of users who actually use this functionality against the greater risk to all users in general. How many users actually need or want to run VBScripts in their e-mail? The real answer is likely to be a small percentage of all users. For those who do, providing an opt-in ability to run VBScripts is a sounder risk engineering practice than opt-out options, where users must reconfigure their software to make it safer (something that few know how to do). Currently, by default, most applications are configured for maximum functionality and minimum security.

The second speculative risk made by the vendor was including scripting engines in Internet-enabled software. The combination of allowing untrusted content from the Internet to interface with and control Internet-enabled applications is inherently dangerous. Finally, giving desktop components (such as ActiveX controls) the ability to be scripted from untrusted Internet content is a dangerous risk. Most programmers will enable maximum functionality without consideration of the risks posed by malicious content. Allowing controls to be scripted opens the doorway for malicious content arriving from Internet applications to control the rest of the desktop. All of these risks illustrate speculative risks taken by a software vendor in providing more functionality or features. In addition, the buffer overrun vulnerability shows a speculative risk to release software before it has been properly analyzed for this common software security vulnerability.

The sum total of losses due to these new features or bugs is in the tens of billions of U.S. dollars. These losses are absorbed by businesses that consume and use the software, not the software vendor itself. The software vendor's risk is one of negative public reaction. Judging from the lack of accountability and the voracious appetite of a feature-hungry public, chances are that this trade-off in providing functionality over security will likely persist in the future. The risks from code-driven attacks are discussed in Chapter 5, "Mobile and Malicious Code."

Software Risk Management

"If you don't actively attack risks, they will actively attack you!"

Tom Gilb
Software Test Expert

In building Internet applications, it is important to realize the inherent risks of integrating software applications with the Internet. Much like writing software without a design is a bad idea, designing Internet-based software without regard for security risks is an invitation to disaster. The first step to engineering secure systems is reorienting the way we think about software to a risk-based perspective. In many other industries outside of software, safety and security are recognized as necessary and critical parts of the job. On many construction sites, signs of "Think Safety" and "Safety First" are often posted to remind construction workers how important safety is in the course of their jobs. We need the same sort of "Think Security" and "Security First" mentality in the software industry to begin to reorient software programmers and engineers into thinking about the risks their products may introduce into business-critical environments.

There are several key cradle-to-grave risk management activities for software systems that, if followed, can result in consideration of potential losses to businesses, as well as aid in making intelligent business decisions (based on speculative risks) for where and how to spend resources efficiently. These activities are as follows:

- Risk identification
- Planning
- Design
- Test
- Independent validation and verification
- Monitoring and maintenance

A risk-management-driven process to engineering Internet applications begins by identifying risks with respect to threats, vulnerabilities, and consequences. Initially, consider pure risks of the e-commerce system—that is, the potential downside from security violations. Once the threats, vulnerabilities, and consequences are identified, then a business decision can be made about what speculative risks are acceptable.

Risk Identification

The risk is the potential downside of what will happen (consequences) if a threat exploits some vulnerability in your system. It is instructive, then, first to identify what are the threats to the system and ultimately to the business. For instance, if the system were subject to a denial-of-service attack, would the business be taken offline? Obviously, the consequences of a business being offline could be significant in terms of both lost revenues and lost customers. Is the threat strictly from the outside (the untrusted Internet), or are there insider threats from employees who may have access to the system who should not? Is there a threat of data theft? That is, is the data of some value that would motivate an adversary to steal it? Is there competition that might be motivated to sabotage the system? Is fraud a threat? Is there a threat against your customers' privacy? Is there a threat that the system might be used by hackers as a launching point against other sites? Is there a threat of piracy or illegal duplication of digital goods that will result in lost revenues? Is there a threat that a supplier in the supply chain might go down and thus bring the business down as part of a cascading effect? Is the Internet Service Provider, Web hoster, Application Service Provider reliable? Secure?

In considering threats, it is useful to think about the likelihood of the threat. If the likelihood of a threat is close to zero, it may not make sense to plan for it. Conversely, identifying high-likelihood threats can result in maximum return on risk analysis. While there exist few empirical studies on the likelihood of security threats, such as those you might find in actuarial tables in insured industries, one can make rough approximations for various kinds of threats. For instance, what is the current flavor of attack seen in the wild? What do trends from incident response teams indicate as near- and longer-term threats to Internet-based systems? For instance, if you are a major e-commerce provider, the likelihood of a denial-of-service attack is non-trivial. Similarly, buffer overrun attacks are very common. Future threats may be from mobile code in the form of active scripts, e-mail attachments, and live updates. E-mail viruses can cripple not only organizations, but also whole portions of the Internet. If your business provides services to mobile computing devices, with what threats need you be concerned about in wireless computing? If you are a government organization with public visibility and/or anathema, Web defacing is a likely threat. If you are a critical infrastructure service provider, you might consider nation-state or terrorist threats, whereas a small business would not.

Threats and vulnerabilities go hand-in-hand. Generally, threats exploit vulnerabilities in order to breach security and cost businesses. Vulnerabilities are system-dependent attributes that make it possible for someone or some piece of code to obtain access to data or privileges he or she should not have. It should be recognized that all systems have vulnerabilities. It is not realistic for a risk management strategy to be based on a flawless system. Thus, the approach should be one of vulnerability management. A vulnerability management strategy attempts to identify what vulnerabilities are present in the system, how they correlate with threats (and the likelihood of these threats), and the impact or value of losses if the threat were to exploit identified vulnerabilities. In other words, the vulnerabilities a system has should not result in unacceptable losses or consequences based on identified threats. Vulnerability management involves analyzing vulnerabilities, assessing the risk of the vulnerability, and taking corrective action if necessary.

Vulnerability analysis needs to be performed at a functional level as well as at the architectural and code level. A system may be vulnerable to certain threats based on functions that are offered or not offered. If, for instance, a system is vulnerable to eavesdropping where data can be captured in the clear, this may not be of consequence if the data itself need not be private. Therefore, a vulnerability analysis may not recommend a risk mitigation function such as encryption. Conversely, if data confidentiality is required, it is important to choose an appropriate cryptographic algorithm based on the threat. For instance, though a motivated hacker can crack 40-bit encryption, the threat and its likelihood for standard e-commerce activities is miniscule, which makes most standard SSL-compliant browsers and servers suitable for e-commerce. In many financial transactions, such as securities trading, it is important to have strong authentication of parties, logging, and non-repudiation of transactions. A vulnerability analysis will determine whether these functions are provided and whether they can be bypassed.

In addition to functional vulnerabilities, vulnerabilities are introduced by system architecture and implementation. A system architecture that places proprietary information in front of a firewall is vulnerable to certain attacks versus one that places it behind the firewall. Also, architectures that incorporate links to other networks (trusted or not) may introduce new vulnerabilities. The implementation of the e-commerce system in terms of the software applications, the servers, databases, and middleware all will introduce potential vulnerabilities. The vulnerability analysis must continue through the design and implementation phase of the system in order to analyze where vulnerabilities exist in both COTS systems and custom-developed software. The vulnerability management strategy will differ based on whether the component is COTS or custom-developed. COTS systems will require up-to-date monitoring of vulnerability notices from the COTS vendors in order to ensure that appropriate patches are applied to the system. For custom-developed software, vulnerability management will require software analysis for software vulnerabilities.

Finally, it probably need not be mentioned, but all risk management activities need to be performed with respect to the consequences of vulnerable systems and threats. If the vulnerability and threat are of little consequence, then clearly the risk management strategy is to move on to other problems. On the other hand, if the consequence of a denial-of-service attack is a loss of millions of dollars in revenue over a short time period and a loss of shareholder value, then the risk management strategy may call for multiply redundant solutions to mitigate the risk.

Risk Planning

Once the risks have been identified in terms of threats, vulnerabilities, and consequences, the risk planning stage determines the appropriate course of action. The first risk planning activity is to rank-order and prioritize the risks. Risk planning considers the likelihood of the threat against a system vulnerability times the value of the loss. This equation means that not all low-likelihood threats should be discarded and not all high-likelihood threats should be mitigated. For instance, even a remote threat may warrant consideration and risk management if the consequences or loss due to the threat are catastrophic. A security breach of a remotely administered automatic control plant, though it may be considered unlikely, might warrant serious security measures to prevent industrial accidents through online exploitation. Likewise, common probes or port scans from potential hackers may not warrant intrusion response and prosecution if the cost of the action exceeds the cost of the consequence. Thus, a close look at all the risks in consideration of likelihood and consequences should result in a rank-ordered list of risks that may require mitigation.

Once the risks are rank-ordered, resources can be appropriately allocated to manage these risks. Architecting the system according to high-priority risks is important. It is always more difficult and expensive to patch a system after it has already been architected and implemented.

The examples in the preceding section on architectural implications of firewalls, legacy systems, and encryption are considerations when architecting a system to be secure. Architectural considerations will take into account whether risks are strictly external or internal. They may also call for different types of network services such as Virtual Private Networks (VPNs), negotiated protocols, network choke points, and different authentication and authorization services such as PKI, smartcards, and biometrics.

One activity often overlooked in engineering systems is backup, disaster, and recovery planning. It is better to plan for worst-case scenarios than to assume that nothing potentially catastrophic will happen. For instance, if a hacker succeeds in getting administrative privileges on your system and decides to trash the file system, what contingency plans are built in to mitigate this attack? As mentioned before, data- and code–driven attacks are an even more serious threat than hackers. Many of today's e-mail viruses delete all working documents, which can result in the loss of thousands of man hours of effort, if not more. Emergency contingency planning will provide off-site daily backups of files to mitigate the risks of hackers, fire, and natural disasters. In addition, it may be imperative to bring a system back online within short order to prevent further losses in revenue and customer confidence. Therefore, there should be a plan for quick recovery. If someone else is hosting your site, then you will want to find out what contingency plans are in place in case of natural or hacker-induced disasters.

Finally, rather than putting all of one's assets in hardening a system to attack and attack detection, it is important to also consider intrusion tolerance and response. Planning for intrusion tolerance and response recognizes that no matter how well a system is designed, it is likely to be vulnerable, and a very well-motivated hacker will probably find the vulnerability. An intrusion-tolerant system expects that hackers will get past the lines of defense and will plan accordingly. For instance, off-site, real-time auditing and logging can be used to reconstruct the actions of an attacker, not only to determine what assets have been corrupted or stolen, but also to serve as the basis for a prosecutorial case and begin data recovery. Similarly, intrusion response mechanisms will alert system administrators when an attack is in progress to begin to close down access to valued resources and to enable the stealth observation of the attacker.

Security-Oriented Software Engineering

> *". . . any program, no matter how innocuous it seems, can harbor security holes. (Who would have guessed that on some machines integer divide exceptions could lead to system penetrations?) We thus have a firm belief that everything is guilty until proven innocent."*
>
> William Cheswick and Steve Bellovin
> *Firewalls and Internet Security* (Addison-Wesley, 1994)

As with all software development, good design and engineering practices are important for software quality. This point is particularly important for development of e-commerce applications, which are susceptible to attack. Rather than thinking of security as an add-on feature to software systems, security should be designed into the system from the earliest stages of requirements gathering through development, testing, integration, and deployment.

The goal of design for security is to break the penetrate-and-patch mindset that pervades commercial software security today and replace it with a process for finding and removing security-related bugs prior to release. The earlier this activity begins, the better. To give you an idea of where problems in software are typically found, industry studies have consistently shown that over 50 percent of software defects can be traced to poorly written or conceived requirements. Close to 30 percent of defects can be attributed to design errors. Thus, roughly 80 percent of all software defects can be traced to requirements and design—activities that occur early in the software lifecycle.

The cost of finding and fixing bugs in software after release is orders of magnitude more expensive than correcting them early during the software development lifecycle. Surveys performed by IBM, Rockwell, and TRW dramatically illustrate this point. The average cost of finding and fixing a bug in requirements is close to $140. As the bug gets carried into design, the average cost per bug goes up to $455. Now after the software has been released in the field and the bug is found during maintenance, the average cost per bug goes up to a staggering $14,000. This is a 100-fold increase in the cost of finding and fixing bugs in the field rather than in requirements. The moral is to test early and test often.

Good software engineering practices are necessary to develop robust and secure online applications. Activities that mark good software engineering practices are the following:

- Gathering and formally specifying requirements
- Design and analysis
- Adopting good coding practices
- Defensive programming
- Unit testing and integration
- Release engineering
- Third-party validation and verification

Requirements Gathering

To develop secure applications, the software development team must infuse security-driven requirements into these software engineering practices. For instance, requirements gathering has traditionally focused on the functional needs of the end users. These functional needs will also include security properties, such as user authentication and confidentiality and integrity of data. To make the application resistant to attack, the requirements should also specify what the application (and by extension, its users) *should not* do. A specification of undesired behavior not only is useful for preventing security design flaws, but also can be used for security-oriented testing.

Part of the job in designing your software to be both usable and robust is to develop use case scenarios. That is, from a user's point of view, think about how the software application will be used online. Use case scenarios are a common technique in usability engineering, and they are also useful for ensuring that the requirements are complete. In order to "think security" during object-oriented (OO) analysis and design, consider pathological use case scenarios. For instance, do not assume that the user will use the Web form provided by the online application. Rather, consider that a user may alter the form, write his or her own form to send data to the application, or violate field constraints (which might otherwise be checked by a JavaScript). Also, do not assume that "hidden fields" in forms remain hidden. One can see these fields merely by viewing the source in the browser. Consider use case scenarios where hidden fields are altered by the end user. Some e-commerce sites foolishly rely on hidden fields to store pricing information. Simply changing this field in the form can sometimes reduce the price of the good you are purchasing. If you are using scripting languages on the server side that interpret meta-characters, then you will need to ensure that the input received from the client-side is filtered for all meta-characters.

Design

Design is a fundamental practice of any engineering activity. The days of slinging code without some design and analysis are long gone for most commercial software development houses. Design takes into consideration not only the functional requirements, but also other attributes of the code such as modularity, reusability, portability, and testability. While many software engineers often consider the first three attributes in design, they often fail to design their code to be testable. Designing code to be testable involves inserting appropriate "hooks" into the code that make its internal state observable. For instance, adding assertions pervasively in code is a great way to make program state visible and to spot possible problems early during development. Another simple technique used by programmers is simply printing out the state of variables as they are used. More sophisticated programming practices will instrument the code with test stubs to allow unit testing of code. The key point, though, is that program design should also include design for testability in order to make the code more testable and ultimately more reliable and secure.

In any Internet-based software, design must also take security into consideration. As has often been stated here, e-commerce systems must be designed with security built in from the ground up. As mentioned in the preceding section, requirements must take into account not only security properties, such as authentication and confidentiality, but also the types of behaviors a program should not do. The design of the system then will account for security requirements as well as designing robustness into the system, such as exception handlers to ensure that the application will not crash if the operating system throws an exception.

It is important to realize that designs themselves can be tested. This activity is usually called analysis and is often performed in object-oriented system representations. Again, analyzing system designs can result in huge payoffs when performed early, rather than if design errors are found after the system has been released. An ounce of prevention here will save a ton of effort later to patch released systems.

A good design rule is to encapsulate security-critical functionality (such as authentication services) into a small testable kernel of code. The goal is to design the system so that all security-critical functions are easily identified, co-located, and encapsulated in well-defined interfaces. This design rule will permit these security functions to be rigorously analyzed and tested. As an example, rather than spread password checking or authentication services throughout the code in different modules, it should be written once (and thoroughly tested for bugs) and invoked whenever any transactions requiring credentials are necessary. The design must not only isolate the security functionality, but also ensure that it is invoked during security-critical operations.

Once a system is represented in a design, it can be effectively analyzed for vulnerability to attack. The key is to think with the criminal's or attacker's mindset. Remember that the adversary doesn't follow the rules. In other words, attackers cheat. It is important to test designs for resilience to attack. Design is the place to begin contingency planning as well. For instance, good designs will build in redundancy so that if one system goes down, an alternative system can handle the required load. Even geographically distributing replicated systems can result in higher availability. For instance, if portions of the Internet go down in one geographic area (through malicious attack or simple outages), a replicated server on the opposite coast may be able to handle the traffic. The design will need to be able to route requests appropriately, which calls for redundancy management.

While redundancy through replication is a common fault-tolerant strategy, another strategy that can pay off particularly well against a malicious adversary is diverse redundancy. Diverse redundancy is a fault-tolerant design that implements the same functionality through different means. A common specification is used, though different languages, platforms, and even development teams are used to implement the system. One of the key benefits of diverse redundancy is that different development teams will make different errors. Thus, if one implementation is vulnerable to a buffer overrun attack, its diverse twin may not be. One way to force some diversity is to require different language implementations, different compilers, and even different operating systems. The key is that the vulnerabilities are not identical. In replicated systems, the same attack will bring down or compromise all replicas. In diverse implementations, the attacker will have to work at least twice as hard to bring down all redundant versions. Using different platforms (such as Linux and Windows NT) will ensure that a Windows NT-based attack will not compromise a Linux-based system. Likewise, implementing one system in Java and another in C++ will mean that a buffer overrun vulnerability in the C++ implementation will not exist in the Java implementation.

The redundancy-through-diversity approach is not without its pitfalls, however. First, it is expensive. It can be N times as expensive as building a single system, where N is the number of redundant, diverse copies, particularly if distinct development teams are used for each different implementation. Second, errors in specification will likely result in common-mode failures among all redundant copies. That is, in spite of investing heavily in diverse implementations, if the specification itself is flawed, the redundant copies will likely all implement the same flawed specification. Again, spotting errors early can prevent expensive problems such as these. One of the key benefits of the Internet is that it supports just about any platform. This built-in support for diverse and heterogeneous platforms should be leveraged to build robust systems using different platforms and implementations.

Good Coding Practices

Using good coding practices can go a long way toward making your code readable, analyzable, and reusable by others. In addition, it can eliminate a lot of bugs that would otherwise creep up through ad hoc, "cowboy-style" programming. One of the biggest sources of vulnerability in most applications is the use of several unsafe standard C library functions. To name a few, some of the following commonly used C library functions can be exploited by malicious users if they are used improperly:

gets()
strcpy()
strcat()
sprintf()
scanf()
sscanf()
fscanf()

Unfortunately, a whole generation of C programmers has been weaned on using several of these standard functions. The basic problem with them is that they do not perform any bounds checking on the arguments before using them. As a result, using these functions may introduce buffer overrun vulnerabilities in your programs. A more comprehensive table of potentially dangerous C library functions can be found online.[3]

Other good coding practices involve syntax checking. This is related to thinking about pathological use case scenarios, but flipping it on its head. Rather than attempting to come up with all pathological use case scenarios, think about exactly what kind of input is acceptable. In many online applications, this can be specified to a fairly fine level. For instance, if you are asking for someone's credit card number, you know it will have 16 digits, all numerals. It is very simple to perform syntax checking to ensure that what you receive is valid. Even though performing the check at the client side in what is called form validation is good for fixing a problem before it is sent, do not trust that the data has been adequately checked. Again, a user can bypass this checking mechanism and send any data he or she wants directly to the online application. This check needs to be performed at the server in the online application.

Another instance of syntax checking involves checking formatting and ordering of data. For instance, in programming network sockets, the developer of the server piece (who will often write or coordinate with the developers of the client-side piece) will specify the format of packets to be sent by the client. A clever hacker can change the format and order of data sent in packets. Rather than assume that the packets will arrive in the prescribed format, the server-side software should do some sanity checking to ensure that the data is of the specified format. Unfortunately, doing checksums on packets is not sufficient. Freely available software packages allow anyone to arbitrarily change data, format, and ordering of network packets sent to network services (including online applications that process packets). The software package will recalculate a correct checksum on the altered packet; so just verifying the checksum at the server is not sufficient. Since this kind of software is freely available, anyone including hackers can use it to test out online applications and services. Online application developers should certainly use it to test their own software for syntax anomalies and pathological cases.

Another often-overlooked good coding practice that results in many security-related errors is documentation. While many may object that documentation is not a coding practice, it should be. Documentation of code makes code more legible and capable of being examined and analyzed for bugs. Interesting enough, the most effective debugging strategy is good, old-fashioned code inspection. Code inspection by someone other than the code developer can result in finding the most significant bugs (even design bugs). In order to make code readable in the first place, it must be well documented, both within the code and in separate documentation.

Documentation errors are usually errors of incorrect documentation, ambiguous documentation, or missing documentation.[4] Incorrect documentation simply gets the facts wrong, such as the ordering of parameters to a function call. Unfortunately, this type of error can result in exceptions being thrown that can be fatal if not handled. Fixing the problem is even more difficult because the documentation is generally trusted. Ambiguous documentation is one of the most common complaints, as well as cause for security problems and incompatibility. Many Internet protocols as well as software standards, such as the Secure Electronic Transaction (SET) standard, are drafted through a Request For Comment (RFC) process. Ultimately, the outcome from the RFC is a document that specifies requirements for meeting a network service or software standard. Ambiguity in the specification can lead to differing and sometimes conflicting implementations. In many cases, the different implementations of a standard can result in incompatibilities between programs that should be compatible. In some cases, the ambiguity can result in security holes. Ambiguities in network services RFCs (such as the ping RFC) have resulted in different implementations of the same service that have caused denial-of-service problems.

Finally, missing documentation is probably the most pervasive problem. Many times requirements and specifications are just not written. Specifications that live in the head of the developer tend to be fuzzy and non-repeatable. Getting specifications of accepted and unacceptable behavior for an online application on paper will make the job of understanding the application and testing it a matter of execution. Another big benefit of having documentation on hand is that the documentation itself can be tested. Finding bugs in documentation is a lot easier than finding bugs in software without documentation. Typically, the kinds of bugs you find in documentation tend to be significant (remember the cost of bugs in requirements and design phases) and well worth the effort.

Defensive Programming

Arguably, good coding practices start from using safe languages, compilers, and operating systems. Unfortunately, for many different reasons including market dynamics, the software development team does not always have the freedom to make the best choices in all three of these areas. Assuming that the operating system is already chosen, the choice of language in which the application is developed will often influence the security of the application. The preceding section showed several unsafe C library functions. One might assume that C is a bad choice of language. Not necessarily. The truth is that in most cases the C language made these choices (not performing bounds checking in functions) for efficiency reasons. As a result, C programs execute very quickly. The downside is that a lot of checking of safe usage is left to the programmer, who may not always realize how these functions can be misused for malicious gain.

A popular language choice for online systems is Perl. Interpreted languages such as Perl are great for rapidly prototyping software, hence their attraction to the rapid development set. One characteristic of interpreted languages is that they provide powerful constructs for executing system commands. This power is also what makes them dangerous. Perl commands such as eval(), system(), backquotes (`), pipes, and exec() can potentially result in system commands being executed on the Web server at the discretion of an unknown and untrusted remote user. Untrusted user input is often passed as an argument to these calls. If the argument includes system commands, the user may be able to interactively command the server on his or her behalf. Use these commands with extreme caution when processing user input.

While the same types of system commands can be used in compiled languages such as C, they are not as easily constructed or misused as system commands in interpreted languages such as Perl, Python, or Tcl. C, however, provides its own hazards due to its lack of advanced memory management. Regardless of the language used, the cardinal rule in development is to never trust the user input.

Fortunately, defensive programming can add security where powerful language constructs might otherwise fall short. A key defensive strategy is to sanity-check (and sanitize) all program input. As mentioned previously, be sure to sanitize input of special meta-characters. Characters such as the backtick (`) allow input to be executed as commands to the interpreter. Unescape special characters, or if possible, accept only legitimate characters. Do not assume that the length of the input is fixed. Even if the length of the input field is limited in a form, the end user is not constrained to using the form to send in user input. When parsing user input, read only the length of data necessary for the input and ensure adequate memory is allocated for the amount of input to be read.

Another common rule of defensive programming is to check the result of system calls, and function calls in general. Most system calls will return a non-zero error code if a problem results when the call is performed. Rather than ignoring this result, a conditional should be coded that recognizes the problem and handles it appropriately. For instance, null pointers need to be identified before they are used. Along these lines, many system calls will throw exceptions when something is really amiss. If the exception is not caught, then it will likely crash the application, resulting in a denial of service. A good practice is to wrap exception handlers around system calls as well as other people's functions, such as library components. For instance, if a file system read throws an exception, rather than crashing the application, a good coding practice is to catch the exception at the point of the file read and handle it gracefully (such as pop up a dialog box or attempt a reread).

In the preceding section, we learned that a number of standard C functions do not perform bounds checking. A good coding practice would substitute these functions with their safe counterparts. For instance, in the section on buffer overruns earlier in this chapter, the class of strn*() functions was described as safe substitutes. As mentioned, though, some of these functions are not equal counterparts. It is fairly easy to code off-by-one errors in indexing arrays if you are substituting one safe function for its unsafe counterpart. It is important to ensure that indexing is correctly coded and to make sure that you are not falling off the end of an array when you are reading it.

Assertions are as valuable a tool to a defensive programmer as a horn is to a defensive driver. Assertions are usually used during development and debugging to help debug possible problems. Assertions allow the developer to query a program's state, then make some statement or take some action based on a program state. The value of the assertion is that it allows the developer to determine if a function executed correctly, or, said differently, if the program is in a correct state at the point in execution where the assertion is coded. Assertions begin with a conditional statement called the precondition. The precondition checks the state in which you are interested. Usually assertions are coded to check bad states instead of correct states. If the program is in a bad state, such as an error code is returned from a function, then the assertion fires and the body of the assertion executes. The body can be a simple printing statement that records the problem in a debugging log. It is also possible to attempt to affect program state by changing variables or making other calls within the assertion body, but this is a dangerous practice. Inserting side-effecting code within an assertion can have unintended consequences. Assertions are usually removed before the code is shipped for performance reasons.

Environment variables pose a common hazard in many e-commerce applications, particularly in CGI scripts. Environment variables are used by programs to hold the value of certain system properties, such as the full path name to executables and libraries. The problem is, in many cases, that the untrusted end user can set certain environment variables. As a result, it is important to sanity-check and sanitize environment variables from HTTP clients before using them. Use other system environment variables carefully. You should specify explicit paths rather than rely on system environment variables for accessing programs and files. An insider can fool a CGI script that depends on an environment variable to execute a rogue program instead of the intended program.

In addition to these defensive programming techniques, some languages provide safety features that you should leverage when possible. For instance, Perl 5 contains a "taint" module for preventing user-supplied input from being used in system commands. When Perl tainting is enabled, any variable derived from user input (such as command-line arguments and environment variables) is considered tainted (or untrusted). Thus, when a tainted variable is used in a system command such as modifying the file system or spawning a shell, the Perl runtime interpreter prevents the command from executing.

Similarly, Tcl has a safe language interpreter that can prevent untrusted input from compromising system security and integrity. When using application servers for implementing business application logic, strongly typed languages such as Java should be used in favor of C or C++. Java's type safety and advanced memory management can eliminate typical programmer errors in walking through memory that often lead to security breakdowns. Furthermore, Java 2 provides fine-grained access control for Java programs to prevent unauthorized access to system resources.

In short, always expect the unexpected from user input. Employ defensive programming techniques such as sanitizing input regardless of the language used. If you develop using an interpreted language, then use the safe language-interpreter features such as Perl tainting and Safe-Tcl. Use a type-safe language such as Java rather than languages such as C and C++ that give free reign to the programmer to use memory objects in any context.

Defensive programming techniques can significantly aid the developer in writing secure server-side software. Even so, perfection is largely unattainable in software development. In order to provide greater assurance of security, consider using technologies that can "wrap" server-side software in order to limit potential damage from flawed software exploited for malicious gain.

One of the most commonly employed approaches on Unix-based systems is to use the chroot() command in order to effectively cordon off the file system visible to a program. The chroot() function changes the effective root of the file system for a given process to a designated new root. In the case of server-side software, define the new root as the smallest partition of the file system necessary for the program(s) to access. When a process is run in a chroot() environment, it is effectively running in a jail cell to prevent it from causing damage to other portions of the system. While the chroot() environment is useful for preventing auxiliary damage to the rest of the system, it is important to remember that the chroot environment must contain the portion of the file system necessary for the program to perform its function. If the business application logic needs to communicate with critical system resources, such as back-end databases, then these resources need to be included within the chroot environment. In this case, the chroot environment will not protect databases or other included resources from misbehaving software, but it will protect the integrity of other system resources outside the chroot environment. Alternative commercial technologies for "sand-boxing" executing processes are available on the Windows platform.

Another technique for Unix-based systems provides some protection by running CGI scripts with user permissions. The program CGIWrap is designed for systems that allow internal users to write and post their own CGI scripts. While allowing users to post their own CGI scripts is inadvisable for e-commerce applications, if it is a requirement, CGIWrap can be useful for limiting the privilege of the executing CGI process to that of the user. The technique assumes that permissions of users are properly configured on the system so that no user is allowed access to other users' files or to critical system files and programs. In many systems, the Web server is configured to run all CGI scripts under a single account's privileges. Often an account is created for this purpose such as www or nobody. In systems where internal users are allowed to post their own CGI scripts, however, it is inadvisable to allow a user's script to access files owned by other users or other Web server files. CGIWrap enforces the policy that users' CGI scripts can access only files owned by the script's owner. Again, before leaving the discussion of CGIWrap, it is important to reiterate that it is generally inadvisable to allow users to post their own CGI scripts to an e-commerce site.

A more attractive alternative to CGIWrap is the SBOX tool written by Lincoln Stein. Like CGIWrap, SBOX is designed for multiuser Web sites where users are allowed to post their own CGI scripts. In addition to limiting the privilege of CGI scripts to their owner's files, SBOX also can place limits on executing CGI processes on the use of system resources such as CPU cycles, memory, and disk. This feature is effective in thwarting denial-of-service attacks from malicious CGI scripts or poorly written CGI scripts that end up consuming system resources to the detriment of the other e-commerce services. SBOX also allows CGI scripts to be run in a chroot() directory. Thus, SBOX provides wrapping capability of programs that not only limits the file system using chroot(), but also ensures that the CGI scripts cannot infringe on other users' programs and will not deny service to other executing processes. It is important to stress again, however, that e-commerce applications should not be deployed in a general-purpose environment that allows multiple users to upload their CGI scripts. Given that fair warning, if CGI uploading is supported, using tools such as SBOX and CGIWrap can reduce the likelihood of catastrophic security breaches.

Security Testing: "Test Early and Test Often"

Note that on the list of traditional software engineering activities (see the "Security-Oriented Software Engineering" section) unit testing and integration appear pretty far down the list of activities. In fact, though, security testing can and should begin very early. Testing should be an extension of the risk management activities (see the "Risk Management" section) that is applied early in the software engineering lifecycle. In other words, vendors need not wait until they have code to begin testing. Some of the most serious security risks can be tested in architectural and design stages. As stated earlier, one of the great things about having written requirements and specifications is that they can be tested for problems. Of course, finding bugs in requirements, specifications, and designs is significantly cheaper than someone else finding them in the field.

Traditional testing involves generating test cases that exercise the system's intended functionality. Security-oriented testing is directed testing that starts from the risk analysis. That is, security-oriented testing should use risks identified in the risk analysis to direct the tests to attempt to exploit potential vulnerabilities. Many security analysts can examine a system architecture, immediately spot vulnerabilities, then determine which test cases are needed to test whether the system is exploitable. The design of the system will reveal whether certain security attributes have been included as part of the design. For instance, it might be important to install software installation filters on enterprise-critical machines to ensure that untrusted and foreign software is not installed without system administrator approval. Similarly, the design of databases will determine whether proper end-user authentication (check of credentials) and authorization (check of access) checks have been designed. The more testing that occurs early in system design, the more likely robust systems will be developed. The overriding motto for system developers should be "test early and test often."

Once code development has begun, unit testing can begin in earnest. Unit testing involves testing portions of the system even before the system has been completely developed. There is no hard and fast rule on what constitutes a unit. A unit can be a conditional, a loop, an exception handler, a class, a function, a module, a package, a library, or a self-contained program. Often, units are not designed with their own user interface, so a test harness needs to be built to test the unit. In addition, because most units interface with other units (which may not be developed at the time of unit testing), the missing or incomplete units are replaced with "stubs."

The most common strategy for unit testing is to derive test cases to test intended behaviors or functions of the unit. If a specification for the unit exists, test cases can be generated to test expected functionality. In security risk-based testing, test cases should be derived from other criteria:

- Security risks
- Reliability and availability risks
- Exception handling
- Assertions of bad behavior
- Third-party component failures
- Common coding problems

Testing against system risks is what software test expert Chuck Howell calls "the power of negative thinking." The basic idea is to put on a very pessimistic hat and to think of all the things that can go wrong. The goal of the security-oriented tester should be to demonstrate that the software is robust under very stressful conditions, such as when the software is being attacked.

If it is not already apparent, there is a strong correlation between reliability, safety, and security as far as software flaws are concerned. Failures in any one of these dependability properties can result in failures in any of the others. Thus, a software flaw that can result in a program crash not only results in an unreliable system, but also can open security holes, such as vulnerability to denial-of-service attacks. If the flaw is a buffer overrun vulnerability, it will result in program crashes given unstructured data, or it could potentially result in full system compromise given a stack-smashing attack. Similarly, if a nuclear power plant's systems are not secure, its compromise by foreign adversaries or terrorists can lead to catastrophic public hazard risks. Thus, the tester must consider dependability risks in general to address security, reliability, and safety risks in particular. Fortunately, the power of negative thinking can aid in all of these areas.

Be forewarned, however, that the subtleties of security risks make reliability-based testing insufficient for security testing. That is, security testing requires its own focused testing. For instance, when testing systems for security weaknesses, it is more often the case that the tester will observe system "weirdness" than an actual, overt security violation. Different types of system weirdness can point to potential security problems. For instance, the inability of the system to respond to unusual inputs may point to error-handling problems or the lack of sanity-checking input. Another example is buffer overrun vulnerabilities. Most often, buffer overrun vulnerabilities are found not by obtaining root privilege the first time a buffer is overflowed, but rather by forcing a memory segmentation fault and a program crash. How the buffer is actually allocated in memory will determine whether the vulnerability can be exploited to gain unauthorized privilege. The key, though, is that security problems may reveal themselves symptomatically in different ways that will require further analysis of source code to determine if a security problem exists. A detailed source code analysis will then drive test cases that will attempt to exploit potential vulnerabilities.

A commonly applied technique in software testing is code coverage analysis. Code coverage analysis tells you which portions of your code have been executed (covered) from the test cases you have applied. The simplest form of code coverage is statement coverage. Statement coverage tells you which program statements have been executed by the test cases you have run. Statement coverage can be hierarchically organized so that you can see which functions and modules have been tested. More complex forms of coverage analysis exist, such as branch coverage and multiple condition decision coverage (MCDC). The higher the complexity, the more test cases required to satisfy the coverage condition. The Federal Aviation Administration (FAA), for instance, requires MCDC coverage on avionics flight control software.

Although code coverage is useful for identifying which portions of code need to be tested, it should not be oversold for security analysis. For instance, simply executing code does not mean that you have analyzed it for security risks. Thus, reaching 100 percent statement coverage does not mean that the program you have tested is secure. It means only that you have executed all the statements in the program. Instead, code must be analyzed against security risks and specific types of known software flaws, which are discussed later in this section. Instrumenting software with assertions of unsafe or insecure states can be useful during coverage testing to determine if any security policies have been violated during testing. Probably the most useful benefit of coverage analysis is simply knowing which portions of the software have not been tested. In other words, code coverage analysis should be used to determine what code needs to be tested, not to reach some level of confidence in its security.

Unfortunately, there is no canonical set of tests to run to determine if a system is secure. If there were, it stands to reason that a tool could automate security testing. As a result, the best approach to security testing is to use the security risk assessment to drive the testing. This will involve mapping security risks to test cases and code—a non-trivial exercise. Remember that your adversary must do the same. The point is to stay ahead of the adversary. Usually, just by thinking about security risks and how they apply to the implementation, you can get a substantial head start over the hackers, who will not have as much information as you will about your own system.

Aside from system- and application–dependent testing based on particular security risks, there are some fairly generic types of security-oriented testing activities. For instance, consider the set of unsafe functions described in the section, "Good Coding Practices." Obviously, you want to avoid unsafe functions; however, this is a good starting point for finding potential problems. For instance, it is fairly easy to scan code for any of the unsafe functions using pattern-matching commands such as grep on Unix. Better yet, the ITS4 software tool developed at Cigital will do this for you automatically (see www.cigital.com/its4/). Once the dangerous functions are identified in the code, you can replace them (carefully) with their safe equivalents, or they will need to be tested to ensure that they cannot be exploited.

Common Software Security Problems

Other types of generic testing can be performed to identify common security hazards in software. For instance, the following is a list of software problems that can lead to security hazards:

- Buffer overrun
- Default configuration/misconfiguration
- Unpatched software
- Race conditions/time-of-check-to-time-of-use
- Hidden features/unknown functionality

- Unusual/unexpected interactions
- Inconsistent behavior/different implementations
- SUID root programs
- Inadequate input sanity checking
- Poor random-number generators

The two most common software security hazards are buffer overrun vulnerabilities and misconfigured software. Buffer overrun vulnerabilities were discussed in detail earlier in this chapter. Misconfiguration is more pervasive than buffer overrun vulnerabilities and the single biggest reason most Internet systems are vulnerable to attack today. One of the biggest reasons most systems are misconfigured is that, by default, out-of-the-box systems are configured for maximum functionality and minimum security. As a result, when a system is first turned on, installed, or run, it is often configured to give the user maximum flexibility and ease-of-use rather than configured by default to be most secure. For instance, many network servers are chock full of different network services that listen promiscuously when the server is booted up. If you are unaware of what network services are running by default on your server, you probably will not realize that you are offering certain privileged services to people who do not need access to them. For example, many Unix servers are delivered with RPC services that allow remote users to run command shells and other software programs interactively on remote machines. Although this is excellent for internal and authorized users, it can open up vulnerabilities to outside untrusted users. RPC services have also been notoriously buggy and vulnerable to buffer overrun attacks.

Another major vulnerability with misconfigured network servers is global file sharing. Unix supports file sharing through NFS mounted drives, Kerberos, and YP (Yellow Pages) services. Windows supports file sharing through NetBIOS services. File sharing is frequently turned on to facilitate ease of data sharing with remote machines. The problem is that if global file sharing is enabled, anyone on the network (including remote Internet machines talking the same protocol) can gain access to critical and confidential files on your machine. If read and write privileges are enabled, then there is the potential for severe damage from a hostile entity scanning ports for file shares. Likewise, if you do not need to offer NetBIOS, BIND/DNS, News, IRC, or FTP services, these services should be disabled at the box, and all requests to these services from untrusted sources should be controlled or blocked by firewalls.

Aside from shutting down services that need not be offered, even offered services themselves must be configured. For instance, FTP servers must be carefully configured to ensure that file uploads are either disallowed or carefully controlled and that FTP clients do not gain access to files on your network for which access should not be granted. Web servers are notoriously misconfigured as well. Many times, files live in the document root of Web servers that should not. One well-known example is a shopping cart software application that stored credit card numbers of customers in a flat-file format database. This file was placed by default in the document root of the Web server. As a result, anyone who knew the name of the file could freely access all of a site's customers' credit card numbers simply by typing in the name of the file in the URL of his or her browser.

One can fault the software vendors for releasing software with minimal security settings; however, software must be configured according to the security needs of the user group. The security needs are captured in a security policy, and this will vary from site to site. Thus, rather than attempt to guess at security policies, vendors release software that will work out of the box with minimal configuration and leave configuration for security as an exercise for the user. Unfortunately, software configured this way will often open up security holes in your site, unless it is reconfigured. This problem is known as the "deadly defaults" and is discussed in detail in *E-Commerce Security: Weak Links, Best Defenses* (Wiley, 1998) in Chapter 4.

Conversely, it is also easy to argue that vendors should implement an "opt-in" strategy for most unsafe practices. For instance, downloading and running active content such as Web scripts, ActiveX controls, Java applets, Office 2000 document links, and executables should require the user to opt in to this capability (a safe practice that requires user intervention) rather than the current opt-out practice that requires a user to go through myriad menus in order to figure out how to disable these potentially unsafe actions.

Leaving security practices to users is generally a bad practice, as most users are not security-aware enough to make good security decisions. While most of the software security problems on this list can be addressed by the software vendor, one software problem that is left to the end user, or more appropriately to the system administrator, is the problem of patching software. As a result of bad software, the patch has become the ubiquitous solution. When a problem in software (generally one with serious ramifications such as security holes) is discovered, the software vendor fixes the problem by releasing a software "patch." It is up to the installed user base of the flawed software then to apply the patch. One of the biggest software security problems is unpatched software installations. That is, even when a security hole is known and a software patch is released, it is often the case that the software does not get patched, leaving the installation vulnerable to attack. Unpatched software represents a critical vulnerability in Internet-based systems. Unfortunately, fixing the problem requires widespread cooperation on an Internet scale.

A race condition is a term used by software security analysts to describe a programming-caused phenomenon in which an adversary attempts to gain privilege by "racing" a program to gain access to a privileged resource. Time-of-check-to-time-of-use (TOCTOU) flaws create most race conditions. The problem is created when the operations of checking credentials to delivering access to a resource are non-atomic. That is, if these operations are separable (non-atomic), then an adversary can switch the resource for which access was granted to another, more privileged resource. The classic example is that a program checks the credentials of a user to write to a file on the system. Assuming that write permission is granted, a race condition will exist if there is a delay between the time access is granted to the resource and the time it is used—that is, when the file handle is granted. During this time, an adversary—for example, the user—can switch the file (or more likely link the file) to a more privileged file, such as the system password file. In a certain sense, it is a bait-and-switch tactic. That is, the user baits the program into allowing a write to a file he or she should be allowed to write (such as on the local file system), then once access is granted, he or she switches the file to a link to the system password file (for which access would not have been granted). If the access check is performed atomically with the resource usage, then the race condition will not exist. Work by University of California at Davis researchers resulted in a Perl script that will analyze programs for TOCTOU flaws.

A common source of vulnerability in programs is hidden features or unknown functionality. This problem is particularly acute in today's component-based environments where a large part of software development involves using other people's software components. The risk is that the third-party software component you may use may contain unknown or even hidden functionality (such as Trojan horses). Thus, you may develop a system that unknowingly has Trojan horses or simply some additional functionality that was not documented. Later, an attacker may exploit this functionality. A common example is programmers leaving in debug functionality. These are functions that were inserted to help programmers debug possible problems. A well-known example was the sendmail debug bug that allowed anyone connecting to port 25 of a system running sendmail to enter a debug user ID and gain root access to the system. This problem is also common in CGI scripts on Web sites. Many debug functions and/or development scripts are often moved to production Web systems inadvertently. A common debug function is to print out all environment variables and even print out the script source. In the hands of an adversary, this information can be a gold mine for finding potential vulnerabilities.

Unknown features in third-party components are related to the risk of unusual or unexpected interactions between components. The problem is often caused because developers of a software product cannot consider every environment in which their software will run. All the programs that run on the machine, their configuration, and their usage define the environment. Like snowflakes, each desktop machine or device provides its own unique and dynamic environment. Component frameworks make unknown and unexpected interactions more likely. For instance, the COM/DCOM component framework allows previously distinct and independently developed applications to communicate, embed, and drive each other. It is hard for developers to anticipate how a given program will be used by another, and this is the heart of the unknown interactions problem. A prime example is how VBScripts can be used to command Microsoft applications. Little did the Microsoft developers think that untrusted VBScripts—that is, viruses—would one day be used to command Microsoft Outlook to send out malicious payloads in e-mails to all members in the user's address book. Another example is interactions between scripts and Java applets. Interactions between JavaScript and Java applets can together break the Java and JavaScript security models where individually either could not.

One of the most frustrating vulnerabilities and most difficult to debug problems is caused by different implementations of the same system specification. Unfortunately, this is a fairly common problem. One example was described earlier in reference to RFCs on Internet protocols. Different implementations of the same protocols (such as the ping program) can result in vulnerabilities on certain systems. This problem cuts across the board of software applications. Different implementations of the JavaScript interpreter and the Java Virtual Machine have led to vulnerabilities. Astute hackers leverage these differences for malicious gain. One of the problems of today's software is that unless it is working correctly, it tends to present a security hazard or denial-of-service problem. Currently, we don't have a fail-safe mentality in programming so that we develop systems that, even when they do not function correctly, they still perform safely.

The risk of SUID root programs is one of giving more privilege to a program than it needs. SUID root programs run as superuser on Unix systems. These programs are prime targets for attack because, if successful, a buffer overrun attack can give the attacker superuser or root privileges on the system. Some programs must run SUID root in order to gain access to privileged ports or privileged data on the system, such as the system password database. These programs must be carefully tested and analyzed for security flaws. One of the larger problems is in-house-developed software or scripts that run SUID root for convenience. Some developers or system administrators will run a program SUID root to get around access control obstacles rather than designing a better solution. The problem is created by the desire for convenience over security and good design. The consequence is that access control mechanisms designed to protect resources are defeated, and a new, potentially vulnerable SUID root program now runs on the system.

Inadequate input sanity-checking has been discussed in detail in the section *Defensive Programming*. The key is for developers to start thinking about the range of input they might receive versus the range of input the program functionally needs to accept. Most attacks attempt to leverage software flaws by trying unusual and unexpected input. By sanity-checking input before it is processed, a lot of attacks can be nipped in the bud.

Poor random-number generators are a pervasive problem in cryptography, and one that has been around for a long time. Even so, the problem still persists. Fundamentally, it is very difficult to produce random numbers on a deterministic machine—that is, a computer. That is why random-number generators are actually called pseudo-random-number generators (PRNG). PRNGs are often used in generating seeds, or initial constants used to seed a cryptographic algorithm. Because cryptographic algorithms are necessarily deterministic, once the seed is known, all subsequent cryptograms can be deterministically predicted with knowledge of the algorithm and the clear-text input. Therefore, it is imperative that the seeds be sufficiently random that they cannot be easily guessed. A lot of problems in crypto implementations come in using a PRNG incorrectly, in developing a PRNG in-house, or in using a flawed PRNG.

To give a recent example, PGP 5.0, the popular Pretty Good Privacy open source encryption package, has a flaw on certain Linux installations that might allow an attacker to guess the seeds correctly.[5] Normally, PGP asks the user to generate a source of randomness such as typing at a keyboard or moving the mouse. The randomness comes from the time between keystrokes or mouse movements. In addition, PGP uses a randseed.bin file as an additional source of randomness. A problem arises in an option of PGP to bypass these sources of randomness and to use the /dev/random utility on the machine for random information. This non-interactive option is used when generating a large number of keys. The problem is rooted in the way the data from /dev/random is processed by PGP that is not sufficiently random enough to prevent an attacker from guessing the key that is subsequently generated.

Another prominent example of random-number generation problems is illustrated by how Cigital researchers cracked an Internet gambling site's shuffling algorithm in a way that allowed them to predict every subsequent card picked from the deck with 100 percent accuracy.[6] The site was playing Texas Hold-em poker online in real time and, ironically, published its shuffling algorithm written in Pascal to show the fairness of its approach. The algorithm revealed several flaws that could be used to a malicious player's advantage.

Players play against each other while the site shuffles the deck and distributes the cards. The shuffling algorithm was flawed in several respects. First, it used an integer-based PRNG, the Pascal Randomize() function, which takes as input a 32-bit seed and produces 32-bit numbers. The shuffling algorithm starts with an ordered deck of cards and then uses the PRNG to randomly reorder the deck. In a real deck there are 52! (factorial) possible shuffles of a deck, or approximately 2^{226} possible unique shuffles. The integer-based PRNG uses 32-bit integers, which means it can produce just over 4 billion possible seeds. This means that only 4 billion possible shuffles can result from the shuffling in practice—much less than 52! shuffles. In other words, searching the space of 4 billion ordered decks of cards is significantly easier than that of 52! shuffles.

With PRNGs, there is nothing random about the sequence of numbers it produces once the seed is known. The next integer it produces is completely determined by the last number it produces, and ultimately by the seed it uses. Thus, the key to generating reasonably random numbers from a PRNG is to use randomly generated seeds (sounds like a chicken-and-egg problem, right?). The way that Randomize() generates initial seeds is based on the number of milliseconds on the system clock that have expired since midnight. This makes the problem of predicting the shuffles significantly easier. Because there are only 86,400,000 milliseconds in a day, this means that you effectively have to search through just over 86 million shuffles—again, much less than 4 billion and much, much less than 52! shuffles. By synchronizing with the system clock on the server generating the pseudo-random number, the Cigital team was able to further reduce the number of possible combinations down to approximately 200,000 possibilities. Searching through this set of shuffles is trivial and can be done on a PC in real time. In fact, the Cigital team wrote a program that on five cards being drawn from the deck will show exactly the cards that will be drawn by opposing players, and it will even tell the malicious player whether to hold-em or fold-em.

These examples clearly show that e-commerce software must be designed and developed diligently with security risks in mind. Software forms the key weak link in e-commerce systems today. Developers of Internet applications need to bring the kind of mentality and approach to system development that is a hallmark in other mission-critical areas such as safety-critical and fault-tolerant systems.

Fair Warning

It is apt to end this chapter with words of caution and a summary of the state of software from security expert and commentator Bruce Schneier.

The following is an excerpt from an essay he wrote on "Why Computers Are Insecure."[7]

> *Suppose a software product is developed without any functional testing at all. No alpha or beta testing. Write the code, compile it, and ship. The odds of this program working at all—let alone being bug-free—are zero. As the complexity of the product increases, so will the number of bugs. Everyone knows testing is essential.*
>
> *Unfortunately, this is the current state of the practice in security. Products are being shipped without any, or with minimal, security testing. I am not surprised that security bugs show up again and again. I can't believe anyone expects otherwise.*

This chapter built on the notion that security is a software problem. Rather than simply bemoan the problem, this chapter presented a risk management-oriented approach to software security. The approach uses risk management to drive design and development of Internet-based software in a software engineering style methodology. While the vast majority of today's Internet software is developed on Internet time without regard for software security risks, the economics of computer security losses, combined with product liability, will likely drive the software vendors on to the right track, as we have seen in other essential software environments. As software vendors, we can use good security engineering practices to differentiate our products from the shoddy products released by vendors who don't care about quality or security. As businesses, it is our responsibility to demand high-quality, safe, and secure software from software vendors. As consumers, it is our responsibility to push back on software vendors and e-commerce sites that do not protect the security of our business transactions and the privacy of our data.

Notes

1. In written testimony to the U.S. House Science Committee, Subcommittee on Technology, hearing on 10 May 2000.
2. See "Microsoft Security Bulletin (MS00-034)" online at www.microsoft.com/technet/security/bulletin/ms00-034.asp.
3. G. McGraw and J. Viega, "Make Your Software Behave: Preventing Buffer Overflows," IBM DeveloperWorks, www-4.ibm.com/software/developer/library/buffer-defend.html.

4. F. Cohen, "Eliminating Common Software Security Faults," *Software Development*, May 1998, www.sdmagazine.com.

5. See CERT Advisory CA-2000-09 at www.cert.org.

6. See "How We learned to Cheat in Online Poker: A Study in Software Security," ftp://ftp.rstcorp.com/pub/papers/developer_gambling.pdf.

7. B. Schneier, "Why Computers Are Insecure," RISKS Digest, 20:67, http://catless.ncl.ac.uk/Risks/20.67.html.

Weak Links in E-Commerce

"Using encryption on the Internet is the equivalent of arranging an armored car to deliver credit-card information from someone living in a cardboard box to someone living on a park bench."

PROF. GENE SPAFFORD
CERIAS, PURDUE UNIVERSITY

By this point in the book, you will have a finer appreciation of the role software plays in the security of e-commerce systems. In this chapter, we take a systematic look at the primary software components that make up e-commerce applications and provide an overview of the risks to each of these components. As you have heard before, e-commerce systems are only as strong as their weakest link. Many times, by force of habit and the influence of marketing campaigns, we tend to focus on the strongest links and overlook obvious weak links. For instance, firewalls and encryption give us a good, but often false, sense of security. The expression "there are many ways to skin a cat" applies equally well to breaking the security of computer systems. There are many ways to get both around and through firewalls. If the system administrator does not account for these various methods and places too much faith in the security of the firewall, then the security of the system or the data the administrator is responsible for protecting may be compromised. Similarly, we place a lot of faith in strong encryption algorithms and protocols. If the secret phrase or password that decrypts the transmission can be easily captured (for instance, by a client-side Trojan horse program) or if the decrypted document can be captured, then the security of the whole system can be compromised.

In this chapter, we systematically analyze e-commerce applications from end to end for risks and vulnerabilities that, if exploited, can result in a complete compromise of security. While new risks will develop as new technologies emerge, the systematic approach to analyzing the risks described here is applicable to new systems. This approach should help focus attention away from the hype of new feature functionality to an examination of potential risks introduced by new technology. The goal of this chapter is not to say these are the definitive risks you need to be worried about, as much as to point out that every system will have risks to its security and privacy that need to be systematically analyzed, and ultimately addressed.

A secondary goal is to continue to fight the vendor hype that *your* e-commerce system will be secure if you use this particular vendor's technology. We have seen this type of hype time and again with "secure" protocols that, in fact, protect the confidentiality and integrity of data only over the data transmission link. Similarly, a common vendor practice now is to "secure" your e-commerce application by adding security properties to it, such as encryption, authentication, and non-repudiation services. While such products might generally add some security property, they should not be oversold, and you should not be lulled into a false sense of security. Rather, it is important to understand what security they do provide and what other risks are. If nothing else, remember that cryptography and security are not synonymous. Rather, cryptography is often a necessary but insufficient component of a secure system.

For instance, consider an online application that uses encrypted tunnels such as a Virtual Private Network (VPN) in order to send data to and from both parties to the transaction. Sounds secure, right? Consider now that the Web-based application inadvertently, or potentially maliciously, sends a worm or Trojan horse over this encrypted tunnel to your Web client. The worm or code will certainly be encrypted, then decrypted and run on your machine. Unfortunately for you, the encrypted tunnel provides no security against this code-driven attack. Code-driven attacks are discussed in more detail in Chapter 5, "Mobile and Malicious Code."

In the rest of this chapter, we describe the components involved in e-commerce transactions, the weak links in each, and the methods for mitigating these risks. Although the issues of security and privacy in e-commerce are complex and involve non-technical factors, we contain the discussion to the software risks that can affect security and privacy in e-commerce.

Breaking E-Commerce Systems

In order to make a system more secure, it is sometimes necessary to break it first. That is, we must find out where the vulnerabilities in a system are in order to strengthen it. In this section, we do exactly that. Before we begin to break an e-commerce system, we must first get into the right mindset. Typically, when software programmers develop an online system, they are thinking about developing to a specification of desired features and maximizing performance in terms of throughput (requests handled per second), response time, latencies, and other traditional performance related measures. When considering the security of the system, though, we must think with a criminal's or cracker's mindset.

The first rule of the cracker's mindset is that there are no rules. Now you can throw the system specification out the window (well, not so far that it can't be retrieved for feature function testing). Crackers will cheat. The goal of cracking is to get around the way people normally use a service (such as authenticated access) by using the service in a way that it is not expected to be used. In other words, crackers will change the rules of the game midstream in order to gain access to resources they should not have. Of course, hacking or cracking is not that new. Crackers have long been defrauding phone companies by finding ways to gain access to long distance services without going through a billable account. Also, realize that crackers, like water, will follow the path of least resistance. Whichever areas are perceived to provide the strongest security or most resistance to cracking will likely be ignored. If you are using SSL to encrypt Web sessions between Web clients and your Web server, a cracker will likely not try to break the encryption stream as there is likely an easier way to get at the same data, once it is decrypted and stored in the clear.

Third, crackers go where the money is—sometimes literally, sometimes not. In other words, crackers will typically try to crack into a site if there is some reward for their effort. Sometimes the cracker is motivated by money, but often by fame and notoriety. The point is, crackers are not motivated by the mundane. The level of protection you provide should be commensurate with the value of the resource you are protecting. For instance, if you are hosting a Web site that publishes the menus for local restaurants, you may not run the risk of a full-scale denial-of-service attack, or even of crackers trying to break in. It simply is not as attractive a target as, say, a bank's online transaction Web site. Similarly, we typically don't bother encrypting most e-mails because most potential snoopers are not interested in our e-mails. On the other hand, if you are sending out sensitive e-mails that someone in your office or on the Internet may be motivated to read, you should consider using one of several commercial and free encryption packages.

Finally, it is important to remember that security is a chain that is only as strong as its weakest link. Crackers will naturally attempt to attack the weakest link. In practice, cryptography does not form the weakest link—at least in appearances. In a system where the components are not equally strong, crackers will be directed toward the weakest link. This fact also forms the premise of "honey pots," where a site deliberately sets up a sacrificial machine with appealingly vulnerable services in order to track and monitor potential crackers. In e-commerce systems, because crypto is often perceived to be the strongest link, crackers are directed toward cracking host-side services and client-side content. As a result, it is important to maintain strong host security, both inside and outside of firewalls. One side effect of corporate firewalls, unfortunately, is that system administrators tend to relax host security. The resulting effect is that once a cracker makes it through or around the firewall, he or she can leverage the trust relationships between machines inside the firewall to compromise many machines. The "crunchy on the outside, soft and chewy on the inside" problem is pervasive in enterprise IT systems.

Case Study of Breaking an E-Business

Consider an e-business application and how a cracker may go about disassembling its security for malicious gain. Online investing has become very popular for several reasons. Now, rather than waiting for quarterly statements in the mail or dealing with a phone menu, you can quickly view the status, balances, and the current value of investment holdings by visiting the Web page of your portfolio manager. Even better, if you like to be able to buy and sell equity shares on demand, you can establish online Web-enabled brokerage accounts with most of the major investment banks. Figure 4.1 shows a simplified workflow diagram of an online investing application that enables users with established accounts to view portfolio holdings, cash balances, update the stocks tracked, and even conduct online trades. The key benefit of the online application is that once an account is established, there need not be human intervention, phone calls, or forms to sign to perform simple functions, such as checking today's value of a technology portfolio, or even to perform more complex functions, such as selling shares in a stock short. For the on-the-go investor, these online applications will be migrating to the browsers of wireless handheld devices and utilizing mobile code technologies such as WML Script to automate much of the client-side processing, such as setting preferences.

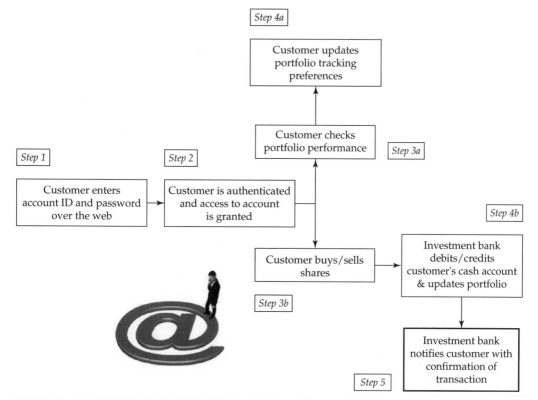

Figure 4.1 An online investing application.

The workflow diagram in Figure 4.1 shows how the online transaction is intended to proceed. E-business application developers use diagrams like these, often called workflow or use case diagrams. They show how the e-business is intended to be used.

We are now going to think with the cracker mindset and see how this online application can be broken. First, it is helpful to look at a sample network architecture that implements the online application. Figure 4.2 shows an example network architecture of the system that implements the online investing application shown in juxtaposition, along with example exploits. The system consists of the end users' client machines, the Internet, routers, firewall, front-end Web/e-mail servers, application servers, databases, and workstations.

Now consider the many ways a cracker could break this online application. Figure 4.2 shows one example scenario, though there are many

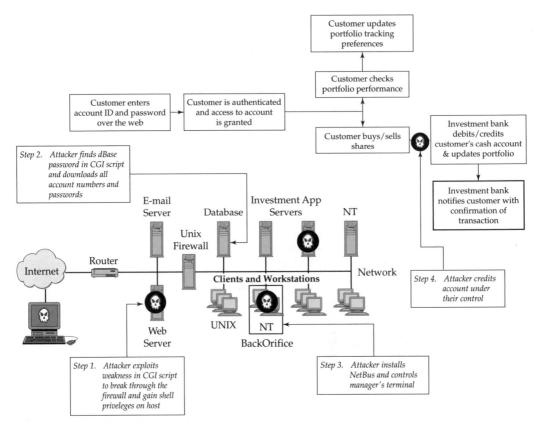

Figure 4.2   Breaking an e-business.

that could be executed in practice. In step 1 of the attack, the cracker uses the Internet and a Web browser to misuse one of the CGI scripts that implement the application on an application server machine. The CGI script could just as easily be a development CGI script inadvertently left on the server before going to production, a default CGI script from an application server distribution, or a script that implements flawed logic of the online investment application. Exploiting CGI scripts is a common method that crackers use to gain shell access to Web servers. CGI script vulnerabilities are discussed later in this chapter. The vulnerability need not be in a CGI script, either. Application servers can be implemented in Java, C, C++, Perl, or Python in various application server frameworks. The key is not so much which language the business application logic is developed in, as much as the vulnerabilities introduced by the complex logic often implemented at this middleware layer. One of the key problems in the development of application middleware, in general, is poor input sanity-checking. The cracker can exploit the lack of input sanity-checking to feed the application server unexpected input used in system commands to gain shell privileges on the machine.

Though application server misuse is a common way of breaking into systems, there are many other ways to gain that initial access in step 1 of the attack. For instance, the Web and mail servers may be running any one of several network services such as ftp and BIND/DNS that may be misconfigured. The Web and mail server software themselves may be vulnerable to attack. Most of the popular commercial Web and mail servers have recent and long histories of being vulnerable to buffer overrun attacks, which often permit full system root shell privileges on the host. Once the attacker gains system privileges on an internal host, he or she can exploit the web of trust often woven between machines on a local network to gain access to other machines on the network. This is precisely what the attacker does in step 2 of the attack illustrated in Figure 4.2.

Once the attacker has access to the various file systems on the application server, he or she can often view source code of CGI scripts or other application middleware to discover customer account numbers, passwords, and even database administrator passwords for accessing the back-end databases. From here, he or she can download important and confidential client information stored in the database. In step 3 of the attack, the attacker leverages the internal privileges he or she has gained to plant backdoors to get back into the system unnoticed. A suite of software, commonly known as a "rootkit," is available to crackers that allows them to not only get back into a system unnoticed, but also to erase their tracks in audit logs. In the example shown, the cracker installs a rogue remote administration program known as Back Orifice, which gives the cracker the ability to remotely administer the network with the same privileges and power as the authentic system administrator.

At this point in the attack, the cracker has assumed total control of the e-business. The attacker has many options including: (1) blackmailing the business with threats of discrediting it, (2) defacing the Web pages, and (3) working in a stealth manner to uncover proprietary business information, confidential client information, or even subverting the application for personal gain. Step 4 of the attack illustrates the last case, where the attacker credits a cash account under his or her control. The cracker must move quickly enough to grab, so to speak, sufficient loot before traditional back-end auditing mechanisms discover the discrepancy in transferred funds. While this scenario is conjured, there have been real cases, including one involving a leading multinational bank where significant sums of money were, in fact, transferred to accounts by a cracker who broke into the bank systems in the pre-Internet era. Since then, there have been rampant speculation and rumors that leading banks have been extorted significant sums of money by crackers claiming to have gained access to internal systems.

Unfortunately, defending against attacks is harder than launching attacks. As mentioned earlier, there are many ways to skin this cat. It takes only a single flaw or overlooked vulnerability for a cracker to compromise a system completely. While defense-in-depth is a popular strategy, the reality is often that multiple layers of defense fall like a house of cards when a single hole is exploited. The problem is known as an asymmetric attack problem, where it is much more difficult and costly to defend against an attack than to launch an attack. The number of flaws that can be exploited in today's IT infrastructure to leverage security compromise is staggering, when considering all the different platforms and devices that make up current IT infrastructures. Compounding the problem is the fact that a cracker can work in relative anonymity using a $500 computer and modem to launch attacks. Even worse, crackers can work from any number of Internet kiosks available in airports, malls, cafés, and even laundromats. As crackers get more sophisticated, attacks will be launched from mobile devices that can roam in and out of different geographic zones and then be discarded—making tracking of the attacker next to impossible.

E-Commerce System Security

In spite of the fairly bleak picture painted here, businesses can effectively manage the risk of crackers. As in many other security domains, the security posture or stance assumed by the business is critical for deterring and thwarting crackers. To use a physical-world analogy, consider a burglar who intends to break into homes in a nice neighborhood. As the burglar scopes out potential targets, he or she will notice some houses with burglar alarms—complete with conspicuous signs of the alarm systems—and some without. In all likelihood, the burglar will pass on the houses with the burglar alarms and move on to the other, less well-protected targets. Thus, the security stance assumed by the owner plays an important role.

Every business must first determine what its desired security stance is. The security stance is documented in its security policy. System administrators use the security policy to configure the business's systems, routers, firewalls, and remote access solutions. Without an explicit security policy, there is no way to determine what the security stance of the business is, how to configure its systems, or even if a security breach has occurred. The security policy represents the desired security posture of the business. Once the security policy is developed, the actual security posture of the business must be assessed. That is, the system must be evaluated from a security point of view to determine how well it meets its security policy. Usually, there is a difference between the desired stance and the actual stance. This difference is the security gap between where the organization would like to be (secure against particular threats) and where it actually is in practice.

The process of developing a security policy and evaluating the business's systems against that policy will identify not only the gaps between the actual security stance and the desired posture, but also gaps in the security policy. It is important to have an independent party, preferably a third party, evaluate the security stance of the organization. A third party can fairly assess whether the organization's system upholds the security policy. If the group that develops the security policy and/or the system configuration is also responsible for evaluating it, chances are the evaluation may be biased, and potential vulnerabilities may be overlooked.

Who's Protecting the E-Commerce Applications?

In this chapter, we'll examine e-commerce systems from different views. First, consider the view of e-businesses in Figure 4.3. The diagram shows two e-businesses communicating over the Internet, perhaps performing business-to-business types of transactions.

The layered view of the e-business shows the lowest layer of the e-business to be the networking layer. At the networking layer, we worry about the reliability, integrity, and confidentiality of the data that runs over the "pipe." We worry about this because the Internet is a public switched network, meaning that any number of third parties may have access to the data that traverses the nodes of the Internet on the way from the data source to its destination. Also, the Internet Protocol (IP) is a connectionless protocol, which means there is no dedicated circuit between source and destination. As a result, packets sent during a given session may in fact take different routes to their destination, depending on traffic congestion and rerouting algorithms. Because the

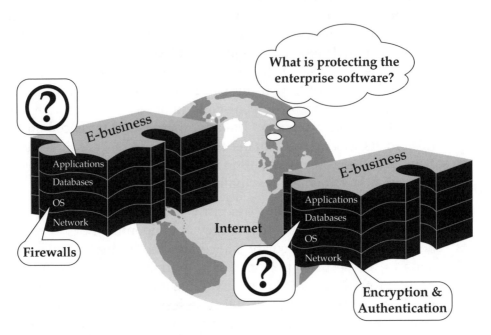

Figure 4.3 Layered view of e-businesses.

Internet Protocol (IP) is an unreliable datagram protocol, the networking layer includes a connection-oriented reliable transmission layer such as TCP (transmission control protocol) that ensures that dropped or lost packets are retransmitted and that bit flips that may have occurred during transmission (for instance, over wireless networks) are corrected.

The combination TCP/IP services provides for reliable and robust delivery of Internet packets. TCP/IP, however, does not provide "secure" connection services. Typically, this means that there is no guarantee of confidentiality, identification, or even delivery of packets sent from one Internet host to another. Because Internet packets will often traverse several Internet nodes from source to destination, it is possible that packet contents can be intercepted by third parties, copied, substituted, or even destroyed. It is this risk that most people citing Internet risks of e-commerce have decried, while missing the more substantive risks of e-commerce dealing with server- and client-side security and privacy. Fortunately, we have good solutions to the data confidentiality problem. Cryptography techniques developed decades ago by mathematicians can provide very strong guarantees for data confidentiality, authentication of parties, and integrity of data sent during the transmission. Furthermore, digital signatures can be used to sign received mail in a "return receipt" application that provides guarantees of delivery of e-mail. Thus, as shown in Figure 4.3, we can use encryption services to protect data transmitted over the network.

The operating system, or platform, that hosts the e-business applications lives on the networking layer. In a layered model, the services of one layer use the services of the lower layer and provide services to upper layers. The network layer is often thought of as a core portion of the operating system; however, from a layered services point of view, it is fine to think of the operating system software running on top of the network layer. Operating systems are notoriously rife with software flaws that affect system security. Chapter 5 in *E-Commerce Security: Weak Links, Best Defenses* (Wiley, 1998) discusses this topic in detail. Operating systems are vulnerable because commercial operating systems today are immensely complex software systems. For instance, the Windows 2000 operating system is purported to have more than 50 million lines of source code. It is impossible to catch all software design and programming errors that may have security consequences in a platform this complex. Even though Unix operating systems have been around for the better part of 30 years, new flaws in operating system utilities are found on a weekly basis across all the different Unix platform variants.

Security holes in the platform are critical by nature. That is, if the operating system itself is vulnerable to exploitation, security provided by the application can be potentially compromised by holes in the platform. Another way to think of the operating system is the foundation on which applications are built. Cracks in the foundation make for weak security at the application layer. As Figure 4.3 suggests, firewalls provide protection against operating system flaws. One of the key roles of firewalls is their ability to shut down services offered to logical domain addresses. Using Internet domain addresses, the firewall administrator can partition Internet addresses into "trusted" and "untrusted" domain ranges. For instance, any Internet address outside of the company's domain can be considered untrusted. As a result, all operating system services such as remote logins can be shut down to everyone outside of the company's domain. Even within a company, the domains can be partitioned so that certain subdomains are trusted for access to certain machines, but others are not. The key benefit then of firewalls is their ability to restrict access to the platform through offered services. As a result, firewalls can make it easy to "hide" operating system flaws from untrusted entities.

Even so, firewalls are vulnerable to data- or code–driven attacks through offered services. For instance, an attack through SMTP (mail) or HTTP (Web) will not be stopped by a firewall if the firewall is configured to let e-mail and Web services through, which after all are necessary for e-commerce. These types of attack are discussed in more detail in Chapter 5. Second, firewalls will not stop operating system exploits from insiders or the trusted entities who are offered access to the platform. For the purpose of this discussion, however, it is important to realize that firewalls, if properly configured, can close down exposure to a significant number of platform vulnerabilities simply by failing to offer access to platform utilities and services to untrusted outsiders.

Now we can see from Figure 4.3 that we have reasonable protection services against network- and platform-based attacks against e-businesses. The key question is what protection do we have against application and database attacks? We call out the database layer separately in the diagram because of the importance of its role in e-commerce; however, for all intents and purposes, we can consider database attacks in the category of application attacks. In other words, who or what is protecting our online businesses from application-based attacks?

This is a critical question that has yet to be addressed by the industry. So far the Internet industry has largely skirted the question. Why? Because there is no simple solution. Let's first examine the importance of the problem. What is so important about the application layer in the first place? In other words, if I have a firewall, a Secure Sockets Layer (SSL)-enabled Web site, and digital certificates/signatures in place, why do I need to be concerned with application security? The reason is that the applications *are* your online business. That is, the online applications define and distinguish your business from every other business. The front-end Web servers, back-end databases, and platforms are fairly standard and uniform from business to business. The online applications, though, are what make your business unique. The Web pages (which should also be unique) are merely packaging for your online applications. The online applications capture your business application logic. As a result, this software is going to have to be custom-developed either in-house or outsourced to an e-business development group.

Furthermore, because online applications are becoming increasingly sophisticated, the software that implements the application logic has become incredibly complex, requiring component-based and object-oriented paradigms such as Enterprise Java Beans, CORBA, and DCOM/COM services. Collectively, these are known as application servers. The key point, however, is that because the application logic is custom and complex, it is often rife with errors in implementation or logic that can be and is often exploited by crackers.

Again, it is important to emphasize what we mean by application security so that it is not confused with other marketing hype. By application security, we mean this: Is a given online application resilient to attacks? We do not mean this: Does the online application authenticate end users, does the application encrypt transaction data, does it provide non-repudiation of transactions and guarantees on service? These are all questions of varying importance depending on the application. The latter questions address characteristics of the transaction, not properties of the software. As we emphasized in earlier chapters, security today is a software problem. In the rest of this chapter, we address this problem in some detail. First, we provide a different view of e-commerce systems than the layered view described previously, and we describe vulnerabilities in the different software components and strategies for managing these risks.

Components and Vulnerabilities in E-Commerce Systems

Figure 4.4 shows a generic *n*-tier architecture of an e-business, together with a summary of the types of vulnerabilities and risks to each of the major components. Using the Internet, Web clients (running on PCs or hand-held devices) interface with a front-end Web server, a middle layer of business application logic, and back-end databases, ERP system, supply-chain management software, and even some legacy systems that are now brought to the Internet.

In this section, we break out the major components found in e-commerce systems and analyze their vulnerabilities and risks to both businesses and consumers.

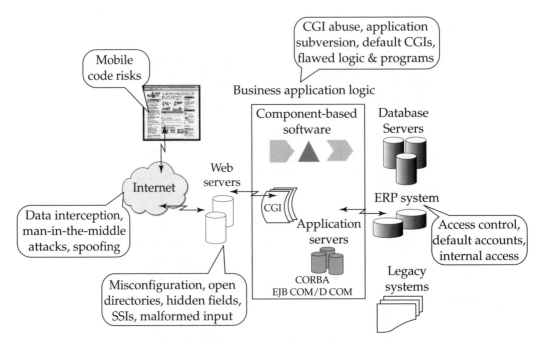

Figure 4.4   Client/server *n*-tier architecture of an e-business.

Client-Side Risks

Most e-commerce is performed using standard Web browsers and mail clients. Increasingly, more e-commerce is being performed on hand-held mobile devices such as Personal Digital Assistants (PDAs) and cell phones. The security risks particular to the wireless devices are covered in Chapter 6, "Security Issues in Mobile E-Commerce." Client-side security risks are mainly from malicious mobile code such as Web scripts, ActiveX controls, and hostile Java applets. Mobile code security risks are discussed in detail in Chapter 5. Another major risk in client-side software is loss of privacy. Your computer and its related software carry and can glean a great deal of personally identifying information (PII). For instance, your browser gives up a lot of information about your computer (name, IP address, browser type, version, company name) and sometimes about yourself, particularly if you have enabled some of the auto-form features of certain browsers. Browsers also are used to track your movements through the Web. For instance, every Web site you visit will typically get a record of the last site from which you visited (often called the referrer site). Banner ads that appear in browsers also track which sites you visit to create a profile of your Web usage.

A class of more insidious programs, known as spyware, can send information about your computer usage out to specific sites, often without your knowledge or approval. One of the key risks with client-side software is that you simply don't know what the programs are revealing about yourself and to whom. A simple principle is that a program should not be sending out any data from your machine that you do not know about. An audit of many of the programs on your machine might reveal that quite a few are in violation of that principle. While most spyware programs are written to provide marketing data for software vendors to more effectively profile and target their customers, some are specifically written to spy on your usage activity. SpectorSoft markets a spyware tool known as eBlaster to people who suspect their spouses are engaging in illicit online affairs. This type of spyware program will spy on user activity, from keystrokes to screen shots, and send a log of the activity out over the network. The point here is not that you need to be aware of your spouse's monitoring your activities, as much as be aware there are serious client-side privacy risks. These are discussed in more detail in Chapter 7, "Privacy in an Online World."

A final client-side risk we mention here is that businesses need to be especially concerned about the risk of malicious executables that run on their user workstations. The desktop machine is like a petri dish for software: It is constantly changing and growing with new software executables—some of an unsavory nature. Malicious software, or malware as it is now known, finds many ways of infecting machines. For instance, one common way of disseminating malicious software is via e-mail attachments. Another is masquerading it as legitimate or entertainment software on a Web page available for download. Users will often upload and download software to and from internal network file shares. The old-fashioned floppy is still a viable way of transmitting malicious software. The Back Orifice 2000 (BO2K) "remote administration kit" is one example of malicious software that, when it runs on your machine, will allow anyone—for example, a hacker—to administer and control your machine remotely. Thus, corporations must closely monitor the software that is downloaded and run on their machines. The risk is that if some malware product were to run on internal machines, the entire network may be compromised from the inside, including loss and theft of data.

Network Protocol Risks

The network risks primarily arise from sending confidential data over the Internet—a public-switched network. Fortunately, most literature you will find on e-commerce security talks extensively, and often solely, about this risk. We won't go into these risks at length. There are any number of good protocols that address the risks of sending confidential data over the Internet. In fact, a few years ago, the list included the following:

- SET
- SSL
- S/HTTP
- S/MIME
- CyberCash

While some of these protocols are still around in one form or another, the industry has squarely decided on SSL as the protocol of choice for secure Web browser transactions. The objective of most secure network protocols is to layer security properties on top of the TCP/IP network layers. Recall that TCP/IP provides reliable and robust delivery of datagrams over the Internet. It does not provide confidentiality, authentication, or strong message integrity services. These are the properties that secure protocols provide. Some go even further. For instance, SET-compliant protocols leave the credit card number encrypted even at the merchant site. The idea is that the merchant does not need to know the consumer's credit card number, and by hiding it from the merchant, a significant portion of credit card fraud arising from merchants can be eliminated. Rather than decrypting the credit card number at the merchant site, it is passed in encrypted form from the merchant to the credit-issuing bank. There it is decrypted, and then the merchant's account is credited the amount of the purchase. The protocol details of SET, SSL, and other e-commerce protocols are described in Chapter 3 in *E-Commerce Security: Weak Links, Best Defenses* (Wiley, 1998), as well as in other books on e-commerce security.

Depending on your online business application needs, you will need more or less of the security properties afforded by secure protocols. For most Web browsing, you will not need to use a secure protocol. The standard Web protocol, HTTP, suffices for most Web browsing. When customers are going to send confidential or personal information to your site, you should consider using a secure protocol that encrypts the data. The *de facto* secure protocol standard is Secure Sockets Layer (SSL), now implemented in every standard Web browser. SSL will not only negotiate a secret session key between the Web site and client to encrypt the data, but it will also authenticate the Web site. The Web site must have a valid certificate endorsed by a Certificate Authority, which the user implicitly trusts (by having a list of trusted Certificate Authorities in their browser). The user can then verify that the Web site he or she is visiting is, in fact, the one he or she thinks he or she is visiting by examining the site certificate once the connection is established. Users rarely do this in practice, but the certificate is available just in case.

These secure properties—that is, encrypted session and host site authentication—serve the purpose for most online commerce applications. Some online applications, though, may demand stronger security services. For instance, online banking and investing applications often transmit very confidential account information and transactions. These types of transactions may require not only confidentiality of the data, but also authentication of the client. That is, before giving access to account information and transactions, the bank will wish to authenticate the user. Common authentication schemes on the Internet include simple user name/password authentication. A much more secure solution is to require strong client authentication using client certificates. SSL supports client certificates, though sites rarely use this capability because it involves requiring customers to obtain a certificate from a Certification Authority.

In the future, e-commerce protocols will need to get increasingly sophisticated to address the burgeoning security and privacy requirements of new applications being brought to the Net. For example, as criminal, medical, disease, and patent databases begin to migrate to the Internet, the protocols developed for accessing them need to consider the security and privacy needs for both the database owner/maintainer and the client/requester. Today, the progress in genetic diseases is developing astonishing information about the likelihood of developing deadly disease in the future based on your genetic DNA sequence. While this often raises moral and ethical questions of how much information about future potential disease should be revealed to doctors and patients, it also raises the specter of this information getting into the wrong hands once the information is brought to the Internet.

Consider the case of a doctor querying an online genetic disease database with her patient's DNA sequence. The online application attempts to match the DNA sequence with potential diseases the patient might develop in the future based on the patient's genetic makeup. Now consider that the database is maintained by a commercial entity such as an insurance provider, unbeknownst to the patient. The patient does not wish the database maintainer to know either the query or the result. That is, she would not want the database maintainer to know her genetic sequence so it cannot do its own searches, nor would she want it to know the disease that is returned as a result of a query because that information can be used against her for both insurance and employment purposes. Likewise, the database maintainer may not want to know either the query or its result, as it may put the maintainer at risk for lawsuits should the information inadvertently get leaked. Furthermore, the database maintainer may wish that the contents of the rest of the database remain private from the inquirer. That is, except for the specific result returned to the inquirer, the inquirer should not be able to ascertain any other information that resides in the database. This requirement helps protect the commercial interests of the database maintainer so the database cannot be easily duplicated or queries cannot be made without a cost-tracking mechanism. To support this dual model of secure and private information access, e-commerce protocols need to be developed and commercialized that not only encrypt data in transmission, but also consider the security and privacy needs of both parties to the transaction.[1]

Another e-commerce application area that will require different security and privacy requirements on e-commerce protocols involves applications that accept e-cash or digital coin payments. Currently, most online payment schemes use either credit or debit cards. Most online payment systems are account-based, in that payments are made from an account of credit with a bank. Payments are made either with online verification of funds or offline with batch payments at the end of the day. A number of applications, particularly small or micropayments applications, are being created that do not want or need the overhead of an online account-based transaction. Traditionally speaking, many commercial ventures, services, and products do not require customers to have an account or line of credit. For example, vending services and parking meters are coin-driven services. In many cases, the customer may wish to pay with cash simply because he has no desire to have the transaction tracked by a third party, such as a bank or a creditor.

Newer online applications for micropayments will include downloading articles from selected publications for which no subscription is required. Whatever the application, customers are demanding cash-based alternatives to the current account-based system for making payments. The key security and privacy concerns are with ensuring that e-cash cannot be multiply spent (that is, minting your own e-cash) and preserving (potentially revocable) anonymity in transactions. While several protocols have been developed with these goals in mind, none has reached commercial success or adoption by the vendor community. As mobile e-commerce begins to drive more traditionally cash-based transactions (such as parking meters, vending machines, and ticket booths), these new digital cash-based protocols may begin to be adopted by wireless vendors.

Regardless of the network protocol used for your e-commerce application, the key thing to remember is that attackers will attempt to breach the easiest obstacle in their quest to obtain system privileges and unauthorized access to data. If the security provided by the network protocol is perceived to be strong, attackers will look for alternatives around the network security. For instance, the following types of standard attacks from the cracker's toolkit will, by-and-large, bypass the security provided by most e-commerce protocols:

- Man-in-the-middle attacks
- DNS attacks
- War dialing
- Exploiting software vulnerabilities in network services such as FTP, Bind, SMTP, and HTTP servers
- Internal access
- Leveraging trusted hosts
- Brute-force crypto attacks

In summary, it is important not only to select the appropriate network protocol for your given online application, but also not to be lulled into a false sense of security because a "secure" network protocol is being used. Instead, good security engineering will consider vulnerabilities in other components of the system described here that are more attractive targets to determined crackers.

Business Application Logic

The business application logic pictured in Figure 4.4 represents one of the key areas of vulnerability in e-commerce systems. The business application logic defines each particular business's offering. That is, the program logic encodes what the online business is offering in terms of products and services. It also defines the look and feel of the Web site and provides all of the interactive features, such as dynamic Web pages, personalized Web pages, and online transaction capabilities. As such, the software that implements the business application logic must be custom-developed for each particular site.

In contrast, most of the other software components of a Web site are commercial off-the-shelf (COTS) software. For instance, the Web server, back-end databases, and supply-chain logistics software are often purchased off the shelf from software vendors. With COTS software, largely, the end user or organization has no control over the code and therefore is not responsible for coding bugs and fixes. Software bugs in COTS software are usually independently discovered and reported. The software vendor then releases a patch, which the end users are responsible for applying. Thus, in the case of COTS software, the consumer or purchaser of the software is responsible for staying on top of software patches. The most important task in securing COTS software systems is to make sure that (1) they are properly configured for a secure installation[2], and (2) that the software is properly updated to the current version and patch level.

Because business application logic is custom-developed, it is developed with in-house staff or, more frequently, the development is outsourced to an e-business site developer. Regardless, the business application logic represents a key risk area in e-commerce systems for several reasons. First, the dynamic and interactive nature of e-businesses, coupled with increasingly sophisticated online services, requires a significant amount of software application development to code the business application logic. As a result, the application servers tend to be very complex pieces of software, very likely to contain flaws, and susceptible to the interactive kinds of attacks launched against Web sites. While application servers and their development platforms offer the potential of industrial-strength, reusable software components, errors in design and implementation of business application logic can compromise the security of the e-business.

Traditionally, the middle tier of software is implemented on Web servers using the Common Gateway Interface, or CGI. CGI scripts are programs that run on the Web server machine as separate processes from the Web server software. These general-purpose programs are invoked by the Web server in response to user requests. The CGI script's main function is to process user input and perform some service (such as retrieving data from a database or dynamically creating a Web page) for the end user. Because CGI scripts process untrusted user input, the security risks associated with the CGI (and other forms of middle-tier software) are extremely high. Many attacks against Web-based systems are implemented by exploited CGI scripts. While CGI scripts can be written in any general-purpose programming language, they are most often written in Perl, C, Tcl, and Python.

More recently, component-based software (CBS) is making inroads in e-commerce applications. The idea of using CBS is to develop, purchase, and reuse industrial-strength software in order to rapidly prototype business application logic. Two of the more popular component frameworks for e-commerce applications are Enterprise JavaBeans

(EJB) and Java 2 Enterprise Edition (J2EE), which support component-based Java. Other component models include the Object Management Group's (OMG) Common Object Request Broker Architecture (CORBA), and Microsoft's Common Object Model (COM) and Distributed COM (DCOM). The component frameworks are the "glue" that enables software components to provide services such as business application logic and use standard infrastructural services, such as naming, persistence, introspection, and event handling, while hiding the details of the implementation by using well-defined interfaces.

Business application logic, when coded in CBS systems, usually runs in application servers. The application servers provide the infrastructural services for particular component models, such as EJB, CORBA, COM, and DCOM. They also provide an interface for the business application logic to back-end services such as database management, enterprise resource planning (ERP), and legacy software system services.

In addition to supporting traditional CGI functions, component-based software is expected to enable distributed business-to-business applications over the Internet. The component-based software paradigm also supports good software engineering (see the next section). The Unified Modeling Language (UML) supports object-oriented analysis and design for component-based frameworks. In addition, as the market for component-based software heats up, many standard business application logic components will be available for purchase off the shelf.

While the benefits of component-based software are numerous, they pose security hazards similar to those of CGI scripts. Component-based software enables software development in general-purpose programming languages such as Java, C, and C++. As such, they execute with all the rights and privileges of server processes. Like CGI, they process untrusted user input, and because component-based software can be used to build sophisticated, large-scale applications, the likelihood for errors is arguably greater than for simple CGI scripts. Regardless of the implementation—CGI or application servers—the security risks of server-side software are great, and therefore server-side software must be carefully designed and implemented.

The key risks in the middleware layer of e-commerce sites are these: misconfiguration of the CGI, default/development CGI scripts left on the production server, CGI misuse, application subversion, flawed logic, and programming errors.

CGI Script Vulnerabilities

CGI scripts are often targets of attackers because they are often misconfigured or vulnerable to misuse. The basic rule of thumb when designing CGI scripts is to expect the unexpected. Or more appropriately, expect the malicious. While you have control over the content of CGI scripts, you have no control over what end users are going to send to the CGI scripts. Also, often overlooked are attacks against CGI scripts that exist on the server as part of the distribution but that are not even used as part of the e-commerce application. Some CGI scripts included as part of the Web server distribution have well-known flaws that can be exploited to obtain unauthorized access to the server. Even if you are not using the default CGI scripts as part of the Web server pages, anyone else can by simply knowing the script names.

One of the most common—yet easily preventable—security hazards is misconfiguration of software. CGI scripts also must be properly configured for security. One feature supported by many Web servers is the ability for individuals throughout an organization to write CGI scripts and have them execute from their own directories. While useful for spiffing up personal Web pages, this feature can also introduce system security hazards. In e-commerce applications, the Web server should be configured to prevent CGI scripts from executing anywhere but in a single CGI directory under control of the system administrator. The script-aliased CGI mode for Web servers ensures that CGI scripts will execute only from an explicitly named directory in the server configuration file. In addition, the CGI script path is not named in the URL to the CGI. Rather, the server "aliases" the explicit path to the CGI script to a choice name such as simply cgi-bin. Thus, running the server in script-aliased CGI mode prevents rogue CGI scripts from executing, and it also hides the explicit path to the CGI scripts.

The CGI script directories also should be properly configured using operating system access controls. For instance, if CGI scripts are written in a compiled language (such as C), the script sources should be excluded from the document root of the Web server, so that they cannot be accessed via the Web. They should be accessible to the system administrator or Web content development group only, and inaccessible to everyone else in the organization. If the script sources fall into the hands of malicious perpetrators, the source code can be inspected for flaws, making the perpetrator's job even easier. Access to the CGI executables directory, frequently called the cgi-bin, should be properly controlled as well. Only the Web server and administrator need access to this directory. Liberal access permissions to the CGI executables directory give malicious insiders the opportunity to place their own scripts on the e-business site.

Most CGI scripts are written in scripting languages such as Perl, JavaScript, and Python. While scripting languages are great for rapidly prototyping systems, they also let the developer write dangerous functionality very easily. For instance, it is easy to construct system commands with user input, a potentially dangerous situation. Writing the same system functionality requires several lines of C code and knowledge of system libraries. The easy accessibility of scripting languages makes them appealing but also dangerous for security-critical applications such as online businesses. It is also important to prohibit access to interpreters from the Web server. For instance, system administrators may be tempted to include the Perl interpreter in CGI script directories; however, doing so provides direct Web access to interactively execute Perl commands—an extremely dangerous configuration.

Finally, account for every CGI program on the server in terms of its purpose, origin, and modifications. Remove CGI scripts that do not serve a business function. View with suspicion and carefully screen CGI scripts that are distributed with Web servers, downloaded from the Internet, or purchased commercially. These steps will eliminate most of the potentially dangerous CGI scripts. Once a stable set of CGI programs is established, make a digital hash of the program executables (for example, using MD5) to enable future integrity checks.

Application Subversion

Application subversion attacks are not often discussed in relation to e-businesses, but they represent a significant threat to most online applications. Application subversion is a form of program misuse. Unlike buffer overrun attacks, application subversion attacks exploit the program logic without violating program integrity to elevate user privileges and gain unauthorized access to data. It is the very complexity of the program he or she is attacking that gives the attacker the leverage to gain unauthorized access. Application subversion attacks use programs in ways that the program's designers and developers did not anticipate. Typically, these attacks are not scripted, but rather developed from online interactive use and abuse.

Most application subversion attacks will attempt to change the rules of the game. For instance, recall the workflow diagram of Figure 4.1. An application subversion attack will attempt to discover ways of short-circuiting paths in the workflow. For instance, there may be a hidden path that lets the user gain access to account information without being authenticated to the particular account. Many application subversion attacks work on the premise that access to all confidential information is not properly authenticated.

Another common kind of application subversion attack is to send malformed input to a program. For instance, many Web pages use forms extensively to drive the application. Often, the data input on the form is checked using client-side JavaScript. An attacker can take advantage of the fact that many online application developers assume that the client is going to use the form and that the JavaScript will properly check all input sent to the site. The attacker can examine the datastream sent by the form, and rather than using the form, he or she can send a modified datastream. Often, an attacker is able to leverage access by placing system commands in the input stream to the online application. If the input stream is subsequently used in a system() call by the online application, the end user may be able to get the system to execute system commands on the attacker's behalf.

Some application developers rely heavily on hidden fields in the HTML document. Hidden fields allow the Web page developer to include information on the page that is not rendered on the page. The end user can see the hidden field data simply by viewing the HTML source. The mistake the application developers make is in first believing that the end user cannot see the hidden fields and, second, in relying on the integrity of the hidden field data for making online decisions. For instance, some online merchants have made the mistake of including pricing information for items in the hidden fields and using those prices to determine the cost of the online transaction. The end user can simply change the pricing in the hidden fields and send lower prices back to the merchants for a discounted purchase.

Another misuse of hidden fields is to redirect application output. For instance, some Web sites include file system path information in hidden fields on their Web pages. This information is used by a server-side script to determine where to read or write transaction information. The attacker, by simply changing the hidden field, can "clobber" files on the file system or read files to which he or she should not have access. In some cases, it may be possible to store a program entered in a form field on the file system to be used later as a means of running a shell on the remote system.

In summary, rigorous software assurance is necessary through the design and development of e-business applications, including front-end Web pages and application middleware. Once the software has been assured to be robust to application misuse and subversion attacks, the system administrator must perform other activities to ensure the security of the e-business middleware:

- All unnecessary scripts or application server programs must be eliminated from the production server.

- Sources to application middleware must be carefully guarded against download or unauthorized access.

- Configuration of the CGI and application middleware is necessary to ensure executable access only to the correct application middleware with the least execution privilege level necessary.

- Sanity-checking of input to application middleware must be done to ensure that only well-formed input is accepted.

Web Server Exploits

Web server security has been talked about and covered in detail, including in Chapter 4 in *E-Commerce Security: Weak Links, Best Defenses* (Wiley, 1998) and *The Web Security Source Book* by Rubin, Geer, and Ranum (Wiley, 1997), among other titles. Rather than rehash the same material here, we highlight some of the common exploits of Web servers used against many e-businesses.

Make no mistake, the key to Web server security is all about configuration. Like other complex pieces of software, Web servers are highly configurable to meet the needs of any given site. By default, most software vendors will configure the software application for maximum functionality and minimum security. Thus, by default, when the server is first started, it is likely more permissive than any given company's security policy would like it to be. The premise for having configurability in the first place is that what's right for one site may be wrong for the next. In order to correctly configure your Web server, you must first develop a policy that defines what access to whom is allowed to which resources. This policy, in turn, is used to configure routers, firewalls, and all public servers, such as the Web server. As mentioned, several books are available that will guide you to a "secure" configuration of a Web server. We use "secure" lightly because configuring the Web server, while necessary, is by no means sufficient to secure the system. The discussion of application server exploits in the preceding section is proof of this.

Once the Web server is as securely configured as possible, it is important to ensure that the Web pages themselves do not open up holes in the security. Many Web page developers fall into some common pitfalls that may compromise the site's security. In the preceding section, we mentioned the problem of relying on hidden fields in HTML for security or business-critical data. Users can abuse the hidden field data to subvert an application. HTML offers other potential vulnerabilities.

One that is most often criticized is Server Side Includes (SSI). The SSI, if enabled (a configuration option), allows server directives to be embedded in HTML. This means that the server will execute any commands embedded in the HTML. For instance, if the following statement was embedded in an HTML document, it would direct the server to display the contents of the system password file:

```
<!--#exec /bin/cat /etc/passwd -->
```

Certainly, Web pages should not be written with SSIs in general. Of course, you might wonder how this might be a risk because the Web pages are under the control of the site. Well, there are many potential ways an attacker might get an SSI in an HTML page. First, the attacker may have found another way into the system (for example, a CGI script exploit), but may want to provide either an easier backdoor or a redundant backdoor in case the CGI script vulnerability is found and closed. The attacker may include an SSI directive within one of the site's HTML pages. Another way to gain access in the first place is to have the server generate a Web page for you with the SSI of choice embedded in the HTML. How might you do this? One way is to exploit a server that generates dynamic HTML depending on the end user's data, preferences, or history. If the Web server ends up using some of the user's data to generate the HTML page, the user may be able to insert an SSI directive in the HTML. A better solution than worrying about whether the HTML pages have SSI directives is to simply disable the SSI such that even if SSIs were embedded, the server would not execute them. Again, this is a configuration option, and like all system configuration files, the Web server configuration file should be protected by both file permission protection and file integrity checks to ensure that it has not been tampered with.

Though SSIs are often highlighted as a major risk, a more common risk is simply putting documents or files in a publicly accessible portion of the Web server. The portion of the Web server that is publicly accessible is called the document root. The document root specifies the portion of the file system that the Web server can read and display to a Web client if requested. Note that the document root can be a superset of the Web pages that are actually displayed when the user clicks through a Web site. That is, there may be documents in the document root that are not linked to from Web pages. This does not mean they are not accessible, however. Simply giving the correct address for the document will result in either displaying or downloading the document to any Web client. Therein lies the problem. Private documents inadvertently placed in a public directory can result in a compromise of business or consumer's confidential information and consumer privacy. For instance, if a database file of credit card numbers is stored in the document root of the Web server for a fictitious company, mycompany.com, the following URL address typed in a Web browser could download the file:

```
http://www.mycompany.com/cardnumbers.mdb
```

This risk is even greater if directory browsing (a configurable feature) is also enabled. Directory browsing allows an end user to view the contents of the file system at a given directory level if a Web page does not exist with the same name. Directory browsing is really a way to explore the file system of another site using your Web browser. You may have inadvertently come across this feature if you "back up" one from a given Web page by removing the page name of the Web page in the URL and viewing its higher-level directory. Attackers can learn a lot of valuable information from viewing the contents of a directory including private files. Furthermore, the browser provides a nice interface, so that by clicking on a file name in the directory structure, the file itself will be downloaded. Again, directory browsing, if enabled, is an open vulnerability and a great way to download private or confidential information.

Finally, another potential vulnerability for an e-business is the use of and dependence on cookies. Because HTTP is a stateless protocol, each new Web page that is visited has no memory of the last Web page that was visited by the user. Cookies are used to "keep state" between different Web pages visited in a given session. Cookies can make an e-business transaction appear to be seamless, sequential, and coordinated. Most people, when discussing the risks of cookies, focus on the client-side privacy risks. While these certainly exist (and will be described later in this book), cookies also pose risks to the businesses that employ them, depending on how they are used. If the information contained in cookies is trusted much in the same way that the content in hidden fields is trusted, then the e-business may be vulnerable to cookie exploits called cookie poisoning. For instance, some Web sites will use cookies to carry authentication information for a given user as the user traverses the Web pages of a site. That is, once the user has authenticated herself, her token of authentication may be carried with her via cookies from Web page to Web page for all subsequent Web pages at the site she visits. Using cookies for authentication is a fairly weak form of authentication. The cookie can be easily stolen (stolen cookies!) by someone snooping her LAN or the Internet, then used to access her personal pages on the Web site. Of course, secure protocols such as SSL can mitigate this risk to a large extent.

Cookies are also used for other purposes that, again, if depended on for critical transactions, introduce new vulnerabilities. The key thing to remember is that cookies are under the control of the end user. Therefore, end users can change cookies in whatever manner they choose. If cookies are used to instruct a Web server where to write a customer-specific file, by changing the cookie value, the end user might be able to clobber other customer files or perhaps even replace critical system files. Similarly, if cookies are used for carrying order information (such as shopping carts), changing the contents of the cookies may corrupt the cart or the transaction, or it could potentially result in an unintended discount to the customer.

The lesson here is that, regardless of the technology used, it is important to examine the features and functions from a security-critical viewpoint. The dependence on a technology and information for security-critical transactions means that the technology and information must be trustworthy, or else it is a vulnerable point of attack. Following a software risk management-oriented approach described in Chapter 3, "Securing

Software," can help identify vulnerabilities before they are released in software and on the Web.

Database Security

Databases have traditionally represented the key intellectual property or item of value to information-based companies. As a result, they have almost always been company proprietary and unavailable to public access. In the Internet model of business, these proprietary databases are being brought to the Internet, often without careful consideration of the risks. In essence, the Web browser becomes the database query interface, often to unknown and untrusted entities.

While there has been much research in database security over the last two decades, the commercial sector has adopted only a couple of key tenets: authenticating and authorizing principals to objects. That is, access to databases is controlled by properly authenticating the credentials of the requesting principal and then verifying which objects the authenticated principal is authorized to access. Thus, any online database application must perform these two functions with rigor in order to protect the most valuable assets of an e-business, as well as their customers' privacy.

While many vendors will tout secure channel access from the Web server to the database, the reality is that there are many pitfalls for e-businesses. The reason why databases are vulnerable in the first place is that a Web interface is being bolted to what once may have been a closed and proprietary interface. Middleware programs such as CGI scripts or application servers will usually mediate access from the Web server to the database. Web servers will provide client authentication functions from simple user name/password dialog boxes to strong client certificate authentication. The needs of the business and the size of the accessing community will dictate which solution is feasible.

In practice, most databases will not store encrypted information. Encrypting data expands its size so much as to make it too expensive to store the considerable amount of data needed to support online businesses. Second, even encrypting the data in the database would not provide that much protection, as the online application must be able to read from and write to the database. Thus, application-based attacks will still be able to get at the data in plain text even if the data were stored encrypted in the database. One of the key vulnerabilities to online databases is from application-based attacks. That is, attacks that exploit the vulnerabilities in the business application logic, described earlier, can often be leveraged into unrestricted access to the contents of the database.

For instance, an attack that exploits a buffer overflow vulnerability in an application server program will usually be able to get command shell access on the remote application server. From there, the attacker will usually be able to find sources to the application server programs such as Perl scripts or even C source code that are used to access the database(s). Because these programs need access to the database, they must also know the passwords used to access the various data partitions. Simply reviewing the source code is often enough to discover these passwords. With password(s) in hand, the attacker can either use the application server program via the Web interface to gain unauthorized access to the database or, more directly, interactively query the databases from the command shell using SQL commands or commands from the database language of choice.

Finally, like the other complex programs that run e-businesses, databases must be securely configured. Basic steps that the database administrator (DBA) needs to take include the following:

- Enforcing Web client authentication to the database
- Enforcing Web client authorization to database records
- Eliminating default database and database platform accounts
- Changing easily guessed passwords
- Configuring and maintaining internal access controls
- Auditing log files for suspicious activity

Account maintenance is a key vulnerability in database management. Often, the database software vendor will create a DBA account with an easily guessed password. Worse, DBAs will use the default account and password distributed with the database installation. Thus, an attacker that has gained internal access or a malevolent insider can quickly gain access to all portions of the database by assuming the identity of the database administrator.

Platform Security

One area we alluded to earlier in this chapter but did not discuss in detail is the platforms that host the different components of e-businesses. The platform represents a potentially key weak link in e-commerce security. The platform, or operating system, represents the foundation of the e-business. If there are cracks in the foundation, there is very little that a strong framework of application software can do to keep the business up. Therefore, it is imperative that system administrators properly patch platform vulnerabilities and maintain the security of the platform itself. As mentioned earlier, firewalls can go a long way toward blocking access to platform vulnerabilities to unauthorized outsiders. However, platform vulnerabilities can undermine the security of the e-business in other ways. Authorized but unprivileged insiders can use known platform vulnerability exploits to yield root privileges on a business-critical machine. Outsiders able to gain user privileges on the platform through smaller holes may then be able to leverage platform holes into severe security breaches.

Some key steps to maintaining platform security include the following:

- Eliminating default accounts generally installed with the operating system
- Changing easily guessed passwords
- Enforcing password expiration
- Killing any unnecessary services that may be running by default
- Applying security patches to the operating system regularly
- Updating the operating system to the most recent version/level release
- Ensuring that file access permissions are properly enforced to prevent insiders from having unnecessary access to critical files
- Enabling audit logging with intrusion monitoring
- Running system file integrity checks regularly

In the age of firewalls, configuring platforms securely has become a lost art. With the plethora of different platforms now running enterprises, most system administrators will punt on keeping up with the latest OS patches and securely configuring platforms under the assumption that firewalls will protect them from all threats. Unfortunately, relaxing host security on the inside can make the job of hopping from machine to machine easy for a cracker until he finds the valuable information he is looking for or is able to wreak maximum damage.

Looking Ahead

This chapter provided an overview of the major weak links in e-commerce systems including Web clients, network protocols, front-end Web servers, back-end databases, application servers, and the platforms on which they run. As you have heard repeatedly, secure network protocols are necessary, but certainly not sufficient, for securing e-commerce. True to the spirit of this book, the vulnerabilities described here are largely based on software flaws that exist in the application layer of e-commerce transactions.

Perhaps the most common vulnerability in e-commerce systems is misconfiguration of software. Unfortunately, the responsibility of software configuration lies with the software consumer. And, in order to securely configure a system, one must develop a security policy that specifies who is allowed access to what. For most COTS software, this is the best we can do to securely configure our systems. Once the system is configured, it is important to get third-party validation and testing of the system. A third-party audit will ensure that the configured system, including routers, firewalls, servers, and databases, meet the required security policy. In addition, they will test the system against well-known, common attacks that you are likely to experience. This type of auditing is what can be considered a "gut check" to ensure that your system is not vulnerable to common attacks such as exploiting RPC services or BIND/DNS vulnerabilities.

Like any software system, COTS software systems also have flaws, many of which are security-critical. It is imperative that system administrators stay on top of the newsgroups and mailings where patches to their system software are released. As a whole, the security and hacker community is very good at finding flaws in complex software systems. The commercial software vendor community is very good at responding to security holes in their software very quickly with patches. To close the loop, the software consumer—that is, the businesses and end users that buy the software—must do their part to download and patch their vulnerable software.

For custom-developed software, which includes front-end Web pages, application servers, CGI scripts, and even mobile content, the developer must ensure that its software is not vulnerable to attack and ensure that any mobile content developed does not infringe on users' privacy. Developing secure software is much harder than patching someone else's flawed software. The key is to follow a software risk management and security engineering approach in designing and developing software, as described in Chapter 2, "Security Is a Software Problem," and Chapter 3. Again, third-party review can help spot critical vulnerabilities in software that are easy for developers to overlook. Unfortunately, spotting errors in code that can lead to security breaches is not easy. It is important therefore to get third-party software experts who understand software security, not just perimeter security.

Finally, looking ahead, in the rest of this book we are going to dive into some depth on selected topics. In particular, in Chapter 5, we will discuss the client-side software risks of running mobile code and dealing with the malicious software threat. With mobile code now as ubiquitous as Web pages and often running unbeknownst to the user, end users face new and serious threats to their security and privacy. The theme of this chapter is continued and applied in Chapter 6, where we address the security and privacy issues raised in mobile e-commerce. Because of the rapid advances in the computing power in mobile and wireless devices, many of the same computer security problems we have in wired e-commerce will apply to mobile e-commerce. Even more, though, mobile e-commerce introduces new vulnerabilities unique to the medium, the methods of performing online transactions, and the devices themselves.

Notes

1. See W. Du and M. Atallah, "Protocols for Secure Remote Database Access with Approximate Matching," in *Recent Advances in Security and Privacy in E-Commerce*, A. Ghosh, editor, Kluwer Academic Publishers, to appear 2001.

2. See Chapter 4 of *E-Commerce Security: Weak Links, Best Defenses* (Wiley, 1998) for securing commerce server systems.

CHAPTER 5

Mobile and Malicious Code

"Given the choice of safer systems or dancing pigs, the average user will always opt for dancing pigs."

ED FELTEN
ASSOCIATE PROFESSOR OF COMPUTER SCIENCE
PRINCETON UNIVERSITY

And there you have it. Most software vendors believe most users prefer neat features over security, which might explain why we continually get new features at the expense of security and privacy. Professor Felten's remarks, though seemingly cynical, are a reflection of some of the early problems Princeton University's Secure Internet Programming team discovered with the Java Virtual Machine (JVM). Many of the holes discovered in the JVM have been so severe as to allow a complete system security breach by hostile applets.[1] Since their inception, Java applets have been used mostly for graphically stimulating diversions or games rather than for business client-side computing.

To drive home the point, we[2] designed a dancing pigs applet Trojan horse (see Figure 5.1) that exploits a hole in the way the JVM signs applets to "hijack" the local Java compiler, a la Ken Thompson's malicious code compiler trick written about in his ACM Turing Award paper.[3] Thompson illustrated by simple example that application source code review is not sufficient to detect malicious code, as a malicious compiler can easily insert malicious code into the compiled executable. Our dancing pigs applet shows that even if you trust your compiler, you can still get burned by Internet content that can effectively replace your trusted compiler with an alternate malicious version.

Figure 5.1 Dancing pigs hostile Java applet.

The dancing pigs applet carries the malicious code in its payload that the user ends up saving when the user downloads the applet from a Web page. This hostile applet targets Java developers, though it could just as easily target the average user. For instance, it could write a malicious program to the user's desktop that the user executes on system startup. In our example, when the user runs the dancing pigs applet, the applet will hijack the Java compiler (javac) by placing an alternate version of the compiler earlier in the CLASSPATH environment variable than the version that should run. This means that the next time the user compiles a Java program, the user will run the malicious compiler rather than the trusted compiler, with no indication that anything amiss has occurred. The malicious compiler does its work silently, infecting all new Java programs compiled by the user. The resulting Java executable will include a malicious code fragment. Thus, every new program the developer compiles will include a malicious code fragment, potentially spreading in a viral manner.

Although the example demonstrates a severe Java VM vulnerability that has since been patched, the reality is that Java is one of the most secure environments in which to run untrusted mobile code. The Java VM defines a very rigid sandbox that gives extremely limited system resource access to untrusted applets and the ability to carefully control access to system resources from signed applets. The Java security problems found to date have been a result of flawed software implementations of the Java VM. Furthermore, the problems were found in a laboratory setting by talented researchers who have carefully guarded the vulnerability information such that the holes could not be easily exploited by crackers until the vendor released a fix. As a result, Java hostile applets or viruses have not been released in the wild, where corporate and individual users' systems would be placed at risk. In contrast, many other forms of mobile code pose a greater risk to organizations and users than Java applets.

Mobile Code

Mobile code is program code that is downloaded, pushed, distributed, or otherwise sent from one location to another where the code can execute. Mobile code generally runs on extensible systems. Or viewed differently, extensible systems use mobile code to extend or enhance their functionality. For instance, most modern operating systems allow their kernel functionality to be extended using loadable kernel modules or device drivers. In a proprietary operating system such as Windows 2000, though you are not allowed to modify the operating system, you can add operating system functionality through device drivers.

Similarly, many of today's desktop applications are extensible. The ubiquitous Web browser provides plug-in modules that allow its functionality to be extended to a wide range of applications, such as the ability to view different multimedia formatted documents, as well as the ability to seamlessly run programs downloaded from the Internet in the form of Java applets, ActiveX controls, and Web scripts. Other desktop applications such as e-mail clients, word processing programs, spreadsheet applications, and even financial planning applications are extensible to run scripts, view HTML pages, and include documents of other formats within containers. Extensible systems have made today's platforms both flexible and adaptable in a marketplace that demands quick releases and continual innovation. Extensible systems, though, have also introduced new risks that their predecessor platforms have not had. In particular, extensible systems allow untrusted and potentially malicious mobile code to transparently download, execute with user privileges, and potentially steal, modify, or destroy data or systems without the user's knowledge or permission.

Mobile code generally executes on an interpreter, virtual machine, or other portable platform. Extensible applications will often use interpreters to run mobile code because interpreters provide an operating-system–independent platform for running mobile code. Regardless of what operating system your machine is running (for example, MacOS, Windows, or Unix variants), the mobile code needs to be written and compiled only once for the application's interpreter or virtual machine. The classic example is Java applets. Once a Java programmer has compiled a Java applet into bytecode—the platform-independent virtual machine instruction language—it can be posted on a Web site and downloaded to any machine running a Java Virtual Machine, typically in one of the popular browsers. Sun Microsystems coined the phrase "write once, run anywhere" to describe the portability of Java applets.

Although Java applets are the example that most often comes to mind, mobile code takes many forms including Java applets, JavaScript, VBScript, VBA macros, proprietary scripting technologies for browser plug-ins and Internet-enabled applications, streaming video, audio files, PostScript files, e-mail attachments, agents, and software updates. Each of these forms of mobile code leverages extensible platforms or applications to instruct the machine to execute the instructions contained in the code. Furthermore, mobile code almost always runs with the privileges and permissions of the user running the code. So, whenever you download mobile code, whether deliberately or not, you are running someone else's programs on your machine with your privileges. This is a key point when it comes to considering the security ramifications. Another key point is that mobile code will often download and execute without the user's knowledge or permission. Every time you surf the Web, chances are you are downloading and running a program someone else wrote whom you do not know or trust. Furthermore, that program may be spying on your activities and data, and it may report to another site.

Realizing the potential for abuse of privileges, many forms of mobile content have built-in security mechanisms to constrain the behavior of untrusted mobile code. The Java security model is a great example. The Java Virtual Machine (JVM) has a built-in sandbox for unsigned (that is, untrusted) applets. The sandbox prevents applets from accessing the file system, other system resources such as the local area network and peripheral devices, other applets, components, and programs, as well as from making arbitrary network connections. Now it is important to realize that the different implementations of the JVM have been flawed in ways that could allow a hostile Java applet to break the sandbox model. In fact, it is easy to historically trace the discovery of JVM flaws with each new release version of a JVM.[4] The fact that there have been flaws in the different implementations of the JVM should not obscure the fact that a fairly rigorous model of constraining the behavior of untrusted Java applets exists in the JVM.

More often, however, there is no model for constraining the behavior of mobile code. For instance, consider the push model for sending out software updates. The push model represents an innovative use of the Internet to download and update software whenever the software vendor releases new patches or versions. The push model of software delivery often turns out to be a scheduled "pull" from the client. Once a software application is installed on a machine, it can use network sockets to communicate back to a network site, including the software vendor's site. Thus, the software can periodically poll the vendor's site to determine if there is a new update available. Anti-virus vendors currently use this capability to update the virus signatures on their client scanners running on everyone's machines.

Vendors of other software products are catching on to this ability to leverage the Internet to update their software. To a greater extent, the notion of extensible applications is changing software development from the days of shrink-wrapped software sold in Egghead stores to versatile software "platforms" being sold with base functionality, only to be continuously updated, extended, and programmed via mobile code delivered over the Internet. Now instead of delivering software with fixed functionality, vendors are delivering software that is programmable or whose functions are extensible. Therefore, software updates can be delivered, often seamlessly without any human interaction required, truly in Internet time.

Better yet, if the application is considered a platform for which third-party software vendors can develop and run code, the range of different functions that the application can deliver to customers will be constrained only by the number of third parties willing to develop for the platform. Browsers are a good example of this kind of extensibility. Browsers are equipped with a number of plug-ins or software modules developed by third parties that leverage the Web to deliver mobile code, sometimes called active content. A plug-in module itself could be a platform to which other third parties write active content. The key is to provide a programmable interface or interpreter and language that other parties can write code in and deliver over the Internet. Providing the capability is not enough. The "platform" must also be installed on enough machines to make it worthwhile for third parties to do development. Key active content technologies such as "flash" content and JavaScript that bring Web pages to life have benefited from having their interpreters included in the standard distribution of the most popular browsers.

In the future, we expect this trend to continue with proprietary scripting technologies. That is, a vendor will provide a scripting platform or interpreter that is shipped with other common desktop applications through sales agreements with desktop application vendors. Once the installed base of platforms has reached a critical mass, a number of third-party developers will write content for the platform. To support this technology, Microsoft has developed an active scripting Application Programming Interface (API) as part of the Windows 32-bit (Win32) platform that supports third-party scripting technologies. Scripts can use the active scripting API to interact with or "script" other components, documents, applications, and system resources on the machine. This core capability provides a basic infrastructure for scripts to control almost every aspect of the system. This is a tremendous capability and arguably moves the vision of Internet-based extensible software forward significantly. Because the security considerations of any given scripting technology are left to the discretion of the scripting technology developer, there is a high probability that this tremendous capability will be exploited by malicious entities writing active content for these active scripting platforms that often provide little to no protection against malicious scripts.

Mobile code today comes in the form of software updates, active content, e-mail attachments, and even software on floppy disks. The risks from mobile code are high. Essentially, anytime mobile code reaches your machine, it runs with your privileges and permissions, meaning it has access to your personal data as well as the ability to modify files, corrupt the system, and send personal data out over network sockets. As technology moves forward, it seems that little thought is given to the security and privacy concerns with new paradigms of technology. While dynamic software updates using push technology can be an enabler to protect us from malicious viruses, it can also be a way to promulgate viruses. If a malicious entity were able to capture and alter the software update pushed to everyone's machines, it would be easy to spread a virus in Internet time on a worldwide scale in a matter of minutes. While digital signing technologies can alleviate this concern to some extent, they are still not widely used in push technology solutions. Furthermore, digital signatures provide little protection against the disgruntled insider who plants the virus or Trojan horse in the software update.

Similarly, active content provides significant risks to users for several reasons. First, active content will typically run without notifying the user that it is running. That is, active content transparently downloads and runs. Second, most forms of active content do not implement a rigorous security model, leaving users susceptible to third-party attacks that develop malicious active content. Third, malicious active content will be able to leverage user rights and privileges to cause significant harm. Current operating system file access permissions provide no protection against code running with your own privileges. Fourth, with the capabilities extensible applications provide and an infrastructure such as the Win32 active scripting API to support third-party scripting technologies, the number and variety of scripting technologies and active content will grow significantly in the future—providing fertile ground for malicious content developers.

Finally, it is important to realize that the networking of computers has made almost all code mobile. That is, even setting aside extensible applications and systems, it is incredibly easy to get new software onto machines. The number and variety of programs a computer runs are constantly changing. Only five years ago, executable attachments to e-mail were unheard of; now they are *de rigueur*. Networked file servers make it easy to share software distributions on an enterprise scale. In the past, to acquire software from public sites, one needed to use special programs to access electronic bulletin boards where program source code was posted. Then, once the code was downloaded, one had to contend with brittle "make" files to compile the code before the program could actually be run. Now, you no longer need to be a technophile to find, download, and run software. The Web browser provides a convenient interface to FTP sites to download and execute precompiled software.

While the Web has made software distribution on a grand scale easy, it has also introduced new risks to corporate networks. Any time software is allowed to install and run on a machine, there is the possibility that the software may be malicious. In the following sections, we first describe the malicious software problem, then describe a particularly menacing mobile code threat—active scripting.

Malicious Code

A study released by InformationWeek Research and Pricewaterhouse-Coopers in July 2000 estimates that the cost of malicious software, or malware for short, will exceed U.S. $1.5 trillion worldwide this year.[5] The impact on U.S. businesses with more than 1000 employees is estimated to be $266 billion, or approximately 2.7 percent of the U.S. Gross Domestic Product (GDP). Most of the costs were estimated to be in lost productivity as a result of downtime and in lost sales opportunities. The study estimates that approximately 40,000 person years of productivity will be lost worldwide this year alone. In recent years, the Melissa virus and its derivatives, the Explorer.Zip worm and its ilk, have made world news headlines and have cost businesses substantial resources and downtime dealing with this malicious threat. In this section, we first present the problem, discuss current approaches to addressing malicious software, and then take a look at future solutions to malware.

First, let's define some of the terminology that is often misused in malicious software. Most people are familiar with viruses, but they do not know the difference between a virus, worm, Trojan horse, Easter Egg, or logic bomb. Informally, we define them here.[6]

Viruses are malicious code that attach to or infect host programs and then replicate themselves. Viruses can infect application executables, or they can run as macros or scripts in an interpreter on some application host. Viruses spread by infecting new documents, applications, or media via the original infected host.

Worms are a special class of virus that use networked computers to propagate to new hosts. Worms have the ability to autonomously jump from machine to machine, using network connections.

A Trojan horse is a piece of malicious code that disguises its malicious intent inside a host program that appears to do something useful or benign. In the background, however, Trojan horse programs are doing their damage, such as corrupting files or stealing information.

An Easter Egg is a variation of a Trojan horse. Easter Eggs are programs within programs that are generally included for entertainment value. One of the most (in)famous Easter Eggs is the Microsoft Excel 97 Easter Egg described in the accompanying sidebar. An Easter Egg that is malicious is, by definition, a Trojan horse.

Logic bombs are overtly malicious programs. The key difference between a logic bomb and a Trojan horse is that logic bombs are not programs disguised within programs. One can receive a logic bomb via e-mail or physical media that upon executing will cause immediate damage. Alternatively, logic bombs may trigger in the future based on some event such as the system clock or some command sequence. Zombie programs such as the client programs used in the distributed denial-of-service attacks in February 2000 can be considered a type of logic bomb that executes when triggered by a remote command sequence.

Attack or exploit scripts are programs written to exploit the flaw in some program for malicious gain. Generally, the program being exploited was not written with malicious intent. Rather, inadvertent flaws in the program can permit malicious entities to take advantage and gain unauthorized privileges. Once an exploit script is written it

Malicious Code Hall of Infamy

Malicious code incidents have made headline news in recent years. What follows is our Hall of Infamy, which represents a sampling of some of the most pernicious and pervasive recent examples of malicious code. These malefactors leverage Internet access through e-mail, newsgroups, Web pages, or IRC channels to wage their attacks. The Internet gives malicious code tremendous scaling factors over prior malware generations both to scale up the number of affected users over multinational regions and to scale down the amount of time it takes to spread infections and cripple networks.

- **Happy 99 Executable Worm.** This worm got its name from the fireworks display it puts on the user's screen along with the message "Happy New Year 1999!!" when run. While this worm was originally spread via newsgroup postings, its most pernicious form of spread is via e-mail. The worm will follow an e-mail with another e-mail with the worm payload as an attachment called Happy99.EXE. To avert executing the worm and infecting others, delete the e-mail and attachment.

- **Pretty Park Trojan Horse.** The Pretty Park Trojan horse is similar to the Happy 99 worm in the sense that it uses e-mail to propagate itself, but it is a bit more insidious in that it also connects to an IRC channel to serve as a remote access Trojan horse for the virus writer. Instead of just following e-mails like the Happy99 worm, this worm will attempt to e-mail itself every 30 minutes to all e-mail addresses in the address book associated with MS Outlook Express. The Trojan horse functionality is that the worm will try to connect to an IRC server over a specific channel. While connected, it can upload information and download commands to act on behalf of an unauthorized malicious entity.

- **Melissa Macro Virus.** The Melissa virus is one of the most infamous viruses in recent times. It is a macro virus that infects Office 97 documents. It first spread on March 26, 1999, through newsgroups, then e-mail, ultimately bringing down many corporate networks. The virus is a macro virus that infects Word 97 documents and templates. The virus sends an e-mail to the first 50 recipients in the user's Outlook address book with a subject line: "Important Message From" (user name is inserted here). Attached to a message that says "Here is that document you asked for . . ." is an infected document that contains a list of pornographic Web sites. The rapid spread of the Melissa virus spurred Congress to hold hearings on this type of virus.

- **Back Orifice 2000.** The Back Orifice 2000 is a remote access Trojan horse that acts on behalf of unauthorized remote users. The victim must be tricked into installing the program on the desktop, or an insider might do so deliberately. It allows a remote user to gain complete control over the machine remotely. For instance, a remote user can reboot or lock up the system, can capture keystrokes or pop up dialog boxes, and copy, delete, rename, create files and processes on the remote system.

- **MiniZip.** The MiniZip worm is a compressed executable version of the ExploreZip worm, which also ravaged corporate networks in 1999. The compression allowed it to evade virus detection engines searching for the signature of the ExploreZip worm. The worm is usually received as an e-mail attachment with a message "I received your e-mail and I shall send you a reply ASAP. Till then, take a look at the attached zipped docs." The attachment, though often displayed with a WinZip icon to fool recipients into thinking it is a self-extracting file, is simply an executable named "zipped_files.exe." Once executed, the virus will erase the contents of all .doc, .xls, .ppt, .c, .cpp, .h, and .asm files, rendering them unrecoverable, unless backups exist. Like its other recent brethren, this worm spreads via e-mail clients.

- **LoveBug.** The LoveBug is among the most infamous of its brethren both for the damage it caused and the manner in which it caused it. The LoveBug is a Visual Basic Script (VBScript) worm that is sent as an e-mail attachment to victims. The subject header of the e-mail is "I LOVE YOU," hence its moniker. Upon opening the attachment, the LoveBug will replace copies of JPEG and other multimedia files with its own script code as well as mail itself out using the Microsoft Outlook mail client to all the e-mail addresses in the victim's Outlook address book. It also has the ability to send faxes over phone lines to recipient fax numbers in the Outlook address book. The LoveBug will attempt to download an executable file from a Web site that will send cached passwords to a predetermined address. Since the LoveBug was first released, there have been a number of variants of this same attack using VBScript attachments sent via e-mail.

- **Morris Worm.** The Morris worm is the father of all worms. Written by Robert Morris, Jr., then a student at MIT, in 1988 this program exploited a flaw in the finger network daemon to spread itself from Unix server to server. It crashed roughly 10 percent of the Internet.

can be widely disseminated and used by malicious hackers or "script kiddies" who need not understand the flaw being exploited to breach the security.

The Malware Problem

Malicious software is software or code fragments intentionally written or removed from a system to corrupt system integrity, violate data confidentiality, or change program functionality without the knowledge and approval of the user.[7] It is important to distinguish malicious software from inadvertently-flawed software. Most computer security violations and losses in practice are made possible by inadvertent flaws in software. In this case, an ill-intentioned person, sometimes called a bad actor, deliberately attempts to exploit an inadvertent flaw in the software to gain unauthorized privilege or access.

Malicious software, on the other hand, is deliberately written to behave maliciously. While most computer security incidents in practice are due to poorly written software, there is a significant rise in the number of incidents due to malicious software in recent years. Furthermore, because the Internet has made distribution of malicious software scalable to global networks over a very short time period, a single malicious software program can have a tremendous effect on the global computing infrastructure—for example, the Melissa virus.

Hacking via inadvertent software flaws on a global scale is much more difficult in a short time period without the aid of malicious software. Thus, we are concerned about the potential of an "electronic Pearl Harbor" scenario in which large parts of the Internet and other critical infrastructures can be brought down by malicious software in a time period too quick for human response.

One of the key problems that enable widespread malware distribution is the problem of unauthorized software proliferation to the desktop. In today's pervasive Internet computing environment, software can migrate to any number of machines without the knowledge of its users. The distribution of malicious software has been a problem for computer networks since the early days of electronic bulletin board systems known as BBSs. BBSs were publicly accessible sites where you could post and download software freely. Even then, it was well understood that untrusted software like that found on BBS sites could be potentially malicious. As a rule of thumb, any software downloaded from a BBS site was not to be installed on a corporate computer system. Rather, this software was mainly for personal use on personal computers at home.

The problem of malicious software has only grown since the days of BBSs. The BBS has been replaced with the Web, and mobile code now seamlessly and sometimes silently downloads and executes on Web surfers' machines. With the rise of the personal computer in the 1980s, malicious code became best known in the form of viruses, which are self-replicating code snippets that can infect common programs. The most common vector for spreading viruses was the floppy disk, which often infected the boot sector of the personal computer.

As the Internet became more pervasive and floppy disks less essential, viruses were spread via shared application documents in e-mail. Macro viruses were invented to demonstrate that desktop applications not only can run code interactively (meaning the application was itself an interpreter), but also can run self-replicating code by infecting templates and subsequent working documents.

The Internet has made downloading and executing of software not only easy, but often transparent to the end user. The Internet has enabled code proliferation on a scale previously unimaginable when programs were shipped on physical media. While many applications provide warning before allowing a user to execute macros, we do not have a defense against preventing users from running unknown executables attached to e-mails.

Unknown programs, often entertaining and clever diversions from work, are attached to e-mails and distributed widely inside and outside organizations. Users end up clicking on attachments and running programs for entertainment without knowing the full behavior of these programs. Many Trojan horses, as well as an equal number of hoaxes, are spread in this manner. Even users cognizant that executing untrusted programs can be dangerous can be fooled into executing programs. Some Trojan horse programs have been disguised as JPEG or GIF attachments when they are, in fact, program executables whose suffix appears to be .jpg or .gif. When they are launched, instead of getting an image, an error box is sometimes displayed (to dupe the user into believing some error occurred in displaying the graphic), while the Trojan horse installs itself and begins its havoc.

A benign version of a Trojan horse is known as an Easter Egg. Typing the following key sequence in a Microsoft Excel 97 spreadsheet will result in a flight simulator being run in Excel:

Open a new blank work sheet.

Press F5, and type X97:L97 in the "Reference" box, then click OK.

Tab once. (You should end up in cell M97.)

Press Ctrl+Shift while clicking once on the "chart wizard" icon.

You are now in the Excel Flight Simulator mode.

The point of the demonstration is that even though a flight simulator was run, it could have more easily have been a malicious software fragment or program that mailed sensitive documents out over a network connection or wiped the contents of all your documents.

Trojan horse programs also exist in consumer devices. A commercial Digital Versatile Disk (DVD) player on the market contains Trojan horse functionality in the form of a secret "Loopholes" menu. The menu allows users to disable three copy protection mechanisms currently encoded in DVD disks. As a result, one can disable the protections that currently prevent one from copying DVD disks to videotape, playing the DVD on a non-licensed player, and watching international releases on U.S. players (and vice versa).

While early DVD players were also known to allow hacks around the copy protection, this product is the first one known to provide a menu to disable the copy protection, through the right sequence of taps on the remote control.[8] The sequence was secret until it was posted to a Web page. The manufacturer claimed to have no knowledge about how the functionality got loaded into the system. This example is a foreshadowing of the types of software problems (or gems, some may say) we are likely to have as software and Internet access become pervasive in all manner of devices.

In addition to attachments, program executables are often downloaded from Web sites on public shareware/freeware sites or as mobile code (such as ActiveX controls). Corporations often frown on downloading and installing programs (to the point of writing company policies prohibiting downloading of software); however, in practice, they have little control over this activity. For one reason, users sometimes do not know they are downloading executables, such as in the case of mobile code that downloads and executes transparently. Second, because e-mail attachments are used as part of the normal course of business, blocking attachments at the firewall is generally not an acceptable solution. Also, because an executable can be disguised as other kinds of documents, firewalling solutions have proven to be ineffective.

Other vectors of malicious code propagation include remote hacks into systems as well as insider attacks. Many systems are vulnerable to penetration because of flawed software. Once a system is broken into, the cracker will often install a "root kit'" that allows the cracker to get back into the system via inconspicuous backdoors. Once a vulnerable system has been hacked, it can serve as a cache for malicious software (sometimes called warez), pornography, and pirated software. Software that may be installed by the cracker includes well-known malicious programs such as Back Orifice 2000 (a remote administration kit for the cracker), NetBus, password crackers, pornography, and viruses. Often, compromised sites are published in underground lists for other junior crackers and script kiddies to find tools, upload and download illegal software, or use as a training ground.

The problem of vulnerable systems is even more acute than possible loss of assets to the victim organization. Many crackers use vulnerable systems as a launching point for attacks against other systems. One reason is that an attacker wants to put as many systems between his computer and the ultimate victim computer to make tracing his origin more difficult.

A good example is the recent spate of distributed denial-of-service (dDoS) attacks against top-tier e-commerce companies in early February 2000.[9] In order for the perpetrators to launch dDoS attacks, a number of other systems had to be compromised first. This step was relatively easy given the number of vulnerable systems on the Internet. Once a server is broken into, a malicious variant of a well-known Unix program (finger) was installed.[10] The compromised server is a zombie computer at this point, performing its functions as normal until beckoned at a later time remotely by the perpetrator to launch a coordinated attack against a target machine.

Therefore, the risks of malicious software run beyond initial damages to an organization's assets. If even one server in an organization's systems is cracked, malicious software is planted and is subsequently used as a launching point against other systems. Not only will the organization be an unwitting party to an attack, but it could also suffer collateral damage after the attack such as the following:

- Loss of reputation
- Loss of stockholder value
- Retaliation attacks from victim organizations
- Law enforcement investigation
- Legal liability for damages resulting from attacks launched from compromised systems

Finally, the infamous "sneakernet" is another common vector for malicious code to infect systems. Sneakernet is the term used for passing software around on physical media such as floppy disks and CDs. This mode of attack requires physical access to the system and usually involves an insider attempting to install software, maliciously or not. Again, while corporate policies may prohibit individuals from installing and executing their own software, we currently have no technology to enforce this policy.

Current Malware Defenses

Today's operating systems are ill-equipped to deal with the threat of malicious software. One of the main reasons is that in most cases malicious software executes with the privileges of its victim. Most operating system security models are user-centric. That is, they provide coarse protection to prevent an owner of one process from corrupting, modifying, or deleting files owned by a different user. This model more or less ensures that your colleagues or people unknown to you cannot easily access or modify your data and programs, and vice versa. On Unix platforms, it also often protects you from removing key system programs.

This model does not protect you from yourself or, more accurately, from code executing with your privileges, which is the usual mode malicious code executes. The key problem in dealing with malicious software is protecting the end user from processes that run with the end user's privileges. This is the problem that today's operating systems do not address. Combine this weakness with pervasive and seamless Internet access throughout the operating system and application layers, and the result is the defenseless state of our computing machinery. We use computing machinery in the broadest sense, as we see malicious software spreading to the pervasive computing platforms of tomorrow: embedded and hand-held devices with Internet access, which will ultimately utilize distributed and mobile computing paradigms.

The current commercial means we have for addressing the malicious software threat are largely signature-based detection tools. That is, the virus detection tools largely work on detecting signature patterns of known viruses in programs. There are several problems with signature-based detection. The most severe is that signature-based detection is reactive. That is, using signature-based detection, one can detect malicious code only after the virus does the following:

- Is out in the wild
- Has propagated to enough machines
- Has caused enough damage to show up on the radar of the virus detection vendors
- Has a signature for the virus, created by vendors
- Has a signature that vendors have disseminated to all the virus detection clients

The time window for the virus to wreak its havoc is quite significant, especially when considered in light of how quickly today's worms can spread. In the interim time it takes to update all anti-virus clients, an Internet-based virus or worm can infect tens of thousands of machines in a matter of hours—much as the Melissa virus did in 1999. Besides being reactive in nature, signature-based detection techniques also suffer from the inability to generalize. That is, they will detect only *exact* signatures of viruses. Slight variants go undetected. Thus, common ways to defeat signature-based detection schemes are to alter or add an instruction (such as a no-op) or shift bits left one on transmission, then shift bits right one on installation. Furthermore, for reasons of efficiency, signature detection schemes will often analyze only a portion of the executable, the portion in which the virus code is known to live. Simply moving the self-contained virus code around the executable can defeat many detection schemes. Approaches that can generalize from known malicious code (or behavior) are necessary to overcome the weaknesses of signature-based detection.

Most malicious software detection techniques require source code for analysis, or they can work with executable binaries. This is a useful distinction to make because techniques that require program source code will be infeasible for most commercial off-the-shelf (COTS) software where source code is proprietary. Software analysis techniques will analyze software either statically or dynamically. Static analysis involves examining the binary executable without actually running it. Static analysis makes predictions of the expected or possible range of behavior of a program. Dynamic analysis techniques involve actually running the program under analysis and observing its behavior under specified input conditions.

The advantage of static analysis techniques is that the full range of behavior for a reasonably small amount of code can be formally understood. The disadvantage of static analysis techniques is the difficulty in fully understanding complex programs, being able to analyze potential security vulnerabilities, and the need to disassemble binaries to an instruction set where enough information is present (including type information) to perform the analyses required to understand the program's behavior. Typical static analyses involve generating control and dataflow graphs. Forward and backward program slicing on a statement or variable can be useful for limiting the amount of code necessary to analyze. In practice, though, program slices tend to be very large, making static analysis still difficult.

While dynamic analysis techniques have traditionally meant testing, the problem of testing any complex piece of software exhaustively is intractable. Furthermore, the lack of an oracle of correct behavior makes testing a difficult task that most commercial developers drop at the first sign of a compressed schedule. Given a security policy, the problem of developing an oracle of secure behavior is much easier. A different class of dynamic analysis techniques that addresses the malicious software problem from a tolerance point of view is monitoring techniques. That is, rather than test a software program to determine whether it is malicious (a halting problem equivalent), the goal of software monitoring is to ensure that if the monitored program is malicious it cannot compromise system integrity or data confidentiality.

In the commercial world, a number of products provide run-time monitoring of programs to prevent security intrusions. The best-known example is the Java Virtual Machine by Sun Microsystems. The JDK 1.0.2 supports a security reference monitor to prevent untrusted applets from accessing explicit system resources. In subsequent release version 1.1, fine-grained access control is supported for signed applets. In addition, products from Finjan, eSafe, Advanced Computer Research, and Security7 all attempt to provide commercial sandboxes for constraining code behavior. Most of these products work by loading kernel modules into the operating system in order to trap requests to system resources that could be potentially malicious.

One of the most significant difficulties with the sandboxing type of solutions is dealing with increasingly multifunctional software. For instance, today's Web browser provides the ability to not only view and download Web documents, but also run mobile code, create and edit files, download and install programs, and send and receive e-mail. Given all the functionality that Internet-enabled software provides, it is hard to write a security policy (to be enforced by a sandboxing solution) that fits all needs. For instance, if a Web browser/mailer were to be run in a sandbox that prevents file access, one could not create, edit, and save files. The end result is that either the policy is completely relaxed or the sandbox is removed, leaving the sandboxing solution useless in practice.

The strength of commercial sandboxes is in protecting users from unknown and untrusted code. That is, sandboxes can effectively constrain code that does not require access to system resources or will not be used for business-critical functions. We could consider such code toys. What kind of protection do sandboxes provide against practical software applications that can be disguised Trojan horses, infected applications, or platforms for malicious scripts or macros? The answer is very little.

The challenge for sandboxing solutions is to restrict not only *which* resources are accessed, but *how* and *when* resources are accessed. For instance, it is necessary for desktop applications to save files to the working document directories, but it is not acceptable for an application to overwrite *all* files in that directory without the user's permission. Similarly, while it is important to preserve the functionality for sending documents over networks, we do not wish to allow a desktop application to arbitrarily send documents over the network to any destination, either. Current approaches do not address this problem.

Addressing the Malware Threat

As the preceding section laid out, current approaches are inadequate for addressing the malicious software threat. Operating systems have built-in controls to protect your files from your colleagues, but not from malicious software. Anti-viral software vendors use reactive signature-based approaches that are not effective against worms that leverage the Internet to spread rapidly. Finally, even advanced approaches such as commercial sandboxes fall down when used in practical multipurpose software applications such as browsers and desktop applications that necessarily need access to system resources.

In a vision for the future, some anti-virus vendors would like to automate the whole process of virus detection to eradicate unknown viruses. As discussed, one of the key problems with current virus detection approaches is that they are reactive. They can detect a virus only after it has caused enough damage to be noticed, isolated, then a signature captured and disseminated. IBM, in cooperation with Symantec, is developing a digital immune system that uses heuristic rules to detect viruses based on tell-tale signs, then isolates the virus and ships it off to a laboratory for analysis.[11] If the virus is known, the laboratory can ship back the cure immediately. This is effectively updating the virus signatures on-the-fly when tell-tale virus behavior is detected. If the virus is not known, then the virus sample is sent to an analysis center where a vaccine is automatically generated, then sent back to your machine to eradicate the virus. Of course, this is still an unrealized vision of the future for IBM's digital immune system. One of the most difficult challenges using this approach is detecting future and unknown viruses. Heuristic rules are notoriously unreliable. As virus writers get more creative and viruses change, writing rules to detect new viruses will be as difficult as obtaining and disseminating signatures of known viruses.

Alternative approaches to addressing the malicious software problem offer hope against the reactive cat-and-mouse strategy currently offered by the commercial anti-virus community. One way to address the malicious software problem is to prevent its execution and proliferation in the first place. By preventing a malicious program from executing, and worms from spreading, a significant bite can be taken out of the malware problem. Or more simply stated, a malicious program that cannot execute is not dangerous. This is the idea behind execution control lists.[12] Execution control lists restrict a user to executing only an approved and known set of applications. This set typically includes all the operating system software necessary to run application software, operating system services, and a set of desktop applications necessary for the user to perform his or her duties. Once the set of programs the user is allowed to run is specified, the desktop is effectively locked down. Thereafter, any new programs that attempt to execute will be rejected.

Why is this approach effective? One of the main reasons is that in today's corporate environments users have complete control over their machines. They can arbitrarily add and remove programs to their machines. While this control is appropriate for owners of individual machines, it is not necessarily so for users of corporate machines. Recall the discussion earlier in this chapter of the many ways malicious content can spread to machines. Users often unwittingly download and execute malicious content. Execution control lists (ECLs) are a technique for locking down users' machines to a set of known and trusted programs. ECLs give control over executable content back to the system administrator, and control over what programs run on the corporate IT infrastructure back to the Chief Information Officer (CIO). This not only will allow the CIO to ensure that malicious content is kept off corporate machines, but also helps the CIO stay within compliance of software license agreements, without monitoring users' behavior and infringing on users' privacy.

When a user attempts to execute a program that is not on his or her ECL, the program execution will be denied; however, an option to request execution of the program can be sent to a system administrator. The system administrator can make on-the-fly decisions about whether the user should be allowed to execute the program or simply defer these decisions until the program can be properly identified. Simply by locking down the desktop machine to a known set of trusted programs, a significant portion of the malicious software threat can be addressed. Furthermore, as new threats emerge—as they do on a weekly basis—a locked-down workstation will be impermeable to these new threats. ECLs provide a proactive defensive stance against the new and emerging malicious software threats to corporate IT systems, thus breaking the reactive cycle of virus detection, isolation, and signature dissemination.

The Code-Driven Threat

The most significant threat of intrusions is rapidly changing from individual-based hack-in attempts to code-driven attacks. This trend does not mean that individuals will not hack into systems or that we should let down our defenses against individual attacks. Rather, work should and will continue to detect hackers breaking into systems. In fact, the commercial sector has responded with a number of intrusion detection tools that have incorporated largely signature-based detection tools. While current intrusion detection tools are sometimes effective at catching hackers, they are ineffective against code-driven attacks.

Code-driven attacks are cyber attacks against computer systems via mobile code. While much attention has been paid to the wily hacker, the most significant threat to our computer systems and data is the threat of code-driven attacks. Malicious mobile code enters systems unimpeded by firewalls. It goes past intrusion detection systems undetected. It can damage our file systems and send sensitive information out over network sockets. It can even spy on our computer and Web usage patterns.

Code that not only damages the user's system, but also spreads itself over Internet connections can quickly bring down very large segments of the Internet and, by extension, the business world. Today's virus and intrusion detection tools are ineffective against countering a threat that can rapidly spread in a matter of hours instead of days. Clever malicious hackers can spend their time hacking into computer systems one-at-a time, or they can write mobile code to automate the process of exploiting a hole, causing damage, then autonomously spreading itself to an exponentially growing number of sites. To defend against this threat, we must build in defenses against not only damage of malware, but also malicious software proliferation.

Mobile code has become both pervasive on Web pages and a threat to Web-based systems. It is difficult, for instance, to browse the Web with JavaScript disabled because Web development has become so heavily dependent on running JavaScript. While Java applets were originally considered the most pervasive example of mobile code, the reality is that Web-based scripts, such as JavaScript, JScript, and VBscripts, are much more pervasive. Unfortunately, the commercial operating system vendors and anti-virus community have given us few protections against the risks of running such code, despite the overwhelming dangers as illustrated by the Melissa-style VBScript viruses.

Another class of mobile code that presents a real danger is e-mail attachments. For instance, the Happy99 and PrettyPark Trojan horses are typically distributed in Win32 executable binary form as e-mail attachments. Once the e-mail is received, the user will typically run the attachment by simply double-clicking on it. Most security specialists believe that user education (that is, instructing users not to run unknown attachments) is the solution to this problem. As these viruses illustrate time and again, user education does not provide enough assurance. Social engineering is typically used to convince users that the attachment is really of interest. For instance, many of these worms are unintentionally sent by someone the recipient knows—a fine way to get someone to open and execute an e-mail attachment.

It has often been said that we dodged a bullet with Melissa. That is, the damage from the Melissa virus could have been much more severe. The truth is that the damage from all of the scripting-based attacks we have seen in the wild has been relatively tame in comparison with the possible damage they could inflict if so programmed. In spite of the relatively tame nature of these viruses, the cost of dealing with them and the losses in productivity and sales—over 2.5 percent of the U.S. GDP— is significant enough to garner the attention of analysts and investors on Wall Street. Civil service and military personnel in the U.S. government have begun to realize that malicious code threatens our very own information-based "new" economy. And yet, we have still dodged a bullet.

Michal Zalewski wrote an interesting essay/cookbook titled "I don't think I really love you: or writing internet worms for fun and profit," which describes a project that he and some of his colleagues have been working on since 1998 called "Samhain".[13] The project involves building a prototype worm that is capable of the following:

- Being architecture-independent—that is, portable across different operating systems

- Being invisible to its victims using process hiding facilities

- Being autonomous, so that it can independently migrate from host to host

- Being intelligent, so that it can learn new exploits and functionality

- Being resilient to detection, network tracing, and reverse engineering

- Being polymorphic to avoid signature detection

- Being programmable, so that it can benignly infect a host, learn about its environment, then maliciously steal its secrets and cause maximum damage

The essay describes the methods for implementing each of these desired properties of a worm, including source code. The worm has been prototyped in an "engine" for the purposes of experimentation. The truth is, though, that there is no rocket science to the work described in the essay. A motivated team could design and develop a worm with these properties without too much difficulty. Such a worm is far more malicious than the current breed of Internet worms that even our current detection and anti-viral systems cannot handle. Thus, the question these developments beg is what defenses do we have against code-driven threats?

Current Mobile Code Defenses

Whereas intrusion detection tools are largely concerned with identifying and stopping hackers or individuals attempting to break into systems, they are ineffective against code-driven attacks. A code-driven attack will typically use an Internet service to send malicious code to end users, who then inadvertently execute the code. Mobile code will download and sometimes run transparently to the user, while at other times, the user is fooled into running the code by social engineering tricks, such as tricking the user into believing the code is a legitimate document sent by an acquaintance.

Code-driven attacks use a variety of different software technologies including executable attachments to e-mail such as binaries and scripts, embedded scripts in HTML mail, Web-based mobile code such as Java applets, ActiveX controls, and JavaScript, Visual Basic scripts, and Visual Basic macros used to drive applications. In addition, Internet chat rooms and newsgroups often serve as an initial dissemination post for malicious code. Finally, code-driven attacks also use more traditional forms of transmission such as ftp services as well as physical media to spread among computers. It is important that our defenses address code-driven attacks regardless of the entry mechanism.

Code-driven attacks find themselves bridging communities of interest with different origins. For instance, the anti-virus community has long been tasked with addressing the malicious software problem. Today's most virulent viruses use the Internet to spread on a scale and time frame unsuitable to current signature-based anti-virus detection tools. Likewise, because intrusion detection tools have traditionally focused on the Internet as the vector of most attacks against computing systems, the intrusion detection community would seem like a more natural fit for addressing the problems of code-driven attacks. Again, the scale and time frame at which code-driven attacks spread are unsuitable for most current intrusion detection tools, which are mostly oriented toward detecting humans hacking into systems—a far cry from the global nature and Internet time scale of code-driven attacks.

Today's approaches to dealing with these forms of malware are not effective. The most common approach to dealing with VBScript viruses is to use a signature-based virus detection tool. Unfortunately, this approach will not detect the next variation of the same attack. Because these viruses spread so quickly, the reactive approach to virus detection is not effective in stopping a Melissa-style virus.

Another approach to stopping code-driven attacks is to disable active scripting within Web browsers and mailers. This is not a good solution because active scripting is used pervasively in Web pages for core functionality. In addition, many active scripting attacks run from the file system and will control other desktop applications. Simply shutting off active scripting capabilities in browsers and mailers will not adequately address VBScripts, JavaScripts, and other scripting technologies (Python, Rexx, Perl) that run directly on the host platform interpreter. Other approaches, such as filtering content at the firewall, have proved to be largely ineffective in the past and will be rendered obsolete in the future by end-to-end encryption.

The reality is this: We are left largely defenseless against one of the most significant emerging Internet threats, the threat of code-driven attacks. While the anti-virus vendor community claims to provide us assurance against code-driven attacks, the truth is that the emperor has no clothes and we are left defenseless against code-driven attacks. At best, we can only hope that the anti-virus community can put out signatures or notices fast enough to protect our systems against code-driven threats. We know from experience that this is not the case. Furthermore, future code-driven threats, akin to Samhain, will silently cross firewall boundaries and execute without requiring user cooperation (such as double-clicking attachments).

Addressing the Code-Driven Threat

The code-driven threat has largely reared its ugly head against the Windows 32-bit (Win32) platform. It is not that the Win32 platform is inherently more vulnerable than other platforms (though some may argue that it is) as much as the ubiquity of the platform in both homes and offices makes it an attractive target. A single code-driven attack can have a significant global impact with high visibility.

One class of code-driven threats that has proven particularly popular, powerful, and troublesome is active-scripting–based attacks. For instance, in August 2000, four of the top six malicious code threats on Symantec's Anti-viral Research Center's Web page[14] were active-scripting–based attacks, including VBS.Stages.A, Wscript.KakWorm, VBS.LoveLetter, and VBS.Network.

Active-scripting–based attacks are developed in code in one of several popular scripting languages (VBScript, JScript, VBA macros, Perl, Python) that run on their respective interpreters. The interpreters reside in various application hosts, including Web browsers, mailers, MS Office applications, and the Windows scripting host. On the Win32 platform, one feature all these interpreters have in common is that they use the Windows Active Scripting interface—a set of well-documented APIs for accessing application and system resources. Active scripts use this interface to access application objects and methods and system resources, as well as to drive other applications.

This interface can be leveraged in order to combat this class of code-driven threats.[15] One approach is to effectively constrain the active scripting capability on the platform to allow benign uses while denying malicious uses. This approach is feasible because the range of possible behaviors for active scripting functionality is much greater than the range of legitimate functionality currently used for Internet-based content. By effectively controlling scripts' ability to access system resources, applications, and documents, this approach can address the threat of code-driven attacks that leverage the active scripting interface.

The approach is effective against the following types of code-driven attacks: e-mail attachments, embedded scripts in HTML mail, scripts that exploit browser holes, scripts that exploit ActiveX controls marked safe for scripting, scripting of MS Office applications, VBA document macros, and other future scripting technologies that leverage the Active Scripting API. The key benefit of this approach is that it is not signature-based. Therefore, it handles a large class of code-driven threats—that is, active-scripting–based attacks, rather than specific instances. As a result, it addresses future and unknown active scripting attacks. While the approach addresses the threat of code-driven attacks from Web pages and e-mail, it is equally powerful against scripts that run from the desktop Windows scripting host.

In conclusion, the code-driven threat to Internet-enabled platforms surpasses the current capabilities of anti-virus and intrusion detection tools. Unless and until we develop defenses that can address the code-driven threat, we will be largely naked to the most significant emerging Internet threat. Techniques such as the one described here can go a long way toward addressing large classes of code-driven attacks.

Notes

1. See *Java Security: Hostile Applets, Holes, and Antidotes* by Gary McGraw and Ed Felten (Wiley, 1996).

2. Credit to Tom O'Connor with acknowledgment to Mark LaDue, Gary McGraw, Ed Felten, and Princeton's Secure Internet Programming team for laying the groundwork.

3. K. Thompson, "Reflections on Trusting Trust", *Communications of the ACM*, 27:8 (August 1984).

4. See *Java Security: Hostile Applets, Holes, and Antidotes* by Gary McGraw and Ed Felten (Wiley, 1996).

5. Global survey of 4900 information technology professionals across 30 nations conducted by InformationWeek Research and fielded by PricewaterhouseCoopers LLP, released July 10, 2000.

6. See also "Attacking Malicious Code: A Report to the IRC," by G. McGraw and G. Morrisett. Available online: www.cigital.com/irc/.

7. J. Bergeron, M. Debabbi, et al., "Detection of Malicious Code in COTS Software: A Short Survey," in *Proceedings of the 1st International Software Assurance Certification Conference (ISACC)*, February 1999, Dulles, VA.

8. D. Greenberg, "Now Showing on DVD: 'Loopholes,'" *Washington Post*, March 24, 2000, pp. E11.

9. See "Distributed Denial of Service Attacks and the Zombie Ant Effect," by J. Elliot, in *IEEE ITPro*, 2(2), March/April 2000, pp. 55–57.

10. Ironically, the first well-documented widespread Internet worm attack known as the 1988 Morris worm exploited the finger daemon.

11. See "The New Hot Zone" by Lev Grossman in *Time Digital*, August 2000, pp. 31–37.

12. See "Execution Control Lists: An Approach to Defending Against New and Unknown Malicious Software," by A. Ghosh and M. Schmid, in *Proceedings of the Information Survivability Workshop 2000*, October 24–26, 2000, Boston, MA.

13. Available online at http://lcamtuf.na.export.pl/worm.txt.

14. Symantec's list of top malware threats is available online at www.symantec.com/avcenter/.

15. See "Code-Driven Attacks: The Evolving Internet Threat," by A.K. Ghosh in *Proceedings of the Information Survivability Workshop 2000*, October 24–26, 2000, Boston, MA.

CHAPTER 6

Security Issues in Mobile E-Commerce

"In the future, everything you don't eat will have computing capability."

BLAISE HELTAI
FLEETBOSTON FINANCIAL CORPORATION

A humorous, but likely prediction of the future. Computers or their successors will be all-pervasive. Just about anything you can think of will have some computing capability. Computers will be woven into the fabric of our society, if not our clothes. They need not have all-powerful microprocessors, either. The key will not be the speed of the processor, but rather the networking ability of the device. Almost all devices will be networked, most likely through wireless networks. They will probably leverage the Internet for interdevice communication. Why put fancy computing capability on a device when the processing cycles can be "outsourced" and results returned via the Internet to the device? The intelligence will be built into the network, rather than the device. Advances in wireless computing will usher in this era. As all our devices, for both personal and business use, become wired—or, more accurately, unwired—the security concerns for wireless access to business assets grow substantially, while the possibility for "big brother"-like monitoring and loss of personal privacy looms large.

By 2004, there are expected to be more than 1 billion wireless device subscribers. The future of e-commerce appears to be headed straight for mobile e-commerce (m-commerce). Today's workers want to be untethered from their desktops, with the freedom to communicate and access information from anywhere at anytime. To this end, current wireless platforms are integrating voice telephony, data, and streaming multimedia in multifunction, rich-content capable devices. Code will be exchanged transparently with data over wireless links. Wireless devices will have the processing power and memory of today's desktop workstations. Wireless devices will have direct access to file servers and network services behind the corporate firewalls. Furthermore, wireless devices will have the ability to ship and execute mobile and itinerant code such as software agents that act on the user's behalf. Even though all these advances in technology give the end user significant freedom and power, they raise serious security and privacy concerns for consumers and businesses. In this chapter, we describe the key security concerns in m-commerce and the avenues for addressing them.

Today, e-commerce is mostly conducted from the desktop using workstations and personal computers. Tomorrow, we expect that a significant portion of e-commerce will be conducted from wireless, Internet-enabled devices. Wireless devices will give users the mobility to research, communicate, and purchase goods and services from anywhere at anytime without being tethered to the desktop. One of the major wireless applications is Web access for research and real-time information retrieval, such as weather, maps, and stock quotes. E-mail will continue to dominate online applications. Innovative online applications, which, for instance, use location reference of end users, will drive forward new areas of e-commerce. In fact, both new and older applications being ported to wireless devices will provide further growth impetus to online commerce and are likely to render current estimates for e-commerce growth overly conservative.

Currently, there are more than 385,000 wireless Internet subscribers (Strategis Group). By 2004, there are expected to be more than 1 billion wireless device users, some 600 million wireless Internet subscribers, and a U.S. $200 billion mobile commerce market. The average cost per minute of wireless usage is expected to drop to U.S. 2 cents per minute in 2004.[1] It is expected that by 2008, the number of wireless Internet devices will outnumber wired devices.[2] While these estimates will likely change wildly in the coming months and years, there is clearly a vast number of current wireless device subscribers worldwide, and a large number of future potential wireless Internet subscribers and applications. Mobile e-commerce will drive the growth of wireless devices and applications. Securing m-commerce will be essential in order to unleash the potentially very large m-commerce market.

M-commerce will be conducted using a variety of devices, such as mobile phones, pagers, hand-held personal digital assistants (PDAs), such as Palm Computing's Palm Organizer and Microsoft's PocketPC, subnotebooks, and wireless notebooks. Furthermore, it is likely that appliances in 300 million U.S. homes, 45 million cars, and other countless non-traditional computing devices will become wireless Internet-enabled in the next decade, making desktop Internet access a relic of the past.[3] Vendors have been promoting novel applications of m-commerce such as paying at cash registers, parking meters, vending machines, and ticket booths. In truth, though, wireless devices will take on the functionality of today's desktop machines and more.

As the form factor of mobile computing devices has gotten smaller, their computing capacity has grown significantly. Today's hand-held devices have the equivalent computing power of their desktop computing counterparts of one generation earlier. This phenomenon, while driving more and more functionality into hand-held wireless Internet-enabled devices, also is driving the security risks we have today in desktop computing into wireless devices. For example, malicious code, long a problem on desktop computing, is likely to be a significant problem in hand-held devices.

Malicious code has already reared its ugly head in Palm Pilots. Two Trojan horse programs have already been written and publicly released for the Palm Pilot: the Liberty Crack and Vapor. The Liberty Crack Trojan horse purports to enable users to convert the free shareware version of the Liberty program to its full-featured commercial version. Rather than being a crack for the commercial version, the Liberty Crack program actually removes other third party applications. Vapor is less pernicious but equally scary. Disguised as an add-on application, Vapor hides program icons from the user giving the appearance that other programs and files have been deleted.

Other forms of malicious code such as viruses, worms, and malicious scripts will become an even greater threat as the devices become more widely used. For instance, the active scripting threat described in

Chapter 5 will apply to PDAs and cell phones that support scripting. This threat is described in detail later in this chapter. Scripting threats have already been seen elsewhere in Japan and Europe with NTT DoCoMo phones and the Timofonica Visual Basic worm. Japanese DoCoMo phone users were spammed with an e-mail message that contained a script called CompactHTML. The script asked the user a question. Regardless of the answer selected, the script would then automatically dial Japan's emergency services number 110. This "prank" has the possibility of paralyzing emergency services in a region. The Timofonica worm spread via e-mail attachments run from PCs, but spammed Spain's Telefonica's cellular short messaging system. The Timofonica worm demonstrates how the interconnectivity provided by the Internet between PCs and wireless devices can be misused for malicious purposes. Also consider that we can already wirelessly exchange Microsoft Office documents between Pocket PCs. Though the Pocket versions of Microsoft Word and Excel do not support macros, it is only a matter of time when scripting functionality will be supported on handheld applications, which will pave the way for macro and other types of scripting viruses and worms.

In spite of the seemingly unlimited potential to drive forward new applications and markets in m-commerce, unless the entire system that supports m-commerce is secured, chances are that the adoption rate will be slowed over consumer concerns of security and privacy. Integrating security and privacy into online m-commerce applications will enable a projected $25 billion dollar market for wireless software, content, and commerce. Consumers appear to be very wary of security and privacy issues, particularly in wireless devices, because snooping wireless conversations is better understood than snooping data packets on land lines. In addition, users keep some of their most personal and confidential information on their personal digital assistants (PDAs) and, as a result, are leery about security and privacy infractions such as inadvertent or malicious data leaks.

Business Risks in M-Commerce

Most industry analysts agree that security and privacy in m-commerce will be critical for widespread adoption. Any perceived lack of privacy will deter consumers from making online purchases from wireless devices or from using location-oriented commerce applications that transmit individual users' locations to remote sites. Currently, many consumers are acutely aware that their cordless phone and cell phone conversations can be eavesdropped at will by curious neighbors with scanners. Most consumers know that their phone number, by default, is transmitted to the other party with their phone call. Some might consider this a convenience for ordering delivery food, some a benefit of knowing who is calling before picking up the phone, and others an invasion of privacy. These perceptions in older-generation wireless devices will affect the way users adopt mobile e-commerce applications unless privacy concerns are addressed forthrightly up-front.

The very reasons businesses are beginning to adopt wireless devices as part of the corporate IT infrastructure are giving rise to security concerns over wireless computing. For businesses, full enterprise integration with application, file, and network servers behind the corporate firewall is a major driving force for widespread adoption of wireless devices. Where the Palm Pilots appealed to individuals for organizing personal appointments, enterprise-enabled wireless companions are more likely to appeal to businesses because of the ability to wirelessly synchronize mail and contacts, the ability to read, write, and exchange desktop application documents, and the ability to use full-featured Web browsers. Many hand-held PCs now come equipped with modems that allow devices to dial into corporate intranets. Some provide built-in support for wireless Local Area Network (LAN) access. The H/PC Pro supports wireless connections to Ethernet networks using IEEE 802.11 wireless LAN standard.

The security risks for businesses in integrating wireless devices into their corporate infrastructure are significant. The problem is best understood by the weak link in the chain analogy. The security of the corporate infrastructure is only as strong as its weakest link. With fixed (wired) devices, system administrators have some measure of control over the infrastructure. With a large number of mobile devices connecting from inside and outside the network, access to resources must be carefully controlled. System administrators must contend with the requirements of remote access to system resources behind the firewall, while still preventing unauthorized access to these same resources. This will require authentication, confidentiality, and authorization mechanisms. Even more, new risks posed by wireless devices will require strong software security mechanisms to ensure safe behavior, appropriate access control mechanisms, and detection and prevention of the proliferation of malicious software.

In addition to contending with the usual Internet security threats in online applications, wireless devices introduce new hazards specific to their mobility and communication medium. For instance, wireless devices can form ad hoc networks where a collection of peer mobile nodes communicate with each other without assistance from a fixed infrastructure.[4] One implication of ad hoc networks is that network decision making is decentralized. As a result, network protocols tend to rely on cooperation between all participating nodes. An adversary can exploit this vulnerability to compromise cooperative algorithms. An adversary that compromises a single node can disseminate false routing information to take down the ad hoc network or, worse, instruct all routing to go through the compromised node.[5]

Similarly, mobile users will roam through many different cells, ad hoc networks, administrative boundaries, and security domains. As the wireless connection is handed off from one domain to the next, a single malicious or compromised domain can potentially compromise wireless devices through malicious downloads, misinformation, or simple denial of service.

In summary, mobile and wireless devices introduce new security and privacy risks to both consumers and businesses. Using wireless devices for m-commerce will result in new vulnerabilities and potentially a new weak link in e-commerce.[6] The security of m-commerce systems is only as strong as its weakest link. In practice, malicious hackers attack weak links rather than waste time on harder problems. Therefore, an effective risk management strategy is to identify weak links and make these stronger, thus making the effort at compromising m-commerce systems more difficult for would-be attackers.

Vendors of wireless devices and systems are beginning to promote their products as the secure mobile e-commerce solution. Before buying into the marketing literature, it is important to understand the risks involved in m-commerce transactions. In this chapter, we explore the technology risks in m-commerce by systematically highlighting weak links in each of the different component technologies involved in m-commerce transactions: the wireless device, mobile code for wireless devices, the communication link, and the wireless content server systems.

The Wireless Device

The wireless device consists of hardware and software, each posing its own security and vulnerability properties. One characteristic often touted as a virtue is the small form factor that hand-held devices have. The virtue is that because they are small, they can be kept on your person, and personal (physical) security measures can be used to keep the devices secure. Another virtue is that because these devices tend not to be shared (either physically, such as shared workstations) or logically (such as shared file systems, at least for the moment), they are relatively secure devices to store very confidential information such as private keys. The small form factor, however, has its own risks. For instance, PDAs are often set down, lost, or stolen. Their small size makes them easier to forget and to steal. As a result, very confidential information can be easily lost or stolen, creating potentially big headaches with certificate revocation and recovering other lost data.

Unfortunately, the perceived virtues of personal physical security may have been taken too much to heart by the device manufacturers. As an example, the user authentication mechanisms on these devices installed by the manufacturers tend to be either trivially breakable or non-existent. As a result, if the device is stolen, the adversary will not have a very hard time logging in and gaining access to confidential data and applications.

The small form factor of the devices also places constraints on the amount of CPU cycles, memory, long-term storage, display, user input mechanism, and peripherals (such as modems) that can be installed with the device. One of the key risks with limited resources is that denial-of-service attacks that consume all available CPU, network bandwidth, and memory are relatively easy to implement. Even inadvertent risks such as bandwidth-hungry applications can quickly bring wireless networks to their knees. Imagine Napster- and Gnutella-like programs downloading music files or software over wireless networks around the clock. Also, because hand-helds are notoriously power hungry (particularly those with color displays), the user will often run low on batteries. If the batteries have died completely, important data in volatile memory can be lost. Perhaps most importantly, though, the physical constraints on power consumption, processing speed, and memory have caused manufacturers to forgo implementing secure technologies in the devices to optimize performance.

The small display size and limited bandwidth of PDAs inhibit the amount and type of information that can be physically displayed to the end user, necessitating special browsers or Web sites for "clipped" content. A small display size might pose unusual risks, such as the user not seeing the full context of transactions if he or she is not aware that paging is needed. The fact that hand-helds do have a display is a significant virtue over smartcards that might require connections with untrusted devices to display transactions. Unlike smartcards, if the wireless device is programmed accordingly, the device's display can be used to inform the user when transactions are taking place and to detail particulars of the transactions.

The platform or operating system that the device runs is equally important to determining security risks. For instance, as of this writing, the Palm OS provides no memory protection for its applications. This failing poses serious threats for each application's own security and privacy. For instance, a trusted application that uses a private key for signing documents can be attacked by a rogue application. The rogue application can attempt to steal the decrypted key in the signing application's memory by interrupting it at just the right time.[7] Other important operating system attributes include access control to files, the ability for untrusted entities to write programs to disk, differentiated privileges (administrator versus user, for example), file sharing over networks, and the robustness and quality of operating system code.

To address these platform risks, the PDA operating system needs to enforce memory protection between applications to prevent one application from spying on another. The second fundamental protection necessary is access control for principals and objects to prevent unprivileged programs and users from accessing confidential data, such as private keys or confidential information in databases. The operating system should also support encrypted tunnels or VPNs to provide confidential access over insecure wireless links. Finally, strong authentication mechanisms should be built in to authenticate the user to the device, such as fingerprint biometrics or simply encrypted passwords.

Application Software Risks

Software applications that run on the platform pose considerable risks to the device and to m-commerce applications. The two significant risks with application software are malicious code and inadvertently flawed code. In Chapter 5, "Mobile and Malicious Code," the topic was discussed at length. Here we explore its use against wireless devices.

Malicious Software Risks

Now with the advent of wireless Internet access to PDAs, malicious code will have a new platform on which to wreak havoc and spread. Some PDAs already offer the ability to exchange files and programs using infrared (IR) links. Most provide the ability to download software from personal computers. Soon, most will be downloading program executables and active content in addition to Web data over wireless Internet connections. Anytime a communication link between intelligent devices is offered, whether it is cellular, fixed-line, a desktop sync unit, an AirPort, infrared, Bluetooth protocols, or competing and succeeding wireless communication standards, you run the risk of downloading, running, and spreading malicious code.

On the PDA or other wireless device, it is likely that code will be pushed to the user, often without his or her consent. The user is less apt to use the device as a general-purpose computer and more apt to use the device to communicate and use online applications. As a result, many feature enhancements, upgrades, and even new software installs will be downloaded automatically without the user's knowledge or blessing, in order to make the experience less PC-like and more appliance-like.

The push paradigm made its splash with PointCast on personal computers, but it has become more subtle recently, embedding itself within operating systems with names like Active Desktop. Many software applications will automatically upgrade themselves, either by scheduled pull or by vendor pushes of new patches and release versions to their installed subscriber base. Although leaving the user out of the loop for downloading and installing software makes software more usable and dynamic, it poses serious risks by providing a new vector for malicious software to automatically download, install, and run. We can expect that the push paradigm will be heavily used for wireless applications.

In many current and future m-commerce applications, digital signing of documents or transactions will be an essential component, both for establishing authenticity of principals and for providing non-repudiation in transactions. In the future, courts may consider digital signatures on documents to hold the legal weight and authority of hand-written signatures on physical documents. Malicious software can compromise this system by signing documents on the user's behalf without the user's knowledge. Doing so is relatively easy. In many browsers and mailers that support signing, passphrases that unlock private keys for signing are cached by design for ease of use. Malicious software can use the cached passphrase to sign documents without the signatory's knowledge. If digital signatures are legally binding, this can create legal liability for actions the user did not perform. Even without cached passphrases, most passphrases can be decrypted from non-volatile RAM by DES key attacks or by dictionary attacks against login PINs and passwords.

Disclosure of confidential documents or data is one of the most salient risks of malicious software. The user has little observability or control over which data is sent out over the wireless connection. If the malicious software cannot perform a DES key attack on the device itself, it can send the encrypted private key out to an adversary site for offline decryption.

Malicious software also undermines confidentiality provided by encryption protocols and VPNs. When establishing a secure online connection between the wireless device and a server, the data is decrypted typically at the server gateway and at the data reader (browser or mailer) on the device. At either end of the connection, the encrypted data is decrypted and stored in plain text in non-volatile RAM or disk. Rather than attempting to break the secure channel, an adversary need only compromise the device (or the gateway or server) to gain access to the confidential data in clear text. Malicious software serves this purpose well. A malicious application, script, or executable that is downloaded or pushed to the device can read confidential data in plain text and send it out over the wireless link (even over an encrypted channel!) to the adversary's site.

To provide protection against malicious code risks, program install filters should be built into wireless device platforms so that software cannot automatically install and run without the user's knowledge.

Furthermore, software should carry digital certificates of authenticity that vouch not only for the author or publisher of the software, but also for the integrity of the software so that the end user will know it has not been corrupted. The user will be required then to approve all requested new software installations and upgrades.

Just Plain Bad Software

The other serious category of application risks is flawed software. This topic is discussed at length for desktop machines in Chapter 2, "Security Is a Software Problem," and Chapter 3, "Securing Software," and is equally relevant to wireless devices, especially as the application software market grows for wireless devices. Recall that most computer security violations in practice are made by exploiting flawed software.

As the market for PDA application software heats up, more and more applications will be available for the most popular platforms such as the Palm OS, EPOC, and Windows CE. The more ubiquitous a particular platform becomes, the greater the software base will be, and the more likely the platform will be threatened with application-based attacks.

The most pervasive software flaw is the buffer overrun flaw. This flaw is created when the software developer fails to check the length of incoming input buffers before copying the buffer to a stack frame variable. The result is that an attacker able to exploit a buffer overrun flaw can run arbitrary code on the machine, often with superuser privileges. Most buffer overrun flaws occur in programs written in unsafe languages such as C, which do not perform type checking. PDAs are a prime risk because the development languages tend to be C or even assembly. A safer language for wireless application development would be a type-safe language such as Java. Sun Microsystems Java Platform 2, Micro Edition, is expected to be available for the Palm operating system in the future.

Traditionally, most application-based attacks are launched against servers, rather than the client systems. In m-commerce transactions, the client software may be the target of malicious servers. For instance, a malicious server will attempt to gain information about the client, such as type of platform, user, e-mail address, and any software version numbers to reveal potential vulnerabilities. Furthermore, mobile code or active content applications are likely to play a large part in m-commerce transactions. Many attacks against mobile code applications are against the mobile code interpreter, which will typically run on the browser. Thus, a server may attempt to overrun buffers in a PDA browser, an applet may attempt to break type safety, or an active script may attempt to crash its interpreter. Once code is involved in exploiting software flaws, the problem really goes back to the malicious code problem discussed in the preceding section. Malicious mobile code issues are explored in depth in the next section.

Finally, as PDAs are given more and more horsepower, they will likely become servers in some fashion, whether it is to act as a server for distributed applications, as a mail or ftp server, or even as a Web server. The H/PC Pro companion can already run ftp, TFTP, and Web server software. Host-based intrusion detection approaches can play an important role in detecting attacks against these services.

Attacking Wireless Devices via Mobile Code

One of the most interesting developments in wireless devices is the ability to send and execute mobile code. In the wired world, mobile code is used pervasively in Web pages. The risks of active scripting against desktop computers are only now beginning to be understood and appreciated (see Chapter 5). Scripting will have ample uses in the wireless world, too, and will pose even more significant threats. Client-side processing in wireless devices is attractive for reducing the number of communication hits necessary on the extremely bandwidth-limited wireless links. For instance, client-side form validation reduces unnecessary server-side error reports and reentry messages. Furthermore, some server-side processing can be offloaded to clients using mobile code that will increase the availability of servers to more simultaneous connections. Third, scripting will be pervasive in wireless Web computing for the same reason it is ubiquitous in wired Web pages: Web page development leverages JavaScript heavily for display functions and client-side transaction processing.

Ever since the spate of Melissa-style malicious VBScripts hit the Internet in 1998, the problem of mobile scripts has begun to become appreciably recognized. Unfortunately, the commercial anti-virus industry can muster only a reactive approach to fighting active scripting threats, as described in Chapter 5. Although the e-mail viruses released to date have been mostly VBScript-based, there is no reason why the same types of attacks could not be launched using JavaScript. In the following sections, we describe the threat of WML scripts to wireless applications and devices. We use WAP-enabled cellular phones as our case study. Like most communication protocols, WAP is a layered protocol usually implemented as a network stack in devices. The service at any given layer is provided to the service of the layer above it, while it derives services from the layer beneath it. The layered model of WAP aligns with the ISO/OSI 7-layer model for network communications from the Wireless Datagram Protocol (WDP) up through several protocol layers to the Wireless Application Environment (WAE).[8]

Most wireless security discussions have focused on the Wireless Transport Layer Security (WTLS), which sits above the Wireless Datagram Protocol. Like SSL, WTLS provides authentication and confidentiality services for wireless connections. It does not provide any assurance against malicious content that runs on the device, nor for online application exploits of WAP servers. For this reason, we focus the discussion on the WAE layer, and specifically on WML scripts that run in the application layer of wireless devices.[9]

WML Script

WML Script is the wireless equivalent of JavaScript. More accurately, WML Script is based on JavaScript and uses similar syntax and constructs and provides semantically equivalent functions. WML Script, however, was specifically developed for capability-limited WAP-enabled wireless devices. WML Script is designed to be loaded from Wireless Markup Language (WML) pages—the wireless surrogate for HTML derived from XML. The primary reason WML and WML Script were developed was to work with the limited display, bandwidth, processing, and storage capacities of wireless hand-held devices, such as cellular phones. While WML Script is optimized to work with the bandwidth- and capability–limited facilities of WAP-enabled devices, it is designed to attempt to replicate JavaScript functionality as much as possible. In addition, specific libraries are distributed with WML Script engines to provide access to device-specific facilities, such as telephony functions.

One of the main reasons for using WML Script is to provide a uniform interface to wireless applications and functions, independent of the device brand. Until recently, most functions available on cellular phones were native and built in by the manufacturer. For instance, voice mail, call management, and personal address books, among other myriad functions, were device-specific and varied by manufacturer. Given the number of different phone manufacturers, these differences present significant challenges to wireless phone service providers in terms of both compatibility and usability for wireless customers.

The industry is now quickly moving to provide these features via WML Script using the WML Script interpreter as the standard development platform across different manufacturer's devices. The idea is that the interface and functionality for these different wireless services will be the same regardless of which particular brand of wireless device the customer chooses. This also would make it possible to use different phones without requiring the user to reprogram personal preferences, data, and functionality.

Security Risks of WML Script

Like the developers of the wireless device platforms, the developers of WML Script have ignored the lessons learned from past security problems with JavaScript and other mobile code technologies. The security risks associated with WML Script are based on a fundamental lack of a model for secure computation. The WML Script specification does not call for the distinction most JavaScript interpreters make between trusted local code and untrusted JavaScript downloaded from the Internet.[10] As a result, WML Script is given the same amount of access whether it is downloaded from a trusted service provider, is built into the phone, or is downloaded from untrusted sites. The lack of access control for WML Script means that the types of attacks that can be launched using WML Script will be limited only by the imagination of malicious script writers.

For efficiency reasons, WML Script is compiled into a WML Script bytecode, which is downloaded by the client, and run on a WML Script virtual machine, or interpreter. Though the wireless industry uses the terms "bytecode" and "virtual machine," these should not be confused to embody the same type safety properties of Java or to enforce a sandboxing mechanism.[11] Indeed, WML Script is not a type-safe language, nor does the VM or interpreter appear to enforce any kind of sandboxing mechanism to prevent WML Script from accessing persistent storage or making network accesses.[12] In fact, a WML Script can download remote WML Scripts using standard URL requests. Though URL domain/path checking is performed before a script can be downloaded and run, the check is a server-side check and will not prevent client-side damage from a malicious script. Furthermore, WML Script can be pushed to clients (using scheduled pulls from Web pages or other WML scripts) unbeknownst to the device owner.

Unlike the JavaScript interpreters in most desktop browsers, the WML Script virtual machine currently does not appear to have a mechanism for preventing access to persistent storage on the device from untrusted scripts.[13] As a result, personally identifying information kept on the device is susceptible to unauthorized disclosure from malicious WML scripts that can download, read the personal information, then ship it off to other sites. Given the limited amount of storage capability on phones currently, this may be the least interesting of attacks.

More interesting attacks will involve online application duplicity and e-mail virus attacks. Consider that many online applications require users to authenticate themselves using an account identifier and pass-word. Using WML Script, an attacker can send the user an e-mail with the account holder's favorite banking page. The WML script can be used to rewrite all the links on the page to redirect the user to a page under its control where it can ask the user to reauthenticate, grab the user name and password, then forward the user on to the real bank page. The malicious site can then use captured user accounts and PINs to its own malicious advantage. Another example of up-and-coming WAP applications will be the ability to charge purchases in real time (for example, buying movie tickets) to their wireless phone bill, to e-cash stored on the phone's smartcard, or to an online account of credit with a bank. WML Script will be used heavily for these types of online transactions for processing the client-side portion of the transaction. Malicious WML scripts will have the ability to falsely ring up charges or potentially offload money from smartcards or bank accounts.

Because WML Script can access persistent stores, it will be fairly trivial to write WML scripts that can destroy user data stored on the device. As the persistent store sizes grow and more applications are ported to WAP-enabled devices, such as document processing applications, the value of the data stored in persistent storage will grow, giving virus writers more incentive to write damaging scripts.

Script worms will also be written that use Web, chat room, and e-mail capabilities to spread via cell devices. Initially, these worms will simply propagate from phone to phone, consuming precious wireless bandwidth and possibly running up phone charges for end users. Because access device storage is not well constrained, in the future, they will behave maliciously by shipping off or destroying valuable personal data.

Another interesting area for malicious scripts to exploit is telephony applications, much as the DoCoMo CompactHTML worm did. WML Script provides access to telephony functions through the Wireless Telephony Application Interface (WTAI).[14] Access to the telephony facilities of the phone allows online service providers to do the following:[15]

- Accept/initiate calls
- Send/receive text messages
- Add/search/remove phonebook entries
- Examine call logs
- Send tones during calls
- Press keys on keypad during a call

Realizing the potential security risks of WML Script accessing telephony functions of the phone, the Wireless Telephony Application (WTA) services rely on a couple of assumptions to provide security.[16] First, it is assumed the user will visit only trusted WAP gateways wherein a WTA server may run. The WTA server is simply a server that delivers WML Script over WAP connections to access the WTA functions on the phone. If the user hits an untrusted WAP gateway that sends WML Script with WTA functionality, it is possible for the WML script to make random phone calls, send personal data through a phonebook, or even erase a phonebook. Hence, the security model here is that the user should hit only trusted WAP gateways. If WAP-enabled devices and services grow as predicted, this assumption will rapidly become untenable, as many vendors will launch sites with their own WML pages and WML scripts.

The second assumption made for secure functionality is that a user will securely configure his or her device, not to give blanket permission for any WML script to access the WTA functions. In fact, there are three permission types available to access WTA functionality: *blanket permis-*

sion to access all functions within a WTAI library, *context permission* to run a given WTA function within the current execution context, and *single action permission* to access a given WTA function once.[17]

Finally, it is worth mentioning that the WTA specifications do not define any default permission settings. Rather, these settings are determined by the mobile service provider. If history is any indication, service providers will preconfigure devices with liberal permissions to permit access to their own scripts without regard for other potentially malicious scripts.

In summary, the WML Scripting capability built into WAP 1.2-compliant devices will provide a fertile breeding ground for the current generation of malicious scripts that run unabated in wired platforms. Furthermore, without any foundational security model, the severity of attacks against wireless devices will increase as these devices become more critical to users and businesses in both storage and processing of confidential information.

Wireless Network Risks

Much work has been performed in communications security over the last several decades, starting with information theory and including the latest advances in elliptic curve cryptography. In spite of the maturity of the field, wireless devices pose new and significant threats to Internet-based commerce because of the nature of the communication medium they use.

The nature of wireless networks makes them vulnerable to attack. Each wireless device serves as its own node in ad hoc dynamic networks. Mobile devices are autonomous units that roam from network to network. Unlike fixed-wire networks, in wireless ad hoc networks, the physical network need not be attacked, nor is there a fixed network infrastructure that can be physically protected with bricks and locks or logically protected with firewalls and gateways.

Rather than an attacker needing to pursue a target, targets can come to attackers in wireless networks simply by roaming through the attacker's zone. Wireless devices pass through many different untrusted networks from which service is derived and data is exchanged. Information can be stolen or altered without the end user knowing any better. Service can be, and is often, easily denied, inadvertently or not. Transactions can be interrupted, then reinstated, often without reauthenticating principals. Requests can be redirected and malicious code surreptitiously downloaded together with expected Web data.

As users roam through various untrusted networks, connections are handed off from one zone to another. During hand-offs, connections may be interrupted mid-transaction. Simply "refreshing" a browser to reestablish the connection may inadvertently introduce risks. For instance, the new zone may be a malicious one that reestablishes a connection with a malicious entity whose purpose it is to capture account and password information. Reestablishing connections and transactions without authenticating principals on both sides of the transactions can be dangerous. Most Web sites currently are not configured to deal with intermittent service failures, as are common to wireless connections. Most vendor implementations of SSL do not reauthenticate principals or recheck certificates once a connection has been established within the current session. Attackers can use this vulnerability to their advantage in wireless networks.

The wireless network is ripe for man-in-the-middle attacks, well known to the fixed-wire Internet. In man-in-the-middle attacks, an attacker will interpose its site or service between the end user and the intended destination site. Often, the attacker's site will give the look and feel of the intended site. For instance, if the user were to check CNNfn regularly for stock quotes in and around airports, a malicious user can alter directory naming services (DNS) in ad hoc networks around the airport to redirect all CNNfn requests to its site. Because secure DNS is still not implemented and deployed in practice, it is not very difficult to compromise the DNS, simply by establishing your own DNS server that other people necessarily trust. Providing the same look and feel of a Web site is easy because it can be duplicated perfectly simply by downloading the site. The insidious part of the attack is in discreetly changing dynamic information—such as stock quotes—to benefit the malicious entity.

The wireless medium also provides excellent cover for malicious users. Because wireless devices roam in and out of wireless zones, have no fixed geographic point, can go online and offline easily, and have much of the capability of wired devices, the devices and their users can be difficult to trace. As a result, attacks from wireless devices will likely become the preferred *modus operandi* of attackers for launching attacks against fixed networks.

Much is made of cryptographic algorithms and protocols over wireless networks. Without doubt, mobile e-commerce will require confidentiality, integrity, and authentication services provided by cryptographic protocols. To do without is foolhardy. To believe that these protocols provide the panacea to m-commerce security problems is dangerous. The examples given in earlier malicious code show how confidential data sent over encrypted channels can be easily compromised from within.

It is important to remember that while all crypto protocols may look identical off-the-shelf, it is what is underneath the hood that matters. It is very difficult to design a solid crypto protocol, but it is even harder to implement it robustly. Flaws in the software that implement crypto protocols often make it easy enough to break crypto algorithms without resorting to brute-force attacks against ciphertext. Poor use of pseudo-random-number generators (PRNGs) as well as use of flawed PRNGs commonly undermine even good crypto algorithms.

As is often the case in crypto protocols, the use of the protocol gives the perception of stronger security than the actual implementation. In general, crypto protocols are assumed to be secure until someone finds the card that brings down the house of cards. It is very difficult to tell from looking at ciphertext how strong the crypto algorithm is. It requires analysis of the algorithm, design, and implementation to find potential problems. Often, commercial encryption protocols are closed source and not available for peer review. As a result, crypto protocols are assumed to be secure unless proven otherwise. The upshot is that consumers feel more secure when using "secure" protocols in m-commerce, which is good for the industry. It also has the effect of giving a false sense of security when there are so many other weak links in the system. Strong perceived security will redirect the resources of adversaries to other weak links, as discussed in the preceding sections.

Wireless Content Servers

One of the major risk areas in m-commerce is the wireless content servers themselves. The servers present ideal targets for adversaries because they are single points of failure where valuable data and services are concentrated. Most servers are vulnerable to denial-of-service (DoS) attacks as the distributed DoS attacks against the largest e-commerce sites in February 2000 vividly illustrated.[18] The risk of denial-of-service is even greater for wireless content servers. Today, single wireless content servers provide access to and translation services for a great number of Web sites, making them an ideal target for DoS attacks.

Targeting a server makes more sense than targeting many individual clients. The return on investment is greater. Breaking into a single server has yielded more than 300,000 credit card numbers of customers of an e-commerce site. If one wanted to compromise the integrity of a financial institution, what better way than to break into its Web site and simply vandalize its Web pages, let alone gain access to its customers' online accounts?

In m-commerce systems, the small display size of hand-held wireless devices makes translation of standard HTML Web pages necessary. The Wireless Markup Language (WML) was created for this purpose. Currently, most cellular phones make requests for the limited number of WML-formatted sites. HTML to WML translation services have grown in demand as more customers are clamoring for access to their favorite Web sites. When wireless devices such as cellular phones make Wireless Application Protocol (WAP) requests for a particular HTML page, a translation service can translate the requested HTML to WML and return the trimmed Web pages in WML format to the phone over the WAP connection.

This layer of indirection potentially opens up other vulnerabilities in the system aside from the denial-of-service vulnerability mentioned previously. For instance, in order to support Secure Sockets Layer (SSL) sessions, a secure session must be established with the WAP gateway using the Wireless Transport Layer Security (WTLS)—the wireless SSL surrogate. The connection request is then made to the HTML Web site, presumably over SSL. The connection must be encrypted and decrypted at the WAP gateway, opening another single point of vulnerability for attackers to gain access to confidential information.

Last Word

In this chapter, we present several new risks in mobile e-commerce systems. One of the main goals of this chapter is to dispel the notion that m-commerce systems will be secured simply by using off-the-shelf encryption protocols or software packages. Instead, this chapter highlights several weak links in m-commerce systems. As in most e-commerce systems, the system is only as strong as its weakest link. Furthermore, the weakest link actually directs the efforts of adversaries for reasons of efficiency and return on investment.

While many of the risks of desktop e-commerce will pervade m-commerce, m-commerce itself presents new risks. The nature of the medium requires a degree of trust and cooperation between member nodes in networks that can be exploited by malicious entities to deny service as well as collect confidential information and disseminate false information.

Encrypted communication protocols are necessary to provide confidentiality, integrity, and authentication services for mobile e-commerce applications. The protocols themselves present their own unique risks, as discussed earlier. Perhaps the greatest risk of encrypted communication links is the false sense of security they give wireless users and purveyors of mobile e-commerce.

Probably the most significant risks for m-commerce systems are from malicious code that will begin to penetrate wireless networks and from flawed software that runs on both wireless devices and m-commerce servers. Malicious code has the ability to undermine other security technologies such as signing, authentication, and encryption because they run resident to the device with all the privileges of the owner. As agent-based commerce becomes an integral part of m-commerce, it will be difficult to distinguish malicious agents from benign ones. If agents are given the authority or proxy to act on behalf of the device's owner in both a commercial and a legal sense, then the ramifications of malicious code attacks grow even more significantly.

M-commerce servers are particularly vulnerable to application-based attacks because of the growing complexity of the software that runs these systems. Software flaws in the middleware layer are likely to be exploited by determined adversaries and their disciples as they get published in underground lists. The servers are particularly rich targets because they represent single points of failure and the highest return on investment for an attacker's efforts.

In summary, the best strategy for securing mobile e-commerce is a risk management strategy that begins by identifying weak links. Once weak links are identified, the threat understood, and the consequences of attack quantified, effective software risk management will concentrate efforts on design and assurance activities in m-commerce software systems.

Notes

1. B. Zerega, "The 3G Force", *Red Herring*, August 1999, pp. 84–88.

2. T. Lewis, "Ubinet: The Ubiquitous Internet Will Be Wireless," *IEEE Computer*, 32(10) (October 1999): 126–127, 128.

3. Ibid.

4. Y. Zhang and W. Lee, "Intrusion Detection in Wireless Ad-hoc Networks," in *Proceedings of the ACM/IEEE MobiCom2000*, August 2000.

5. Ibid.

6. A.K. Ghosh, *E-Commerce Security: Weak Links, Best Defenses* (New York: John Wiley & Sons, 1998).

7. D. Balfanz and E. Felten, "Hand-Held Computers Can Be Better Than Smart Cards," in *Proceedings of the Eighth USENIX Security Symposium*, USENIX Association, August 23–26, 1999, Washington D.C.

8. WAP Forum, *WAP Architecture: Wireless Application Protocol Architecture Specification*, Technical Report, WAP Forum, April 30, 1998. Available online: www.wapforum.org.

9. WAP Forum, *Wireless Application Environment Specification v.1.3*, Technical Report WAP-190-WAESpec, WAP Forum, March 29, 2000. Available online: www.wapforum.org.

10. WAP Forum, *Wireless Markup Language Script Specification v.1.2*, Technical Report WAP-193-WMLScript, WAP Forum, June 2000. Available online: www.wapforum.org.

11. G. McGraw and E. Felten, *Java Security: Hostile Applets, Holes, and Antidotes* (New York: John Wiley & Sons, 1996).

12. See endnote 10.

13. Ibid.

14. WAP Forum, *Wireless Telephony Application Interface Specification*, Technical Report WAP-170-WTAI, WAP Forum, July 7, 2000. Available online: www.wapforum.org.

15. WAP Forum, *Wireless Telephony Application Specification*, Technical Report WAP-169-WTA, WAP Forum, July 7, 2000. Available online: www.wapforum.org.

16. C. Arehart et al., *Professional WAP* (Birmingham, UK: Wrox Press, Ltd., Arden House, 2000).

17. Ibid.

18. L. Garber, "Denial-of-Service Attacks Rip the Internet," *IEEE Computer*, 33(4) (April 2000): 12–17.

CHAPTER 7

Privacy in an Online World

"You have zero privacy anyway . . . Get over it."

SCOTT McNEALY
CEO, SUN MICROSYSTEMS

Scott McNealy's comments set off a firestorm among privacy advocates. Just the same, his comments on the folly of privacy protection resonated with a cynical attitude toward privacy among many of the digerati. The comment reflects the sentiment that there is no sense trying to close the barn because the horse has already bolted. There is so much data being collected about you all the time, from your purchasing patterns on your credit card/check card, the calls you make, your physical location when your cell phone or wireless device is on, your online browsing habits, to your shopping habits when you use your club card that there is very little left in our lives that remains private. For now, we rest comfortably at night with the belief that there is no way that all these disparate data collectors are in collusion to fit all the pieces together. But, if someone did have access to all this data, they could get a fairly complete picture of nearly every detail of our lives. With data mining technology growing in sophistication, data warehouses growing in size, corporate acquisitions increasingly valuing database profiles of users, and custom mass marketing to the individual being the holy grail of online marketing, chances are that one day in the near future a company will be able to assemble all the different pieces of our lives captured in bits in our ever-digitized world.

Simson Garfinkel's *Database Nation: The Death of Privacy in the 21st Century* (O'Reilly, 2000) provides an eye-opening indictment of how pervasive data collection is in our lives. In this chapter, we focus on privacy issues in e-business. While it is hard to argue that privacy is a consumer issue, increasingly, it is also a very real business issue. Businesses that fail to heed the call to respect consumer privacy will lose business to those good e-businesses that do. Privacy is the new hot button issue in online commerce, and especially so in mobile e-commerce, where the privacy issues are magnified. One of the biggest issues in online privacy is simply not knowing what information is being collected about you. Most people, when informed and given a choice, do not have much issue with the types of data collection currently practiced. Most privacy issues stem from fear, uncertainty, and doubt (FUD, in business speak) with what some faceless and nameless big brother knows about you. In this chapter, we attempt to demystify the uncertainty surrounding privacy in e-business and provide pointers to tools and practices that give you greater control over your personal information. Informed users and forthright businesses are more likely to reach a mutually acceptable agreement regarding collection and usage of data. Companies that are forthright about data collection and protection can use privacy protection as an opportunity to build stronger relationships with their customers.

The Security-Privacy Relationship

Unfortunately, many people use security and privacy interchangeably. While they are related, it is useful to understand their distinctions and their dependencies. Privacy refers to aspects of individuals or entities that the owner wants to remain confidential from third-party interests. These aspects include data, properties, and behavioral characteristics such as the schedule we keep and our shopping habits. Data includes all documents the individual wishes to keep confidential. Properties include those defining aspects of the individual or entity, such as physical attributes and preferences, such as religious faith.

When people talk about security, they often mean data confidentiality. Clearly there is some relationship between security and privacy. In order to have privacy, we must have security. That is, if there is to be any hope of privacy, the aspects that wish to remain private must have security measures in place to keep them private. This applies both to individuals wishing to protect their privacy and to corporations that collect privacy-related data. Corporations that do not have a secure infrastructure cannot ensure that the confidential data they collect can be kept private. Likewise, individuals who wish to keep their data private (for example, files on their computer's hard drive or their Web browsing habits) cannot expect these aspects to remain private if they do not have security provisions to keep these particular aspects private.

There is clearly a dependency relationship between security and privacy, but it is not symmetric. While one must have security to ensure privacy, by no means does having a secure infrastructure imply privacy. For instance, even if a company that collects personal data stores it in an ultra-secure facility, the company may at any point in time choose to sell or otherwise disseminate this data, potentially violating the privacy of the individuals whose data it collected. Even though this point may seem obvious, it is important that one not confuse boasts of security with an expectation of privacy. Likewise, boasts of privacy should be viewed with skepticism unless the entity can demonstrate it has the capability and will to secure the data. A laudable privacy policy by a company that cannot protect its data is not worth the HTML in which it is written.

In summary, security and privacy, though distinct, are intricately related. Though security and privacy are often used interchangeably, it is also foolhardy to talk about privacy without security, or for companies to talk about security while ignoring the privacy implications of the data they collect from their users and partners. Although they should not be used interchangeably, one should not be considered without the other.

Online Privacy Policy

Most e-businesses are keenly aware that it is politically correct, if not imperative, to have online privacy policies. What is unclear is what these policies should say and how they should be implemented and enforced. To develop a meaningful privacy policy, it is important to start with consumers' privacy concerns. These will, in turn, guide the development of basic privacy policies that companies will need to implement. From a customer perspective, there are at least four main privacy concerns:

- What information is collected about users
- How collected information is used and for what purpose
- How collected information is secured, shared, rented, sold, or otherwise disseminated
- How much personal information about an individual can be collected, aggregated, stored, and ultimately used

These concerns really highlight the amount of uncertainty about business practices in collecting and using personal data. The lack of published information, and often the lack of knowledge about existing data collection and use practices even within an organization, gives rise to much of the fear surrounding privacy. Privacy involves not only confidentiality of data, but also privacy of behavior. That is, an important privacy concern with many folks is the right to be free from profiling of habits, such as the types of purchases we make, the hours we spend online, the stores we go to, and other personal preferences. Most people accept that companies profile their employees inside corporate networks (to detect intruders, for instance), but do companies have the right to profile consumers shopping at their site? Do they then have the right to sell these profiles? Who owns this data, and is the data covered by contract? These are important questions for which we still do not have definitive answers.

The following are examples of privacy concerns in everyday computer usage:

- When I surf the Web from work and send out e-mail, what information about my online usage is my employer collecting?
- What information about my Web browsing habits are stored in cookies, and with whom is this information shared?
- When I register my computer online with the manufacturer or the operating system vendor, what information is collected about my computer?
- Which applications on my machine is my registration information shared with?
- When my hard drive starts spinning arbitrarily and my modem lights start flashing, who is using the network?

Again, most privacy concerns stem from uncertainty over what's going on behind the scenes and the lack of published information about data collection practices. Basic tenets of online privacy require the following:

Notice. Companies need to declare explicitly what data they are collecting and for what purpose. Embedding these notices in the style of esoteric software license agreements will not work.

Choice. Customers should be able to review their personal data and make changes as desired.

Opt-in basis. If possible, users should have to opt in for collection of personal data, rather than having to opt out of data collection or being given no choice at all.

Compliance. Privacy policies without enforcement or verification of compliance are simply a promise—and, more often, a public relations ploy. In addition to policies, procedures need to be implemented to ensure compliance and, preferably, third-party verification.

These four basic tenets of privacy should serve as a guide for businesses to maintain good privacy practices for their customers. Serving notice of what data is collected will go a long way toward dispelling the fear, uncertainty, and doubt created by privacy concerns. The mistake some sites make, though, is to put their privacy policy in complicated legalese form like those found in software license agreements. As everyone knows, nobody besides overly gung-ho lawyers actually reads these agreements. If the intention is simply to protect your company from a legal standpoint, a legalese-type document might serve the purpose. If the purpose is to inform your customers and build a relationship based on trust, the privacy policy needs to be communicated in language a 12-year-old child can understand.

Giving users choice to both review and amend their privacy data is a very progressive step that some forward-thinking companies are beginning to adopt. Microsoft provides this capability on one of its Web sites. The idea is to provide full disclosure of what data is actually collected about individual users, then to allow the user to correct any errors in the information. The benefits of this approach are numerous. Customers will know exactly what data is collected, eliminating a lot of uncertainty. Second, with the ability to change the data online, customers will be able to correct mistakes, businesses will have more accurate data, and a trust relationship can be built between business and customer.

One of the most contentious issues in online commerce is the practice of opt-in data collection versus opt-out. An opt-in stance is a privacy-friendly approach that requires the customer to give the site approval to collect his or her data. Opt-out policies, used by the majority of sites, collect data on customers by default. They also allow the customer to request no data collection. In other words, the customer has the choice to opt out of the default data collection practices. In either case, the customer is given some choice in the matter of data collection, but the distinction is what data collection practice the business follows by default. The least privacy-friendly policy is to collect customer data without the customer's knowledge and approval, nor provide the ability for the customer to opt out of data collection. Unfortunately, this is the status quo today in online commerce. For many businesses, establishing an easily accessible and understandable opt-out policy is good enough for both businesses and consumers. The real problems in privacy stem from when customers do not know what data is being collected about them and do not have any recourse to examine, change, or stop the data collection practices.

Developing a good privacy policy is one matter of importance; compliance is a separate one, and one that has been largely ignored by businesses. Many e-businesses are savvy enough to develop sound privacy policies. Compliance with the policy is an entirely different matter. In many cases, online privacy policies are merely a public relations ploy to assuage concerns over privacy. What happens behind the scenes can bear little resemblance to the letter and spirit of carefully drafted privacy policies. In other words, having a privacy policy without implementing its stated practices is simply false advertising. Most people see the logic in this argument. Compliance with privacy policies, however, is often difficult to assess.

In some cases, breaches of stated privacy policies are egregious and discernible even without third-party auditing. For instance, a survey conducted for the California HealthCare Foundation of the 21 most popular online medical sites found several breaches of their own posted privacy statements. Breaches included sharing personal and identifiable customer information with third-party sites, such as advertisers and advertising banner placement sites. Some sites carry advertisements from third parties that are forms requesting personal information. In many of these cases, it is difficult to distinguish who is asking for the information (the site you are visiting that has the privacy policy or the third-party advertiser) and where your personal information is actually going. Then there are cases of inadvertent data spillage between the hosting site and third parties such as advertisers. In March 2000, Intuit, the maker of popular financial planner Quicken, acknowledged that sensitive financial information customers entered in mortgage and credit calculators on Quicken's Web site was inadvertently sent to DoubleClick, the ubiquitous purveyor of online banner ads. Online medical advice sites are suffering a shake-out as they begin to move into uncharted territories of keeping patients' medical records online and sharing these with physicians and pharmaceutical firms. Early tests by DrKoop.com have shown that consumers are reluctant to share personal information, such as medical histories, online with people they have not met or do not trust.

The fine print in many privacy policies states that though the site will protect your own data, any data it shares with third parties may be used in any manner whatsoever. To make matters more difficult, some sites reserve the right to change their privacy policies at any time without notifying customers. In perhaps a poor public relations move, Amazon.com recently did notify its customers that it was changing the privacy policy so that customers could no longer prevent Amazon from selling their data to third parties. The change in policy angered many, while leaving others with questions about how the data that has been collected will be used in the future.

Once data is collected and archived, what assurances do customers have that the data will not be shared in the future under a different privacy policy? In an era of mergers and acquisitions, where customer databases are highly valued, these questions are becoming more relevant. For instance, the privacy policy that accompanied data collection under one company may be null and void when acquired by another. Merging firms can also merge databases to pull together different pieces of data about individuals to gain a more complete picture, and to significantly add value to collected data and the companies that maintain the data. A good example was the recent announcement of the merger between DoubleClick and Abacus Direct. DoubleClick is a firm that places ad banners on many different commercial Web sites and in the process creates online surfing profiles for individual users. It uses these profiles, together with information on which ads a customer has already seen, to determine which banner to place on a Web page the customer is visiting. Abacus Direct markets consumer purchasing data to offline catalog firms. Abacus has a large database of residential names and addresses. The merger between these two marketing media magnates would give the capability to merge their respective consumer databases. A database merger would effectively tie together offline personal information with online collected information, adding tremendous value to marketers for data collected online and offline. The large public outcry over the merger of these databases and scrutiny from the Federal Trade Commission has held off the database merger plans for the moment. But once the brouhaha simmers down to a dull roar, will DoubleClick merge the databases under the radar of the watchful public eye?

These cases bring up the need for compliance and third-party verification of privacy policies. As the case of medical sites illustrates, consumers do not yet feel comfortable with the privacy, confidentiality, and security of the data that is collected about them. Trusted third-party verification of Web sites' adherence to privacy policies can bridge the trust gap between consumers and online businesses. The most significant attempt at third-party verification has come from industry itself, rather than a government body. TRUSTe places its seal of approval on many Web sites to show that it has reviewed and approved the site's privacy policy. In theory, when a customer visits a site with the TRUSTe seal, the customer should be able to trust its privacy practices. The value of the seal, however, has been undermined by privacy incidents involving companies whose Web pages bear the seal. For instance, RealNetworks came under fire when its jukebox software collected the personal listening habits of users who downloaded the software and sent them to RealNetworks without notification or choice. The RealNetworks site bears the TRUSTe seal. Though TRUSTe does not cover privacy breaches due to application software, the distinction between Web-based collection and software-based collection was lost on most customers. Similarly, six of the medical sites found to be in violation of their stated privacy policies in the California HealthCare Foundation study bear the TRUSTe seal. Another potential problem with the TRUSTe seal program is that sites that obtain the seal pay for it. This model introduces an inherent conflict of interest, where the certifier has a financial interest in giving a seal of approval. As of this writing, TRUSTe still has yet to revoke a seal on one of its approved sites, in spite of several well-publicized privacy violations of member sites. One of the key problems is that TRUSTe, like other approval seal organizations, merely reviews and approves privacy policy. At the time of this writing, it, like others in its category, does not have the ability to audit and enforce compliance of the business with its policy.

Without independent third-party audit of an organization's compliance, consumers have little basis to trust whether the privacy policies are actually being enforced. Often, the businesses themselves do not know whether they are in compliance of their own privacy policies because data collection tends to be a technical matter rather than a policy matter that an executive can grasp. For instance, many businesses by default collect information about from where users are visiting because Web servers automatically log this information. Thus, even though they may have no intention to collect data and their privacy policy may reflect this stance, the actual practice is highly dependent on the technical implementation details.

To date, the U.S. government has let industry police itself regarding privacy policies. The current perception is that industry has not been doing a good enough job, particularly in the areas of notice, choice, and compliance. Though industry is loath to have the heavy hand of government involved, to some extent that may be inevitable, particularly in industries that are regulated offline, such as health care. New regulation, such as the Health Insurance Portability and Accountability Act (HIPAA), is designed to ensure strict accountability standards in the handling and dissemination of patient medical records. The punishment for HIPAA violations includes jail time for company executives. Thus, compliance will be particularly important for some regulated industries, and this will likely spill over into other Internet industries. Ironically, having a good privacy policy can place a business at risk if it does not also stay in compliance with its policies. For instance, the U.S. Federal Trade Commission (FTC) has considerable leverage to prosecute businesses that fail to adhere to their published privacy policies.

What We Know about You

As we have stated here often, one of the biggest problems that gives rise to most privacy fears is simply the lack of information about what information is actually being collected about you. In the online world, this problem is made worse because of the nature of the medium. First, consider the privacy consequences of shopping in person at your traditional brick-and-mortar retailer. When we buy something from a merchant in person, we know exactly what information we are giving up, even if we haven't considered all the consequences. For example, when paying by credit card or check, we give up our credit card numbers, account numbers, identity, and sometimes our social security number. This information might be more than you want to give if you are concerned about profiling of shopping habits and the possibility of the retailer profiling your shopping habits. In many states, drivers' license numbers are predesignated to be your social security number, unless you request otherwise.

With a social security number in hand, a resourceful individual or company can learn quite a lot about you including address, birth date, maiden name, occupation, earnings, and credit history. Social security numbers are used so pervasively as personal identifiers in the United States—far beyond the scope of the original intention of tracking earnings for social security administration—that they have become an unofficial national identifier. Many consumer profiles are tracked using social security numbers. In fact, identity theft, where someone else is able to masquerade as you possessing legitimate papers and credit cards with your identity, usually starts by stealing or misusing social security numbers. The number of incidents of identity theft has risen so dramatically as to become the fastest growing crime in the United States, prompting many calls for legislation for protecting identities and clearing credit records and police records tarnished by identity theft.[1] The Computer Risks Forum has covered identity theft for years.[2]

To make it even easier for retailers, many grocers have created club cards that are required to be presented at check out to be eligible for discounts on goods. Though they are pitched as a savings tool, the cards are really the means for grocery retailers to track the shopping habits of their customers. In order to receive the card, you must fill out a form that may include all kinds of personally identifying information including the names of members in your family and your address. When you present your card, the items you purchase are recorded in your profile. As you can imagine, by recording your grocery purchases, a pretty good profile of the way you live and your purchasing habits can be established—for better or worse. If the grocery store sees significant preferences for one brand of bread over another, it can use this information to stock up on the preferred brand and stock less on the unpopular brands. Similarly, you may have noticed that register-issued coupons printed on the fly are often based on what you actually purchase. Interestingly enough, the coupons will sometimes be issued from competing manufacturers to persuade you to buy their products next time. Some people feel a little uneasy about someone keeping track of their personal shopping purchases. Herein lies the rub of the new generation of commerce. In order to get discounts, one must "join the club" and give up personal information. Fortunately, this is an opt-in system. You can always forgo the discounts, which over time can add up to substantial savings, in order to preserve your privacy. You can pay by cash if you want even more privacy. The balance between privacy protection and data collection will in the future likely lie in this form of bartering personal information for some kind of reward. With club cards, the choice is clear: Give up personal shopping habits in return for savings. In online commerce, the choice is still not this explicit.

When you consider all the different types of electronic transactions we conduct on a daily basis, the number of different ways we can be monitored is staggering. Consider the following partial list of electronic monitoring compiled by *Time Magazine*:

ATM machines. Every time you withdraw money from a machine, a record of your location at a particular time and date is created.

Prescription plans. When you use your company's prescription plan to offset the cost of drugs, your employer may have access to the types of drugs you are taking and therefore be able to infer the types of illnesses you may be suffering from.

Cellular telephones. Because cell phones transmit radio waves on specific frequencies, anyone with a radio frequency scanner can monitor your conversations. Web-enabled cell phone surfing has its own privacy risks, too. Service providers Sprint PCS and AT&T Wireless transmit the phone numbers of cell phone owners to the Web sites they surf to on their Web-enabled phones. Cellular towers can also be used to triangulate your position if your cell phone is on. Some highway traffic management systems are considering using the number of cell phones per road area as a measure of traffic to replace cameras and helicopters for traffic reporting and forecasting.

Credit cards. We use credit cards to purchase just about anything. Your credit card transaction history provides a fairly complete picture of your life. Credit card histories are available to law enforcement officials, and credit histories are available to any number of merchants.

Phone calls. By default your phone number is broadcast with the phone call you make, unless you punch in the code to block your phone number.

Electronic toll collection. Transponders placed in cars are becoming the norm in areas with toll roads on busy commutes. The idea is that rather than stopping to drop coins, you can drive through the toll booth with the transponder that sends your account number to the receiver in a booth. The toll is automatically deducted from your account, and your credit card is charged to periodically refresh your prepaid balance. Therefore, a record of when you drive through specific toll booths is created. Discretely placed receivers can record your movements throughout a city. Look for transponders to move us through metro underground systems quickly in the future.

Surveillance cameras. Big brother is alive and well. Smile, you're on candid camera! From highways to convenience stores, public buildings, banks, private buildings, public squares, and even homes, surveillance cameras keep a record of our physical presence and enable remote online monitoring.

Employee badges. Once used solely to gain access to a building, now electronic badges, like toll transponders, note the times we enter and leave a facility, as well as our location throughout the facility.

Online monitoring. A business has the right to monitor all your computer usage from its machines: from keystroke monitoring to e-mail monitoring to Internet usage. Other people besides your company may also be monitoring your online usage. This is the subject of the rest of this chapter.

When shopping online, we generally have little idea about what information is being sent to the sites we visit. Unlike shopping in person, where you actually know what information you are giving up and have some choice in the matter, Web sites collect all kind of information about us without our knowledge or approval. A lot of this problem is due to the nature of the medium we use in online commerce, rather than malicious intentions of e-businesses. To get a more complete picture of where privacy concerns are, we take a systematic look at e-business transactions using the same elements as shown in Figure 4.4; however, rather than highlighting the security weak links, we highlight the points of exposure for private data. Figure 7.1 shows a generic *n*-tier architecture of an e-business with different privacy risks highlighted at

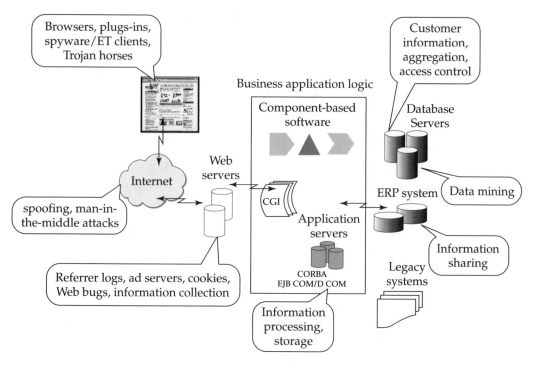

Figure 7.1 Privacy risks in e-commerce components.

different components in the architecture. In the following sections, we discuss privacy risks and techniques for capturing and processing private data at each of the main components in this architecture.

Client-Side Privacy Risks: The Mole on Your Desktop

The computer right in front of you might be your biggest privacy risk. Programs that run on your machine—whether on your desktop computer or on your handheld PDA—share more data about you than you might suspect. The main privacy risk in Web-based commerce is information given up by your own browser, voluntarily or not. Anytime you hit a Web site, the site can glean all kinds of information about your system from the information your browser sends. From your IP address that is sent with every packet, the site can learn what domain you are browsing from, whether it's your Internet Service Provider (ISP), your company, or your own domain. A simple reverse lookup on your IP address gives this information and more. It can also tell the name of your computer if it is assigned a host name within the domain. If the domain is your own, the registration information listed for that domain is also available, which will include point-of-contact names, addresses, and phone numbers. Complete specifications of your system can also be obtained from every Web site request including your operating system type, browser type and version, processor type, screen specifications, and even the types of active content you will accept including Java, VBScript, and JavaScript. Armed just with the system specification, any given site can determine whether you are vulnerable to any number of potential malicious code exploits that could further compromise your privacy.

While browsers give up information about you and your system, it is often the case that users voluntarily divulge much personal information. For instance, many online shopping sites request users to "register" with them. The upside is that once a personal profile is registered with the site, you will have fewer hassles in the future when transacting with the site. It will already know your mailing address, preferences, and sometimes even your credit card number. As a result, you need not fill out the same tiresome forms over again every time you purchase an item at the site. Great convenience, but you have also given up much personal information that the site can rent or sell to other sites. Some browsers take the additional step of setting this up for you automatically. Simply enabling autocomplete for forms in your browser will allow your browser to share your information with sites that interact with the autoform bot. This feature is certainly an enabler of e-commerce by saving the customer the hassle of filling out forms at every site he or she visits. In fact, a great many online transactions from a willing buyer are simply never completed because of trouble filling out the forms. As a result, many customers are inclined to use autocomplete features in Web browsers to save them the trouble. With this much personal information being shared with who knows how many sites, the practice of automatically sharing personal information with online sites should be carefully considered.

Spyware and E.T. Programs

Clearly, Web browsers share a lot of information with sites we visit. There may be other software programs on your machine that are secretly reporting information about you, your software, and your online habits over Internet backchannels. This class of software, called spyware, is becoming increasingly prevalent. Any software that employs the user's Internet connection without his or her knowledge or approval can be called spyware.[3] Spyware will generally report particular information back to the home office over the user's Internet connection, though direct dial-ups to a server are also possible. Spyware programs are sometimes called E.T. programs (after its movie namesake) because they "phone home," usually with some data you might not expect. Wireless devices may become targets of spyware programs in the future, particularly once always-on Internet connections from cell phones and PDAs become more generally adopted.

The spyware program problem traces its origins to Microsoft's online registration wizard, first released with Windows 95. When you first turned on your Windows 95 machine, the registration wizard would attempt to dial Microsoft's site to electronically register you with Microsoft, much as many manufacturers ask you to register via postcards for large appliance purchases. Going beyond its call of duty, though, the registration wizard scans your hard drive to compile a list of other installed programs and sends this list back to Microsoft. While you may or may not consider the list of installed programs confidential data, the more fundamental question this E.T. application begs is why does Microsoft need this list? Some critics contend that Microsoft collected this information for competitive business intelligence so that it could determine which competing products users were buying and perhaps leverage this information to market Microsoft's products to these users. This marketing practice has similar characteristics to how register-issued coupons at grocery stores are printed. The data collection practice, though, raised larger concerns that if Microsoft was engaging in this practice with its registration wizard, where else was it collecting data? Because Microsoft wrote the operating system and much of the desktop applications, some have speculated that it is possible that Microsoft is sending out data silently over network connections. An interesting footnote to the story is that after the uproar died down, Microsoft didn't change its practice, and the registration wizard in current Windows versions still performs these same checks, but asks your permission before sending this data back to Microsoft.

Other software vendors noticed the trail blazed by Microsoft, and a new industry of E.T. applications was born. Today, more than 22 million people are believed to have downloaded E.T. applications.[4] Many users have experienced the strange phenomenon of hard drives spinning seemingly arbitrarily when no one is at the keyboard and extra flashes of the modem lights, indicating some data transfer. While hard drives can start for many different reasons unrelated to E.T. applications, when data transfers arbitrarily occur over the modem, it makes one wonder why. Is there some program running that decides to use the network connection to send data out? We notice this only because we happen not to be using the computer or network at the moment. Consider programs that stealthily use the network while you are using it as well. An extra flash of the modem lights is indistinguishable from your normal network activity.

Most vendors of software caught in the act of phoning home justify the practice by claiming the data collected is used in aggregate form to understand the market for their applications. The standard defense in privacy-related breaches is that no personally identifying information is collected, although unique identifiers are often collected along with the data in many cases. Richard Smith, a privacy and Internet sleuth with the Privacy Foundation, caught RealNetworks in the act of sending data out over the network connection. RealNetworks' RealJukebox software lets users download digital music from Internet sites to play on their computers. In addition to downloading music, RealJukebox also sent the user's music selections back to RealNetworks, together with a unique identifier. Therefore, RealNetworks was able to collect a profile of music preferences associated with each unique identifier code. RealNetworks' defense is that the data was collected without associating it with the individual's name. Users who download Real-Networks' software must register with RealNetworks, which means that RealNetworks could associate the unique identifier associated with the RealJukebox software with the identity used in registering for the software. Though it claimed that it did not match users' identities with their unique identifier, the uproar over the data collection practice convinced RealNetworks to disable the E.T. component of the application.

Though RealNetworks took the heat on the RealJukebox product, it is worthwhile thinking about the other software products you use. Nearly any software product that is Internet-enabled runs the risk of compromising your privacy. For instance, the new Microsoft CD Player (version 5.0) that comes with the Windows 2000 platform has some nifty features whose privacy implications are eerily reminiscent of RealJukebox. For those of you familiar with the Microsoft CD Player that was distributed with earlier Microsoft operating systems, you'll recall that the original Microsoft CD Player does not know the name of the CD or its musical tracks when it first plays the CD. You have the option of painstakingly entering the title, artist, and name of every track on the CD. Then the next time you play the CD, the CD Player will recall this information. Of course, if you play the CD on a new or different machine, you'll have to reenter this information. Well, the new Microsoft CD Player distributed with the Windows 2000 platform goes a long way toward putting us out of our misery. Rather than painstakingly entering the information for each CD, the CD Player gives you the option to download the information from either of two Internet sites: Tunes.com or Music Boulevard. It works like a charm. The title, artist, and musical tracks are instantly downloaded. The beauty is if you go to a new machine with the same version CD Player and an Internet connection, you'll still be able to download this data, obviating the need to enter this information by hand multiple times. While the benefits are clear, you can probably see where we are going with this. If Tunes.com is receiving every request I send to download music information, then it can compile a pretty good record of my musical tastes—something that I may not care to share with it or anyone else with whom it might share this information. Besides, because this service is free, what does Tunes.com get out of this? Maybe it gets exactly what it wants—a musical interest profile of the millions of Microsoft users who will play CDs. The Microsoft CD Player gives no indication of what data Tunes.com or Music Boulevard is collecting. There is no privacy policy provided with the CD Player. From a privacy standpoint, we care if Tunes.com is building a profile of our musical interests, in which case it will need some form of unique identifier for each individual. Does Microsoft's CD Player send this identifier? Because we know all Microsoft applications know our real identity from the registration, it could send our names as well. The point is, we simply don't know because there is no information provided about what data is shared with this third party. The lesson is that every Internet-enabled software application has the potential to share private information with other parties, with or without your consent.

RealNetworks isn't the only vendor caught in the act of phoning home. One of the most notorious is a company called Radiate, formerly known as Aureate. Radiate serves the software shareware market, where profits are scarce because software is often shared without renumeration. Many shareware developers will ask for a nominal registration fee, but without an organization for marketing, packaging, selling software, and collecting revenue, shareware developers count on the good will of their users to voluntarily send in registration fees. One alternative model for collecting revenue on shareware is to embed advertising banners within shareware software. This model is exploited by Radiate in more than 400 different shareware software applications. Popular shareware software applications GO!zilla, Free Solitaire, and GetRight come embedded with an adbot E.T. package included by Radiate. In order to effectively target ads to users and to serve up different ads once an ad has been viewed, the Radiate banner-serving adbot reports back to Radiate which ads users click on, the frequency of the clicks, and how long the user views each ad. Therefore, a profile of user's interest can be compiled, and targeted ads can be served up to the users. Sounds innocuous and utilitarian. Privacy advocates, though, argue that profiling users' interests is an invasion of privacy. For instance, data can be collected on whether users click on ads related to alcohol problems, HIV concerns, depression, or pornography. Most people consider these types of interests private and would not want an unknown party monitoring their activities, let alone sharing this data with other parties, such as your employer.

Perhaps most disturbing to those who study E.T. applications is that even after the shareware is uninstalled from the user's hard drive, the Radiate adbot is not; in fact, it continues to phone home on your Web browsing habits. The adbot is started whenever your Web browser is started, and it continues to run for the duration of your Web session, with or without its shareware host. In addition, it reports back to Radiate about all the Radiate family of shareware applications that reside on your disk.

It is the deceptive data collection practices of E.T. applications that tend to raise the ire of the public more than the actual data collected. The Comet Cursor is one such example. Comet Systems cursor software replaces the standard screen cursor with any number of cutesy cursors, such as Peanuts and Pokemon characters that appeal to kids. The free software, which takes only a few seconds to install, is available from Comet Systems or at any one of the 60,000 Web sites that support the technology. While users think they are getting just a cute cursor, in reality they are probably getting more than they bargained for. Every time a user visits any one of those 60,000 Web sites, the Comet Cursor will report the user's unique serial number back to Comet Systems. Therefore, Comet Systems can create profiles for each customer on the sites each visits. The problem with this scenario, even if Comet Systems is not able to associate identities with identifiers, is that data about a customer is being sent from his or her machine over an Internet backchannel to someone else without the customer's knowledge. Other E.T. applications abound, such as zBubbles, an online shopping tool that reports back on your shopping preferences even when you aren't shopping, PKZip, CuteFTP, and SurfMonkey, an application that is supposed to block Internet sites inappropriate for kids, but also sends home their personal information such as the user's personal ID, phone number, and e-mail address.[5]

The spyware problem has interesting parallels with the malicious software problem discussed in Chapter 5, "Mobile and Malicious Code." The basic problem is the same—we just don't know what the software is actually doing. Most software that we download is downloaded in binary form, making it essentially a blackbox, which means we can't look into it to see what it is actually doing. Even for software where source code is available, most people would not know how to determine its functionality. Those software developers capable enough to understand programs usually have neither the time nor the patience to sift through source code to determine its functionality. Most software developers have a hard enough time understanding what their fellow project team members' code does, let alone someone else's. The mere possibility that someone could discover hidden functionality is usually enough of a deterrent to dissuade E.T. application vendors from releasing their software source code. Perhaps for those vendors that do release source code, we should have a little more assurance that at least they are not trying to hide anything. The specter of hidden software functionality, such as spyware and Trojan horses, makes a good argument for open source software.

Spyware Antidotes

Discovering spyware is no easy task, even for privacy sleuths like Richard Smith. We now have tools that can help detect and control spyware programs. The standard tool for the Internet sleuth is the network sniffer. A network sniffer listens promiscuously on the network connection to capture a record of all packets sent to and from the machine being investigated. By examining the log of all packets sent to and from the machine, one can construct the sequence of events that occur as part of an application's network session. The process is painstaking and similar to reading machine code—is not easy, and it requires a lot of patience. Furthermore, if the network sniffer was not listening when the spyware sent off its few packets of data, you won't even detect the data heist. Even if the sniffer was listening, discerning a few packets of data that indicate a privacy violation from the mountain of legitimate network traffic can be daunting, much like trying to find a needle in a haystack. Steve Gibson, another noted Internet sleuth, developed a spyware analyzer just for this purpose.[6] The spyware analyzer simulates a full Internet connection so that traffic from local programs on your machine to the Internet sites to which they attempt can be examined. The simulation creates a makeshift environment so that the suspected spyware program believes a successful connection has been made to the requested home site. The traffic sent to the site can then be examined. Whether this analyzer is more useful than examining packets captured by a network sniffer sent to the actual site is unknown. But it can potentially reduce the noise by eliminating network traffic from all other applications that are not of interest and isolate packets only from the program of interest.

For those of us unwilling to decipher network packets, there are other tools and practices at our disposal that can reduce our exposure and risk to spyware programs. First, as you can see from the Radiate/Aureate saga, use care and discretion when downloading shareware programs. Most of these programs are written by unknown authors or organizations for which you have little basis to trust their software. The reality is that you just don't know what a program might be doing—even programs written by reputable software vendors. When you download programs from shareware sites, you incur additional risk as the developer may not have as much to lose as a reputable firm if it is discovered that it is incorporating spyware in the applications. In the case of shareware, there was a business model to support this kind of activity. As we discussed in Chapter 5, one of the biggest problems with malicious software is stopping its proliferation. Locking down the machine to a set of known, trustworthy programs is one preventive measure.

A second tool that is available from Steve Gibson's site [see endnote 3] is called OptOut. The tool will remove known spyware programs from your machine. This is a good way to begin addressing the problem of known spyware that could be running on your machine right now. But it suffers from the same problem that anti-virus programs do: It can't do anything about spyware programs it doesn't know about that may be running on your machine.

A third tool that is becoming increasingly popular is the personal firewall. While many different software applications call themselves personal firewalls, the type that can be useful for preventing and even detecting potential spyware will have the ability to carefully regulate the network connection. A good example is ZoneAlarm, freely available from Zone Labs.[7] ZoneAlarm lets the user configure exactly which programs should be allowed to use the network connection and lock out any other programs that attempt to use it. So, if a spyware program or DLL attempts to make a connection over the network socket, ZoneAlarm will first deny it, then notify you about exactly which program attempted to make a network connection. Although it will not tell you why it attempted to make the network connection, it will at least give you notice that some program was trying to access the network. If you feel that there is no reason for this program to be using the network, you can bar it from using the network; if you feel it has legitimate reason to use the network, you can allow it. The point of using personal firewalls for this purpose is to let you observe which programs are attempting to use network connections. It is possible that you will catch a stealthy spyware program attempting to use an Internet backchannel by using a personal firewall.

The failure of personal firewalls, however, is that they will not help you detect spyware that is masquerading in programs that use the network for other legitimate purposes. In other words, they won't help you detect Trojan horse functionality in programs that use the network for other legitimate purposes. Web browsers are a good example. Web browsers obviously need network access to download Web pages; but if they are sending off other data that they should not be, such as sensitive files on your system, there is very little that a personal firewall can do about it.

Before casting away personal firewalls, it is worth noting here that personal firewalls are effective for other purposes. Personal firewalls are most often used so that they can protect your machine against hackers that may be trying to break into your system. Today, always-on Internet connections to the home are becoming more common using ISDN, DSL, or ADSL lines. For those of us used to dialing in to an ISP over a slow line every time we need an Internet connection and possibly tying up the phone line, these always-on connections are a blessing, if not necessarily affordable. The downside with always-on connections is that they now become better targets for hackers. If your computer is connected to the Internet for a short time every day, the window of opportunity for hackers to discover, probe, and break into to your computer is pretty small, thus reducing your exposure. If your connection is always on, your computer becomes a target of opportunity. Because most people do not know how to configure their personal machines securely, personal firewalls can effectively protect your machine against offering services it need not be. For instance, a malicious software executable called Sub7 has been making the rounds among many personal computers. The executable is a zombie server that listens inconspicuously on an obscure port on your machine for connections. Malicious hackers will scan computers across large domain segments of ISPs to see if the malicious executable is running. This scan can be performed very easily and requires only a few packets, which can easily fly under the radar of most ISP network intrusion detection systems. If they find a machine with the malicious executable running, then they use its corresponding client to bring the zombie to life. At this point, the crackers can use the malicious executable as a remote administration toolkit to take complete control of the computer and even perform stunts, such as turning the screen to snow or turning it upside down.

A personal firewall will protect against malicious executables in two ways: First, it will prevent any executable from listening to any arbitrary port; second, it will allow requests only to the network services you approve, thus denying requests to network services you may not know about. This second feature is of tremendous value even for legitimate network services that often come enabled with the computer out of the box. For instance, NetBIOS services will often run on advanced Windows workstations. These allow networked computers to share file systems. In most cases, you will not want to share your file system over the Internet with anyone. Some exploits exist to take advantage of these services that run often without the owner's knowledge in order to gain access to users' files. A personal firewall can be configured to block these ports among others. The basic idea of personal firewalls, like their corporate cousins, is to allow only the network services you care about (for example, e-mail and Web services), and deny everything else. Therefore you need not think about every potential service that could be running, such as malicious executables, but rather concern yourself only with the services that you do need. Though this discussion of personal firewalls is a slight tangent from privacy-related issues, it is important to understand the benefits of these tools and to realize that they do, in fact, help protect the confidentiality of the private data you keep on your personal machine.

Network Privacy Risks

The best-understood portion of e-business transactions is the network that transports data between users, businesses, and machines. The network is also the portion of e-business transactions that we pay the most attention to from a security and privacy standpoint, largely due to the fear, uncertainty, and doubt about Internet-based transactions promulgated by the commercial community. Most of us learned to fear Internet-based commerce even before we understood what it involves. The early FUD about Internet-based commerce was that because the Internet is an open network, anyone can capture your credit card numbers and the other private information you send over the Internet. It is certainly true that anyone listening on a node between your computer and the destination computer can capture your packets. It is more likely the case that this would occur on your own local area network, probably at your workplace, rather than on the Internet. The reality is that there is too much traffic at key nodes that route and transmit data (such as ISPs) for them to be in the business of reading your mail or spying on your Web sessions. Some might argue that federal agencies such as the Federal Bureau of Investigation (FBI) or the National Security Agency (NSA) listen promiscuously to networks. Even given all of their substantial assets, they can't examine every packet in every Internet session, nor do they want to do so. If they are listening using, say, Carnivore or Echelon, they are screening sessions for keywords of interest to them that could be indicators of organized crime, terrorist plots, acts of sabotage, or espionage. By and large, most people could care less about what data you send over networks, except perhaps your employer or maybe your spouse. Hence a lot of the stealthy monitoring programs that are written to spy on your data are marketed to and used by employers and suspicious significant others.

In any case, if you are concerned about the privacy of your data sent over public networks, you have several good tools at your disposal.

First and foremost, most Web sites worth their salt will use encrypted sessions when collecting confidential information such as account numbers and passwords. The Secure Sockets Layer (SSL) is the standard secure session layer for Web-based sessions. Two ways to tell if you are in a secure session is to first look for the secure session symbol in your browser, generally a locked padlock in a lower corner of the browser screen, or second, look at the URL of the Web browser. SSL sessions use https:// to set up a secure session. Because SSL also authenticates the site you are visiting, double-click on the padlock to see the site certificate to make sure you are making a secure connection with the site you think you are and to ensure that the certificate is signed by a trusted third party and is not expired.

If you are sending e-mail or confidential documents over the Internet, you should use a commercial-grade encryption package. Many are available—in fact, far too many to describe here. One of the most popular is PGP, or Pretty Good Privacy, created by Phil Zimmerman, now owned by Network Associates. A free version is also distributed by MIT. PGP provides asymmetric cryptography solutions, which means you do not need a shared secret (or password) with the party to whom you are sending the confidential information. Rather, each party to the transaction needs a public and private key pair. You use the public key of the recipient party to encrypt the message. Only that party can decrypt the message using his or her private key, known only to that party. You can also sign documents using your private PGP key. While PGP is popular among the digerati, it has not reached mass adoption because it requires creating keys and having some understanding of how to encrypt and sign documents. Like a fax machine, having too small a community doesn't make public key crypto very useful. If everyone had public/private PGP keys, then encryption would be much easier and perhaps be a regular part of our e-mail transmissions. As it stands, we still largely send e-mail in the clear.

In spite of good crypto solutions available to secure your private data over the network, you will still need to be concerned with some privacy risks, as highlighted in Figure 7.1. The two types of attacks listed in the call-out cloud are snooping and man-in-the-middle attacks. Snooping is precisely the phenomena we were discussing previously of someone listening promiscuously on a network connection such as your LAN. End-to-end encryption can mitigate this risk because the data is encrypted on your desktop before it is sent out over the network. Be certain to know that you have end-to-end encryption. Some VPN solutions that create encrypted tunnels encrypt data only between network servers. Data then passed between network servers and clients are sometimes sent in the clear. Therefore, monitoring programs on the local network will be able to capture your confidential data. Even with end-to-end encryption, snooping risks exist on your own machine. For instance, keystroke capture programs could be running on your desktop machine that enable someone to remotely capture and record your keystrokes. Some earlier versions of Unix workstations had holes that allowed keystrokes to be captured by exploiting lax remote display controls. Software applications have been specifically written to take screen snapshots frequently (such as every few seconds) and send them over the network to a remote monitoring station. This type of software is not that unusual in corporate networks, particularly when they suspect insider sabotage. With screen captures, everything you type is captured and sent over the network. A burgeoning market for monitoring software is playing on the curiosity and fear of suspecting spouses. Many have already loaded these monitoring programs on home machines to monitor what their spouses are doing late at night on the machine. Even if you were using a good network encryption package, the data could be stolen right out from under you before you encrypt it. These types of monitoring packages are more client software risks than network risks. It is important to understand, though, where network protection technologies can fall down on the job.

The second type of network privacy risk highlighted in Figure 7.1 is man-in-the-middle attacks. This is a general category of attack in which adversaries manage to position themselves between you and your destination to capture your data. You might think that end-to-end encryption protocols would take care of this risk, but there are ways to dupe people into falsely creating a secure session. Web spoofing is one such attack, where you lure the victim into believing he or she is making a secure session with the site of interest. In fact, the attack dupes the victim into making a secure session with the attacker rather than with the intended site. It is easy to recreate the look and feel of any site. The attacker can even run an SSL-enabled server so that all connections to the mock site are "secure." While the data is encrypted between your computer and their server, and you notice the locked padlock in the corner of your browser, the data is decrypted by the attacker. Rather than recreating the site, the attacker can forward all queries to the site of interest by using proxies, but he or she can capture your private data along the way. If the attacker was even more mischievous, he or she could alter key data coming back from the site to affect your decision-making process in a transaction. To reduce the risk of man-in-the-middle attacks, in addition to using a secure transport protocol, you should also examine the certificate of the site you are visiting to ensure it is the site you think you are visiting and that it is endorsed by a trusted third party, such as Verisign.

Server-Side Privacy Risks

Even though most privacy risks are thought to occur over the network, as we have discussed earlier, a significant amount of risk actually comes from your own desktop machine. On the other end of the connection, however, is where most of the personal data is actually collected, processed, archived, and distributed. While these components of the server-side system may not be properly considered privacy risks, they are, in fact, responsible for most of the egregious privacy violations we see in practice. In this section, we discuss the machinery responsible for collecting our personal online data.

E-business servers typically have a three-tier architecture. They have front-end servers that provide the Internet network services, such as Web service and e-mail. While front-end Web services are typically what we as customers see, any real e-business has to have a back-end infrastructure that supports the e-business in areas of online transaction processing, supply-chain management, customer relationship management, enterprise resource planning (ERP) software, ordering, inventory management, shipping and logistics, and data mining. The vast majority of these services are legacy systems used by businesses long before they moved their business to the Internet. Regardless, they are the engine of e-business systems. To interface these back-end systems with the front-end Web servers a middleware layer of software is necessary. This is the role of the CGI scripts, application servers, and component-based software that enable e-business transactions. The middleware software actually takes Web requests, such as an online transaction request, processes it, updates back-end systems, and provides a response back to the client via the Web server.

Among all this machinery (okay, software) are tools to collect, process, mine, and disseminate personal data. Make no mistake, processing customer data is an essential part of e-business. Customer relationship management software is critical to identifying repeat customers and ensuring that online transactions not only complete, but complete in a satisfactory manner. The most successful e-businesses have managed to provide excellent customer service by learning the needs of their customers. Repeat customers are the bread and butter of any business. Businesses that fail to keep customers coming back are doomed to failure. Effective data mining strategies on users' Web browsing habits can identify customers likely to purchase products, the types of products they are likely to purchase, and custom-serve Web pages oriented to their particular interests. This cycle of monitoring Web browsing, mining the data, targeting customers based on their interests, and completing the sale is the killer app of online marketing. The more data that is shared with these sites, theoretically, the more targeted and accurate advertising campaigns can be.

CDNow and Amazon.com both maintain individual profiles of personal preferences in music and books. These profiles are aggregated and mined to determine the types of interests users have. The aggregate statistics can be used to make predictions or simply suggestions for books or music a user might like based on his or her current purchasing profile and what other like-minded customers have purchased. For instance, readers of Tom Clancy books might enjoy Nelson Demille's books. If you are purchasing a Tom Clancy book online, Amazon.com may tell you that you should also consider Nelson Demille's works. Once your online profile is established, the business might custom-tailor its content to meet your demographic category. It might serve up a different array of products if it knows you are a 42-year old mother of three than if you are a 17-year old teenager with a generous discretionary allowance. If you define customer service as more closely aligning products with your needs, then an argument can be made that the more personal data a company has, the better customer service it will be able to deliver. The irony is that bigger companies that are in a position to pull together massive databases through mergers and acquisitions will be able to deliver better customer service than the smaller companies without such resources. We typically associate better customer service with small businesses in the brick-and-mortar world, whereas in the e-business arena, more data could result in better customer service.

How do they do it? The front-end Web servers are the primary data collection source. Web servers keep several standard logs such as which pages are hit and how often, the domains from which Web page hits come, the Web sites that "refer" customers to their own Web site via hot links, the search engines used to direct traffic to the site, the search phrases most commonly used on the site, and even statistics on the types of browsers and machines that hit the Web site. And this is just the beginning.

Many commercial sites use ad servers to gain additional revenue from advertising other people's businesses. An ad server will serve up banner ads to users. DoubleClick and Engage are the most popular ad servers, serving more than 20,000 Web sites and hundreds of millions of cookies. Engage claims to maintain 52 million online behavioral profiles with more than 800 interest categories by which it can classify customers' interests.[8] The ad servers will discreetly place a string of code called a "cookie" on your machine if you do not already have one from them. The cookie is a unique identifier that is used as an index into the online database. Cookies are not inherently as evil as they are sometimes purported to be. Cookies were originally invented to accommodate the stateless http protocol. By storing cookies on your machine, a Web site can provide a more seamless experience as you go from one page to the next. For instance, once you have placed an item in your shopping cart, a cookie will "remember" this as you go to check out. Cookies can be and are used for other purposes, such as creating a behavioral profile of Web surfing habits by online advertisers.

Because cookies are merely identifiers, it is hard to know just what the online ad agencies know about us. Whenever we hit a Web site supported by advertising, the ad server will read the cookie from your machine (unless you take steps to prevent this, as discussed in the next section). The ad server uses your cookie to look up your profile and determine which ad to serve to you dynamically, based on your interests it has gleaned from your surfing activities at its member sites. One tangible benefit of this approach is that you don't end up seeing the same ad banners on every page on the Web site. But ad servers will also record which advertisements you have clicked through—the golden egg in online advertising. When you click on an ad, the advertiser has won your eyes and interest. This is also one way advertisers charge fees, based on click-throughs. Not only is the click-through recorded in your profile, but the type of ad and how long you spent at the site are captured. What is more insidious is that if you share other information with an advertiser such as your name, address, names of children, income, etc.—even just once, and even if you didn't realize you were sharing it with an advertiser—this information will potentially become a permanent part of your profile. Now when the ad server reads your cookie, it will be able to associate your online behavioral patterns with this information you have shared, such as where you live. This data, in turn, can be rented to other sites for targeted marketing. The online advertisers can form loose alliances between businesses to pool the data collected at Web sites. In pooling agreements, sharing your name with one member of the alliance results in the advertiser's ability to associate the name with cookies used by all alliance members.

If ad banner cookies weren't enough to worry about, Richard Smith of the Privacy Foundation has spotted and decried the use of what he calls Web bugs.[9] Web bugs are simply invisible banners that still set and recall cookies. What's the point of an invisible banner if it's useless for (non-subliminal) advertising? Well, that's the point of his consternation. The only point of having an invisible banner that tracks a user's Web movements is for stealthy data collection. When you visit a site with advertising banners, you can reasonably make an assumption that there is a third party involved. In most cases, the third party is the advertising agency, such as DoubleClick or Engage, that is setting and retrieving cookies. Web bugs use transparent GIFs so that they are invisible to the user. Even though they may be invisible, that doesn't mean that they can't be fully functional. The advertising agencies still can collect data about your surfing habits as well as identify you even on pages without banners. The problem here is that there is no suggestion that someone is collecting data. Smith likens it to a phone bug that listens in on conversations without making its presence known. The Web bug is deliberately concealed, and some privacy advocates argue that its only purpose is surveillance.

This wealth of information can be used to provide very targeted and effective advertising. While that may be a benefit for many who don't really care to see ads that do not match their interests, others are unsettled by the notion that their online usage is carefully monitored and their identity and personal information might be known while they are surfing a Web site at which they did not volunteer that information. While claims of not collecting personally identifying information is the standard response from companies in the business of collecting online behavior patterns, this stance could change at any point in time, either due to changes in policies, buyouts, mergers, and even bankruptcies.

As long as the market greatly values such data, there will be incentive to collect this data and to correlate it with other databases, online and offline. As technology advances, new methods of collecting and merging data become available, and the value of having rich datasets increases, the battle of online monitoring is sure to increase. Businesses will do well to follow the privacy policy guidelines described earlier for forthright disclosure of data collection and dissemination practices to create a trusted atmosphere of online commerce.

Companies that maintain their own databases of customer profiles will use middleware, as shown in Figure 7.1, to dynamically create Web pages or banners based on the customer's profile or current shopping selections. When a customer revisits a Web site where a cookie has been previously set, the site may know the identity of the user, especially if the user has registered with the site. The site can then use the cookie to retrieve the customer's profile and personal preferences. Depending on the sophistication of the online data collection, the site may use intelligent data mining software to make suggestions for goods to purchase, or it may show Web pages custom-tailored to the customer's demographic profile. This data mining and retrieving logic is implemented in the middleware layer.

Back-end databases store customer profiles as well as aggregate information used to classify the customer for the purpose of creating tailored Web pages. In addition, data sharing and dissemination of customer profiles via network alliance members draw on the data stored in the back-end infrastructure, typically using some out-of-band Internet connection. Thus, customer-profiling activities can add significant middleware logic and back-end infrastructure to an already complex e-business system. For this reason among others, many commercial sites outsource customer profiling to third parties such as DoubleClick and Engage. In the third-party model, Web pages on the commercial site are created so that the banner ads are served up via Web link redirections to the third party. In this manner, the third-party advertising agencies can set and retrieve cookies and serve banners, all without the commercial Web site's involvement, if not complicity. Even though the data collection and retrieval may be performed off-site, it is imperative for businesses using third-party data collection services to understand what data is being sent off-site and to be up-front about it with their own customers.

Protecting Your Privacy Online

Most of this chapter has discussed the various ways that data is collected about your online behavior. If you now think that there may be more data out there on you than you care about, or that you would rather not have a third party collect information about you, or that you prefer Web sites not to know your identity or interests when you hit their Web pages, there is recourse. There are several privacy-enhancing tools available. The EPIC Web site (www.epic.org/privacy/tools.html) is a good resource for privacy literature and tools. Indeed, a burgeoning privacy industry has attracted a lot of money and is aiming to provide users more control over their data and providing guidance on which sites are "privacy friendly." In this section, we briefly discuss the many options you have in protecting your privacy.

The simplest and maybe most important activity you can do is to not volunteer information at one site that you would otherwise not share with others. The most common way people give up information is when they agree to register at a site. Unfortunately, many times, we do not have an option but to register at a site in order to access its services, such as travel services. As businesses are discovering, many people use aliases and other false information when they register in order to protect their true identities. An alternative is to use the tools discussed later in this section that will help create and manage online identities for you. Aside from registration forms, many people participate in surveys and sweepstakes that are great ways for online sites to gather personal information. In summary, if you care about your online privacy, don't volunteer the information in the first place.

Denying the Cookie Monsters

The discussion on cookies should have demystified the privacy concerns surrounding cookies. As we stated, cookies are not inherently evil, and they are, in fact, necessary at many Web sites simply to complete transactions. Not all cookies are used to track your online behavior. Though there have been some problems with the implementation of certain browsers that allowed some sites to read cookies belonging to other sites, the security issues with cookies are minimal. For instance, cookies are text strings that are read, not executed. Cookies do not have the ability to be used as viruses or malicious software. Cookies do raise serious privacy concerns primarily because users do not know what data is being collected by them, how it is being used, and what their electronic dossiers that may include merged information from different sources look like. For these reasons, several tools are available to help you control cookies and deny the mass cookie consumers.

Because cookies are strings of text stored on your file system (your browser has to be able to read them), a first step in taking control of your cookies is to find them. You may have a single file with lots of cookies, or a directory of many cookie files, one per vendor. A draconian step would be to simply delete all your cookie files or, to provide even stronger protection, erase their data, and make the files read-only. Remember that not all cookies are bad. There may be many cookies on your machine that you want to leave alone so that the surfing experience at a Web site is smooth. Web browsers by default allow cookies to be written to and read from your computer. They can be configured to prevent cookies from being written. At the time of this writing, the configuration options allow fairly coarse-grained control, such as allowing cookies or not or prompting you every time a site attempts to set a cookie. The problem with this blunt-edged approach is that not all cookies are bad, and by creating a blanket rule for disallowing cookies, you will make the Web surfing experience very difficult. In fact, you are likely to reenable cookies if you disable them simply because you will not be able to navigate a Web site, or you will become overwhelmed with all the dialog boxes prompting you for permission to set cookies. What is needed instead is a more precise approach to cookies, one in which cookies are selectively cut.

If you look at your cookie files in a standard editor, you will see that they are fairly cryptic to read, even though they are not actually encrypted. A number of cookie editing and blocking tools are available to help you edit cookie files selectively and implement a reasonable cookie policy.[10] The PGP Cookie Cutter (www.pgp.com) application is a free software program that allows users to selectively edit cookie files, allowing you to keep the good ones and eliminate the bad ones. It will also selectively block or allow cookies to be set based on user preferences. Luckman's Anonymous cookie (www.luckman.com/anoncookie/index.html) gives you an anonymous cookie to support anonymous surfing. DoubleClick.com also has an opt-out section that replaces your DoubleClick cookies with an anonymous cookie. Be forewarned, however, that anonymous cookie solutions will result in the same advertisements being repeated over and over again. Other cookie management tools available include Cookie Crusher (www.thelimitsoft.com/cookie.html), which lets you configure preferences for which sites to accept or reject cookies from, and Cookie Monster, which will automatically delete your cookie files at each start-up. Look for browsers to give more fine-grained control over cookie management, if not take the step to require users to opt in for cookies.

Pseudonyms

An alternative approach to blocking cookies or deleting them is to create online fictional identities. This approach has the advantage over cookie-blocking approaches in that it does not break the Web navigation experience. Rather, cookies are still enabled, but your personal identity is concealed through pseudonyms. Pseudonym services create and manage a number of fictional identities for you so that you do not need to remember who you signed up as at any given site.

Several vendors have created software to enable online pseudonyms. Zero Knowledge Systems has developed a service to create and manage multiple identities it calls Freedom Net (www.freedom.net). Rather than surfing directly to the Web sites of interest, the user goes through the Freedom Net where all requests are linked to one of the user's pseudonyms. The user's IP address is concealed to make the Web requests untraceable. Users control how much data they want to share with Web sites through their different identities, allowing different levels of data sharing with different sites. The service is not free, however, and one will need to determine whether the cost of pseudonyms is worth the privacy.

Lucent Technologies has developed similar services, such as the Lucent Personalized Web Assistant (LPWA) and Proxymate, to control information sent to Web sites and to establish online pseudonyms that it uses to automatically fill out Web forms for you. LPWA (www.bell-labs.com/project/lpwa) provides what it calls anonymous, but persistent service. LPWA will consistently use the same pseudonyms every time a user returns to the same site, and different pseudonyms for different sites. You need to go through the LPWA proxy server before hitting the site. Rather than making your Web request anonymous as the Anonymizer does, the LPWA proxy will fill out Web forms with your pseudonym identity information. Using LPWA does not prevent profiling as Web browsing habits will be collected by data collection sites. The data cannot be associated with your real identity, and because different pseudonyms are used with different sites, the profile won't be shared between sites. In a similar effort, Novell's DigitalMe (www.digitalme.com) provides a secure central repository of real or fictitious information that is provided to Web sites via proxy when personal information is requested.

Like most of the problems in privacy and security, anonymous and pseudonym services require a degree of trust. Because the services are able to capture the very information you are trying to hide via their proxies, they could, in fact, collect this information about you and sell it to the very services from which you are concealing this information. The point of these services is to provide trusted third-party services in applications where privacy is important. Rather than having to trust every site out there that may be collecting information about you, you need to trust only one of these services.

One approach that is markedly different, but potentially equally effective, is Crowds (www.research.att.com/projects/crowds), developed by researchers at AT&T Labs-Research. Crowds works on the notion that you can gain privacy by blending into a crowd. Crowds is a Web proxy server that works on behalf of a group—the crowd. Web requests from any member of the crowd are sent to a proxy server, which will then forward it to a random member of the crowd. This member may forward the request directly to the requested Web site or forward it on to another randomly selected member of the crowd. When the Web request is finally submitted, it is submitted by a random member of the crowd, thus preventing the Web site from knowing the true identity of the sender. The interesting aspect of this approach is that there is no identity concealing, thus no need to anonymize requests or create identities. Rather, one's identity is concealed by virtue of the fact that someone else's identity is used on your behalf. That person, in turn, gets the same services from other people in their crowd. The larger the crowd, the larger the number of different potential identities that can make your request. One drawback of Crowds is that it does not conceal confidential information—for example, passwords—that may be in the request that is forwarded through other members of the crowd. If you are worried about confidentiality of data, you will probably want to use a secure or trusted service. Crowds is freely available and requires downloading the proxy server and configuring your browser to point to it.

P3P

The Platform for Privacy Preferences Project (P3P) attempts to build an infrastructure in Web-based sessions to mutually support privacy preferences between content providers and users. The World Wide Web Consortium (W3C) is adopting P3P (www.w3.org/P3P/) as a standard to help promote its acceptance among Web site developers, browser vendors, and users.

P3P provides a machine-readable vocabulary for privacy policies and preferences. The basic idea is to match a Web site's privacy policy with users' privacy preferences to facilitate automatic transfer of information when a P3P "agreement" is reached between the user's privacy preferences and the site's privacy policy. The site's policy specifies in P3P format what data is being collected and how it will be used. In cases where a P3P agreement between the site's policy and the user's preferences is not reached, then the P3P protocol attempts to negotiate alternative terms that will work between the policy and preferences. If an agreement cannot be automatically reached by the policy and preferences, then the user is prompted to determine how he or she would like to proceed. For example, you can specify to be prompted if a site that is collecting your address specifies it might sell this information to third parties.

The system requires users to encode their privacy preferences into several different categories, such as physical contact information, which contains phone number and address data, payment information, which might include credit card numbers and bank accounts, as well as navigation and click-stream data to define what trail is to be left behind when simply browsing sites. Once this data is captured, the idea of P3P for users is that you define who gets access to this data, which can then be automatically transferred to the site, eliminating the need to reenter this data multiple times. Furthermore, because sites will need to encode their privacy policies in the P3P format, this will in theory obviate the need for users to review the esoteric language of privacy policies to determine what data is being collected.[11] P3P also provides a provision for pseudonyms such that users can send the same unique identifier each time they return to a Web site where they have a P3P agreement. A P3P-compliant browser will keep track of the different identifiers used for different sites and send the appropriate one. This will facilitate persistent relationships with sites where users control the information they wish to share with that site.

While the idea appears good in principle, some practical issues are holding up its success. For instance, the vocabulary is fairly arbitrary and does not specify how new categories of data, preferences, and policies are to be added. A secondary issue is that there is not a mechanism to determine compliance with P3P agreements. P3P agreements are social contracts of Web session relationships. If a vendor chooses to violate its policy, there is no provision within P3P to discover this, nor to enforce the policy. The force of law may be the strongest deterrent, though, as businesses may be charged with unfair or deceitful business practices by the FTC or law enforcement authorities. These issues notwithstanding, P3P's biggest hurdle to overcome is achieving critical mass. P3P has the fax machine problem: What good is one fax in the world? Not only do the browser and Web server vendors need to build in P3P functionality, but everyone will have to want to play. That means Web sites will need to encode their policy and mean it. But even more, users will have to participate. It's not a party unless the users show up. Requiring users to participate by filling out forms with personal information might be the biggest hurdle, especially with distrust of vendors and Web sites being commonplace. P3P attempts to carve out a win-win solution for both vendors and users, where vendors get the information they are looking for under constrained and upfront conditions and where users can specify what data they will release. If users do not participate, the vendors will go back to business as usual.

Privacy Is Good Business

This chapter has mainly concerned itself with discussing privacy risks in e-business. As the discussion of P3P should have made apparent, privacy can mean good business from several different standpoints. First, consider that privacy is a business unto itself, one that continues to grow as people's fear of privacy infringements has rocketed to the top of the list of online concerns. Companies such as TRUSTe, which provides its seal of approval for sites, make their money from the companies they approve. Other companies have emerged in this growing business such as Click-Sure, which provides guidance and a confidence rating of e-business practices for consumers, and enonymous.com. Enonymous.com is a competitor of TRUSTe in that it rates the privacy of sites by an audit of the site's privacy policies. Unlike TRUSTe, it is not paid by the sites it rates, thus eliminating a basic conflict of interest. For instance, what site is going to pay for a low rating? Because enonymous.com is not paid by the sites it rates, it can make claims to impartial, unbiased assessments of the site's privacy policies. Enonymous.com's Advisor application notifies customers about the privacy policies of the sites they visit. Other companies that have emerged in this growing industry are The Privacy Foundation, Privista, and the Privacy Council.

As we have often stated, most consumers do not object about the data that is actually collected as much as they do about deceitful data collection practices. Rather than view privacy as bugaboo, businesses can view privacy as an opportunity to build good business relationships based on trust. Businesses that are forthright about what data they collect and how they use it will be able to leverage their openness into establishing a relationship based on trust. If they keep their promises, then the customers will have even more reason to do business with them.

As long as privacy issues remain unregulated, market forces will largely dictate the privacy practices of the majority of businesses. If the market values data collection very highly, then data collection will undoubtedly be here to stay. Businesses that do not pay attention to their data collection practices or that violate privacy policies take on serious business risks. As companies continue to get roasted in the media and on Wall Street for egregious privacy breaches, business will seek solutions that will enable them to be good corporate citizens while delivering maximum value to their customers through personalized content. For businesses, privacy and profit need to go hand-in-hand.

P3P is a good first step in the right direction. While it may not be successful in its current incarnation, the idea is that businesses and consumers can reach agreements on the privacy of their data while providing value-added services. In fact, the future of online privacy might draw on an existing practice that is successful in the brick-and-mortar world. People are willing to release private information in return for discounts, rewards, or some form of compensation. Grocery club cards illustrate this vividly. Shoppers give up detailed profiles of their shopping habits, linked to all kinds of personally identifying information, in return for discounts on groceries. While some may say they don't have a choice in the matter, the fact is that you could forgo the club card, but you will end up paying higher prices. Grocery club card-sanctioned pseudonyms might be a business compromise, where the stores get the information they are seeking on shopping habits of their customers, while customers can maintain their privacy of identity. In the online world, we may be willing to barter our personal information in return for discounts on products or preferential treatment of services. New models of online commerce that support bartering of private information are likely to emerge in an unregulated industry. In the interim, users should be wary of releasing personal information they would not share with strangers, and businesses should use privacy concerns as an opportunity to build trust relationships with their customers.

Notes

1. See www.identitytheft.org for a good resource on identity theft and surviving identity theft.

2. See http://catless.ncl.ac.uk/Risks/ for an online archive of the Risks Forum newsgroup digest, the comp.risks USENET newsgroup for complete postings of computer-related risks, and *Computer-Related Risks*, by Peter Neumann (Reading, MA: Addison-Wesley/ACM Press, 1995).

3. From Steve Gibson's OptOut site: http://grc.com/optout.htm.

4. A. Cohen, "Spies Amongst Us," in *Time Digital*, 5:3 (July 2000): 32–39.

5. Ibid.

6. See endnote 3.

7. See www.zonealarm.com.

8. R. O'Harrow, Jr., "Private or Not?", *Washington Post Online* (Wednesday, May 17, 2000): G22. Online: www.washingtonpost.com.

9. R. O'Harrow, Jr. "Fearing a Plague of Web Bugs: Invisible Fact-Gathering Code Raises Privacy Concerns," *Washington Post* (Saturday,

November 13, 1999): E01. Available online: www.washingtonpost
.com.

10. The Web site www.cookiecentral.com provides good resources on managing cookies with links to privacy-enhancing tools.

11. L.F. Cranor, "Internet Privacy: A Public Concern," *netWorker: The Craft of Network Computing*, 2:3 (June/July 1998): 13–18. Available online: http://www.acm.org/pubs/citations/journals/networker/1998-2-3/ p13-cranor/.